SCHOOLING IN THE LIGHT OF POPULAR CULTURE

SUNY Series, Education and Culture
Critical Factors in the Formation of
Character and Community in American Life
Eugene F. Provenzo, Jr., and Paul Farber, eds.

SCHOOLING IN THE LIGHT OF POPULAR CULTURE

edited by
Paul Farber
Eugene F. Provenzo, Jr.
Gunilla Holm

STATE UNIVERSITY OF NEW YORK PRESS

LC
191.4
.S35
1994

Published by
State University of New York Press, Albany

© 1994 State University of New York

All rights reserved

Printed in the United States of America

No part of this book may be used or reproduced
in any manner whatsoever without written permission
except in the case of brief quotations embodied in
critical articles and reviews.

For information, address State University of New York Press,
State University Plaza, Albany, N.Y., 12246

Production by Bernadine Dawes
Marketing by Dana Yanulavich

Library of Congress Cataloging-in-Publication Data

Schooling in the light of popular culture / edited by Paul Farber,
Eugene F. Provenzo, Jr., Gunilla Holm.
p. cm. — (SUNY series in education and culture)
Includes index.
ISBN 0-7914-1871-5 (hc). — ISBN 0-7914-1872-3 (pbk.)
1. Education—Social aspects—United States. 2. Popular culture-
-United States. I. Farber, Paul., 1935- . II. Provenzo, Eugene
F. III. Holm, Gunilla. IV. Series.
LC191.4.S35 1994
370.19'0973—dc20 93-28209
CIP

10 9 8 7 6 5 4 3 2 1

CONTENTS

CONCORDIA COLLEGE LIBRARY
2811 NE HOLMAN ST.
PORTLAND, OR 97211-6099

INTRODUCTION

Schooling, like other important social institutions, is conducted in a complex field of forces that shape its nature and direction. Attitudes and beliefs about schooling play their part. How people with a stake in the schools—teachers, students, parents, administrators, and other citizens—make sense of it contributes to what schooling is now and what it might become. This book is written in the belief that much more serious attention needs to be paid to how participants in schooling and the public that supports it come to hold their various views about what schooling is and ought to be. There is good reason for us now, as a public, to examine the roots of our ideas, attitudes, and expectations, as these surely affect the quality of our engagement in the issues about and practices of schooling at many levels.

How are views of schooling formed? *Schooling in the Light of Popular Culture* explores an underexamined source of influence that affects the way schooling is experienced and understood in contemporary culture. That source is the flow of symbolic forms comprising mainstream popular culture. This book centers on the portrayal of aspects of schooling—its characteristics, participants, glories, and problems—as they are constructed and displayed in diverse forms of popular culture.

The main assumption of this book is that involvement in contemporary schooling at any level—whether as a teacher, student, policymaker, administrator, or concerned citizen—is conditioned by the sociocultural context in which schooling is understood, a context that is in turn mediated by powerful forms of popular culture. For those with an interest in considering what, for example, schooling is for or teachers are like or the "crisis" in schooling is all about, popular-culture sources affect how and for whom such questions arise and how settled views in response to them become established over time. In this way, popular culture interacts with other sources of influence—such as direct experience, local networks of communication, and more formally disseminated research findings—shaping the social construction of meaning in and about schooling.

This matters for people with diverse connections to the schools. Those entering or engaged in professional roles as teachers or administrators clearly have a stake in how their work in schooling is represented in popular culture. We write as practitioners ourselves, and address this volume first, therefore, to current and future practitioners who would join with us in exploring far-reaching, but often unexamined, factors conditioning school practices and policy. Concerned citizens, parents, and school policymakers also have a stake in the way schooling is treated as a topic of popular culture. For them, this work speaks to two principal concerns. Since their direct ties to schooling are more tenuous, informal sources of insight and information are likely to loom larger for them. In addition, the interests and hopes that persons outside of schooling have for its direction are likewise dependent on the way school issues are represented and resolved within the social context of communication about schooling. Finally, students themselves, including students of education, should not be overlooked, for the meaning schooling has for them is bound up in the attitudes and expectations they have come to hold regarding school experience. We believe that numerous possibilities present themselves for broaching with students issues that are at the heart of school experience by way of exploring meaningful and revealing tendencies in forms of popular culture.

In general terms, this book seeks to foster inquiry addressing the interaction of popular culture and other sources influencing how schooling is understood. Such inquiry brings into view issues that nestle between a pair of important areas of concern and scholarship. One area involves research focused on schooling itself, studies of teachers and learners, curriculum and instruction, new technologies, and so on. This includes the range of traditional educational studies, posing and addressing problems that take school boundaries largely for granted. Increasingly, such a focus is being challenged by a vigorous research tradition that has emerged regarding modern cultural studies. Work on popular culture and, more generally, cultural studies, is burgeoning and redefining the boundaries of inquiry with regard to education (as well as other fields). There is a strong temptation to cross traditional boundaries, rethink the way fields are defined and studied.[1] Such redefinition is long overdue and very promising. But much of this activity is also highly specialized as well, treating issues and problems that have little meaning for people outside of the disciplinary contexts in which they arise. Indeed, some critics have begun to decry the academicization of intellectual fervor focused on popular texts and tendencies.[2] For this reason, this book maintains an explicit connection to the traditional focus of educational studies, on the problems and possibilities of schooling as a locus of concern. We seek to relate school-based concerns to critical aspects of the sociocultural context which, through patterns of representation, frame and influence how schooling is understood and treated. This orientation acknowledges that, as Arthur Danto has suggested, we are in a fundamental sense representational beings, and ways of representing dimensions of our world connect with how we live and act in that world.[3] Our broad purpose in this book is to explore issues that center on the interaction between patterns of representation and of practice, connections at the interface of educational and cultural studies.

The studies in this volume illustrate how powerful and suggestive images and ideas about teachers, learning, and other aspects of schooling are constructed in the "texts" of various modes of popular culture. As a basis for further inquiry, these works describe important tendencies and patterns in the representation of aspects of schooling. This set of studies also provides examples of analytical approaches and strategies for thinking about the meaning of such patterns, raising questions about what mainstream popular culture contributes to the social context of understanding and action in and about schooling.

SCHOOLING AND DEMOCRATIC SOCIETY

We have suggested the value of inquiry at many levels exploring the relationship between popular culture and the schools. Such inquiry need not be esoteric nor highly specialized (although surely it can be informed by work that is). More critical is the widespread need to examine the vital link between forms of popular culture and the enduring place of schooling as a locus of moral and political significance in contemporary society. The interplay of these domains of interest is, in our view, of central importance with respect to considerations of schooling in the context of a democratic society.

Amy Gutmann has expressed succinctly the fundamental challenge of a democratic political culture, that of "conscious social reproduction."[4] At the very least, this notion entails people participating widely and intentionally in the process through which important influences on their lives, especially public institutions, are reproduced and modified over time. The vision of widespread, deliberate involvement in the shaping of public policies that Gutmann associates with democratic values provides a vital standard with which to assess the health of political culture. It is in light of this standard that popular culture warrants the fullest attention. A democratic society cannot be indifferent to the way common understandings of important social and institutional phenomena are formed, modified, and transmitted. The challenge today is to understand more fully why democratic deliberations on matters of this kind are vital and in what ways they are problematic.

Schooling represents an important example of the challenge confronting democratic society. Why are questions about conditions affecting the quality of democratic involvement in and about schooling important today? The general contours of a response are evident. Schooling represents a massive investment of human and economic resources in America. Its precise effect on individual lives is incalculable, of course, but important kinds of influence are readily apparent. These include the significance of what is learned and not learned, insofar as beliefs and skills are concerned, and how such school learning affects the potential for subsequent learning. Beyond this, another kind of influence involves the effects of the hidden curriculum insofar as norms, habits, and expectations are instilled in the young. And schooling maintains a social role as a sorting and selection process connected to the social hierarchy of success and privilege that students encounter after leaving school.

While such effects on individual lives are critically important, they are not the entire story. The ongoing discussion of schooling is itself a central factor constitutive of the culture of which it is a part. The nature of social deliberation and discussion about what does and should take place in schools helps define the nature of the society itself in turn. In contrast to those institutions that are largely managed by powers remote from ordinary citizens, schooling represents a widely contested social territory to which large numbers of people in the culture have immediate access. Schools therefore provide vital sites where public deliberation and compromise can still take place, and in which wider community participation remains possible.

The question of how schooling is addressed by the public is therefore doubly significant. First, it matters how individuals directly involved think about schools because it will affect the shape of lives in a variety of ways, some of them subtle and typically unacknowledged. The second concern follows from this and centers on the viability of democratic political culture. Because schooling has far-reaching effects on the shape of individual lives, deliberations about what does and should take place in schools offer prime opportunities for the building of a healthy political culture. In short, if schooling involves education and not mere training or indoctrination, those involved with schooling—students, teachers, and other participants—must reflect upon what they are doing in schools. And if the society is to preserve and extend its democratic character, there are few sites more conducive to democratic deliberation and participation than its schools. To echo Gutmann, as an avenue of "conscious social reproduction," the quality of public deliberations about schooling may well be read as a measure of the well-being of the political culture as a whole.

Despite the widespread credence of these claims, however, many questions arise as to the quality of discourse about the institution of schooling and the conditions for its improvement. One thing seems clear: If we take a democratic ideal with respect to schooling to mean that all concerned, to the greatest possible extent, strive to examine their beliefs and attitudes about schooling as part of an open, deliberative process of engagement, we cannot be sanguine about the current state of affairs. No one involved in schooling can fail to grasp how far this ideal is from what actually takes place. The image of schooling at the center of far-reaching conversations within communities of care and respect bears little resemblance to the way the topic of schooling is generally discussed.

In a sense, the reason for the discrepancy between longstanding ideal and current reality is not hard to find. Everyone knows schooling inside and out; thousands of hours of acquaintance makes its characteristic patterns and rhythms familiar, a matter of common perception and understanding. What schooling means, what it is for, and how well it functions are subjects about which most people feel competent to speak. Much of what is said about schooling thus exemplifies an air of confidence. Opinions on schooling generally admit of few doubts, little ambiguity. This does not mean that all agree, of course. But from whatever perspective individuals speak about schooling, and whatever observations and conclusions they articulate, a felt need to be circumspect on the topic is rarely evident. Some students know "school sucks," for example. Many business leaders, pundits, and politicians likewise speak with utter assurance about "the school crisis." Schools are not doing what they are supposed to do, whether that means teaching Johnny to read or underwriting America's economic security, solving the social catastrophes of the cities, or whatever. Many concur that the problem is incompetent teachers or entrenched bureaucrats. Others point the finger at irresponsible parents, or a new breed of TV-addicted, junk-fed kids. There is a stridency in discussion about schooling that perhaps even exceeds that which is evident in other domains of public life.

Such stridency may simply be a product of familiarity. But this does not answer the question of why something as vast as schooling, as multifaceted in experience, as socially complex, should so commonly be reduced to the most simplistic, reductive, often dismissive terms. It is, after all, one thing for an individual to speak with self-assurance about particular experiences of school, even to find them emblematic of what schooling means for that person. But it is quite another thing to characterize glibly the whole of schooling one way or another, to pronounce judgment on its status and prospects. Yet this is commonplace.

The result is a babel of voices on schooling. There are numerous conversations one can join, each with its own take on what it is all about. From the variety of perspectives held by students and teachers to the diverse views of conflicting research traditions and interest groups surrounding schooling, fractures exist across the range of groups expressing thoughts on the institution. There is an intriguing paradox here. For while the welter of perspectives and orientations would seem to invite a healthy skepticism about the correctness of any particular view, doubt and openness are rarely voiced. What is lacking is twofold. Within particular orientations, what is lacking is humility: a willingness to be circumspect with regard to one's particular orientation to schooling as a phenomenon. And beyond this, as a society we also lack the ability to converse across the lines of our various positions and interests: a willingness to take alternative readings seriously with regard to the nature of what does or should take place in schools.

The question of why simplistic, formulaic thinking about schooling has such an appeal is thus a vital one. Within the various camps of thought, and between them, there is much to be done in trying to overcome the rush to judgment. What drives the process through which the complexities of schooling are unselfconsciously reduced to a slogan or slight? We would do well to set this question more broadly in the context of issues concerning the conditions for public deliberation. Consider, for example the work of Bellah and his colleagues. A central theme of their recent work, *The Good Society*, concerns the loss of public confidence in the institutions of contemporary society.

> Democracy requires a degree of trust that we often take for granted. . . . [In the United States] we have begun to lose trust in our institutions. . . . The heritage of trust that has been the basis for our stable democracy is eroding.[5]

Many citizens renounce the institutions on which they depend. While sometimes justified by particular circumstances, such renunciation provides no basis for the kind of deliberate engagement that Gutmann describes. It is more likely a recipe for detachment, anger, or cynical indifference.

Aligned with this is the set of changes that have taken place, and that continue, regarding what Habermas called "the public sphere."[6] His focus is on that "domain of our social life in which such a thing as public opinion can be formed."[7] For Habermas, the domain in which citizens may engage matters of general interest and shape public policy is, to the extent that it was realized, a historical achievement. But the very idea of such a domain is now threatened by what Habermas dubs "a kind of 'refeudalization' of the public sphere."[8] Powerful forms of "public relations" in support of policies favoring the interests of well situated individuals and groups increasingly takes the place of "the public use of reason" in determining matters of public policy. In this analysis, we find again that a condition of democratic deliberation is undermined, in this case by the way individual participation in public policy making is marginalized and manipulated.

These remarks capture aspects of an enduring tension that is evident in the deeply ambiguous history of schooling insofar as democratic values are concerned. Schooling has, from the start, been caught up in struggles between conflicting interests, at times responding to widely held democratic impulses while at other times taking sharply antidemocratic turns. This is evident, for example, in school policy struggles centered on the conflicting imperatives of capitalist development and democratic aspirations.[9] Put simply, schooling has functioned as a mechanism of social reproduction, a sorting machine closely tied to, and serving to legitimate and perpetuate, the social hierarchy of power and privilege in American society. But it is also a site where significant gains have been won as individuals and groups have struggled to make schools responsive to the needs of their children.

Public discussion of schooling could build upon an understanding of this problematic past, but rarely does it do so. Concerns of the kinds we have indicated, the crisis of confidence, and the fragility of serious and open public discussion of matters vital to human interests help to account for this. But that is only a start. Perhaps, as Jameson suggests, the vision of democratic deliberation is bound to become merely nostalgic within postmodern culture, a victim of global developments in "late capitalism."[10] Dislocating effects of such developments may indeed fragment human experience to the point at which efforts to define collective interests and promote democratic deliberation are empty, if not absurd. But if this troubling view is to be proved wrong, it is necessary to examine factors that contribute to the impoverishment of discourse about, and erosion of trust in, the institutions of modern society, including formal education. To do so requires inquiry concerning the way that views are formed, at various levels of engagement and interaction, about the central institutions of modern life. The quality of discourse about schooling is contingent upon how schooling is understood, the ways in which the multifarious meanings schooling has for diverse people are formed and modified over time. It is to this topic that we now turn.

UNDERSTANDING SCHOOLING

Coming to terms with how important patterns of social life such as those comprising schooling are understood represents a considerable challenge. Efforts to do so must take into account different and overlapping kinds and sources of meaning and how these interrelate to form what Bruner has recently termed the "folk psychology" with which individuals make sense of their lives. According to Bruner:

> All cultures have as one of their most powerful constitutive instruments a folk psychology, a set of more or less connected, more or less normative descriptions about how human beings "tick," what our own and other minds are like, what one can expect situated action to be like, what are possible modes of life, how one commits oneself to them, and so on.[11]

"Folk psychology" in this sense surely includes a healthy set of understandings regarding the abundant school experience most individuals in modern societies have undergone. The firsthand experience people have as a result of living and working in rule-governed classrooms and schools provides basic sense-making categories for understanding what the nature and purposes of schooling are. But these categories are further developed and informed by auxiliary sources of information and meaning that are brought into relation to them. An account of such sources must include, first, the varieties one encounters of hearsay, gossip, and anecdotal information regarding firsthand experience (the range of tales told about persons and events in school settings). Next, there is the prominent category of informed or expert opinion on the nature of schooling. This includes various forms of insight and opinion deriving from individuals claiming some privileged vantage point, such as school administrators in formal or informal reports, the comments of individuals recognized as experts on educational matters, and research findings published or presented in various scholarly formats and representing a variety of paradigms of inquiry and interpretation. Finally, we encounter references to and portrayals of schooling in the diverse forms and texts of popular culture.

Of the ways in which thinking about schools is stimulated and informed, the category involving representations of schooling in popular culture is perhaps the least examined and least understood. There are reasons to believe this must change. In this regard, an observation of Anthony Giddens is pertinent.[12] Modern society, Giddens suggests, is unique in part because of the extent to which identity formation is tied to events and activity perceived from a distance in space and time.

Increasingly, local attachments and affiliations are being supplanted by networks of remote associations that serve to define and affirm self-identity. As this occurs, the positions we come to and identify with are not the consequence of firsthand experience alone, or local circumstances. Rather, to an increasing extent, who we are and what we believe are profoundly influenced by distant events.

John Thompson has examined this development in close detail, relating it to a historical process he calls "the mediazation of modern culture." He traces the way media industries have

> shaped, in a profound and irreversible way, the modes in which symbolic forms are produced, transmitted and received in modern societies, as well as the modes in which individuals experience the actions and events that take place in contexts from which they are spatially and temporally remote. These developments are partially constitutive of modern societies, and are partiallly constitutive of what is 'modern' about the societies in which we live today. That is, part of what constitutes modern societies as 'modern' is the fact that the exchange of symbolic forms is no longer restricted primarily to the context of face-to-face interaction, but is extensively and increasingly mediated by the institutions and mechanisms of mass communication.[13]

Thompson's observation is important in the present context. When people speak of schooling, as when they address other phenomena of interest, it is increasingly likely that the source and genesis of their view extends beyond traditional boundaries of experience and insight. If tendencies toward crude reductionism and dismissiveness are evident, these are rooted at least in part in distant soil, mediated by images and ideas that have remote sources. The same is true for opinions that show critical insight or sensitivity, where these appear. The mediazation of culture feeds the pervasive tendency to form judgments about schooling writ large and to express these with conviction far beyond what firsthand experience alone would support.

As a result, whatever one's stake in schooling—as a student, teacher, administrator, policymaker, parent, or concerned citizen—what one believes about schooling is influenced in ways that simply did not exist, say, a century ago. And the same is true for all those one encounters, and sometimes contests with, who also have a stake in schooling. So teachers face students who feel "informed" about what teachers, far and wide, are all about, and vice versa. Similarly, relationships among peers and across the various levels and boundaries of institutional life feature this dimension of "knowingness." This comment is written by teacher educators; how often in our contacts with people working in some other capacity involving schooling, or in other fields altogether, are these relationships free of tacit judgments about the work we do? Relationships in and around schooling take place in a context of preunderstandings and expectations that shape, both enabling and constraining in particular ways, the possibilities such relationships contain.

The prejudging of others on the basis of their work or role did not require modern forms of mass media to come into being, of course. But what has changed is the extent to which the mediazation of culture provides people with a sense of connectedness to distant others and the rapidity, across this network of connections, with which one can gain remote affirmations of one's views about how things are (and, always possible, awareness of distant contradictions as well). We expect that anyone reading this book feels quite capable of expressing views not only about this or that local situation of schooling but about the grander picture of what schooling is like. And views of the latter kind are not built up inductively, piece by local piece, but involve leaps of judgment in which modern media play an instrumental role.

This book reflects the belief that what individuals learn at a distance by way of mass media sources is increasingly fundamental to how they think about various aspects of their lives. As Thompson puts it:

> In the course of receiving media messages and seeking to understand them, of relating them and sharing them with others, individuals remould the boundaries of their experience and revise their understanding of the world and of themselves. They are not passively absorbing what is presented to them, but are actively, sometimes critically, engaged in a continuing process of self-formation and self-understanding, a process of which the reception and appropriation of media messages is today an integral part.[14]

The process Thompson describes is deeply connected to how the nature and possibilities of schooling now come to be understood. Inquiry centered on such learning holds promise of entering into a central dynamic of educational and cultural development, as individuals form a sense of self and significant parts of their world, including schooling, in the context of the mediazation of culture.

EXAMINING SCHOOLING IN POPULAR CULTURE

Rich possibilities for inquiry emerge from consideration of how processes of self-formation, schooling, and popular culture intersect. In speaking about popular culture in the context of this work, we will focus on a dimension of this field of inquiry. While we have introduced Thompson's broader focus on the mediazation of modern culture—the entire process "by which the transmission of symbolic forms becomes increasingly mediated by the technical and institutional apparatuses of the media industries"[15]—we will concentrate on the symbolic forms themselves. In particular, we are using the term "popular culture" to refer to the symbolic forms transmitted by various media such as television, film, popular magazines, and music. The descriptive essays included in this book focus on widely distributed examples of such symbolic forms, what Paul Smith refers to as "popular cultural commodity texts."[16]

It is important to be clear on this point, for this focus represents an intentional, and possibly controversial, limitation on the notion of popular culture. As several commentators on popular culture have pointed out, work focusing on the texts of popular culture themselves runs the risk of making unwarranted assumptions about both their received meaning and their impact on the audience consuming them. A tradition of thought originating in the Frankfurt School, and exemplified in the work of Adorno and Horkheimer, has characterized popular texts as essentially ideological in nature, crippling in effect the possibilities for progressive social thought and development.[17] When focusing on the texts themselves, overextended interpretations of this kind are surely possible and do an injustice to the wit and insight of consumers of popular-culture texts and their capacity to construct meanings in their own ways. Such concerns are evident in recent work in cultural studies aiming to redirect attention to popular culture in a broader sense. In this regard, we acknowledge the dimension of popular culture John Fiske describes when he comments:

> Popular texts are inadequate in themselves—they are never self-sufficient structures of meanings . . . , they are provokers of meaning and pleasure, they are completed only when taken up by people and inserted into their everyday culture. The people make popular culture at the interface between everyday life and the consumption of the products of the cultural industries.[18]

Surely Fiske is correct in asserting the insufficiency of popular texts in and of themselves. Their content is not simply conveyed through a kind of one-way transaction, nor is their meaning in use determinable by looking at the texts alone. But care must be taken at this point as well, for, as Collins has remarked, it is possible to romanticize the open capacities of readers to invent fresh meanings for texts and create their own culture.[19] There is, as Thompson points out, a fundamental asymmetry in the communicative process:

> [U]nlike the dialogical situation of a conversation, in which a listener is also a potential respondent, mass communication institutes a fundamental break between the producer and the receiver, in such a way that recipients have relatively little capacity to intervene in the communicative process and contribute to its course and content.[20]

The various contents of widely available popular-culture texts succeed, therefore, as "provokers of meaning and pleasure," to channel and inform the understanding of persons with regard to matters treated in the texts. When particular topics and phenomena are widely encountered in popular-culture texts, attempts to understand them find a resource in those texts. Readers can surely recall examples of how some distant event or state of affairs has come to have a vivid standing in her or his mind by way of television reports, say, or a traveler's tale. This experience is commonplace, and accelerates with the pace of mediazation as daily life is saturated with images and information from all corners of the globe.

Schooling is one such topic, albeit a very large one, likely to be understood in ways that are at least in part beholden to popular images and ideas embodied in widely disseminated texts. The nature and significance of popular-culture texts in the understanding of schooling as a social phenomenon is, however, often discounted and not well understood. Set against other sources influencing the way schooling is understood, whether firsthand experience, hearsay, or varieties of expert opinion, popular culture is likely to be interpreted as something akin to cheap gossip or simply entertainment. This tendency ignores the way that the content of popular culture ultimately can be linked, we suggest, to questions of meaning, power, and pedagogy that are of central and abiding educational significance.

MEANING, POWER, AND PEDAGOGY

This book is addressed to readers representing diverse theoretical and practical interests. This intent is in keeping with the topic itself, focused on the interaction between, on the one hand, cultural forms that are widely distributed and participated in and, on the other, a social institution of some personal meaning to nearly everyone and wide social significance. Three broad questions suggest the scope of issues that arise within this framework.

The first question is how participation in popular culture influences conceptions of what schooling "is" and means. What schooling means for different people and the interplay of elements such meaning making involves are intriguing and significant topics at many levels. Important issues arise with respect to how popular culture enters into the way individuals conceive of the nature and prospects of schooling, constraining and enabling understandings of certain kinds. To what extent are common assumptions about the point and purpose of schooling underscored in popular culture? Be that as it may, popular culture also carries potential for provoking a rethinking of what schooling is about and what it might mean, how it affects people's lives, and why it needs to change. For these reasons, we contend that popular culture represents an underexamined source of influence with regard to the way people, including those who are directly engaged, do and might make sense of schooling in their lives.

The second question is an offshoot of the first. If indeed popular culture influences the way individuals make sense of school experience, the question arises how wider patterns of social interaction constituting the purposes, impact, and future prospects of schooling are affected. This is fundamentally a political question concerning the institution of schooling, and suggests the way popular culture relates to power relations in and around schools. The politics of schooling, understood broadly as involving the ongoing negotiation of contending interest groups concerned with the impact and direction of practice, is bound up in matters of meaning. At various levels—including the classroom, the school, and the larger community—interaction concerning what does or should take place is contingent upon how individuals involved make sense of the situation and of others taking part in it. Popular culture is not likely to be neutral here, but its impact across the many and varied sites at which power relations exist in schooling is unclear. How, for example, do forms of popular culture contribute to the way authority in the classroom is perceived and exercised or the way school policy debates are framed, conducted, and settled? Inquiry at many levels is necessary in order to understand how various forms of popular culture function as a factor in the power relations schooling unavoidably involves.

Finally, as the comments above suggest, there is reason to ask how the interaction of popular culture and schooling does or might affect pedagogical relationships, those centered on patterns of teaching and learning, in schools. As popular culture contributes to the process through which people make sense of schooling and how schools are governed, it very likely conditions pedagogical possibilities in wide-ranging and largely uncharted ways. For this reason, popular culture presents both challenges and opportunities to those who care about teaching. Aspects of popular culture may be quite corrosive with regard to the conditions for fruitful pedagogical relationships in schools, for example, by fostering stereotypes about, and undermining the morale of, teachers. But just as society creates and consumes images and ideas about schooling, it provides teachers in return with numerous texts and artifacts to explore with students, opening up a space for discussion about the familiar world and how it is represented in popular forms. There is great potential here for critical reflection as pedagogy takes account of the interaction between school experience and popular culture.

These three questions involving meaning, power, and pedagogy suggest both the scope of issues that the studies in this volume bear upon and the range of perspectives that link them. Potentially vital contributions to schooling at every level, and to democratic culture concerned with what takes place in schools, open by way of inquiry exploring the range of questions popular-culture studies involve, raise, and help to frame. For this reason, we hope to engage a wide array of readers in a process of inquiry, examining popular culture and its possible role in the formation and critique of beliefs and attitudes about schooling.

The collection of studies is divided into four sections. The first examines popular-culture texts created for and circulating primarily among an adolescent audience. Teen-centered films set in schools, rock-and-roll lyrics about school experience, and the presentation of educational matters in *Seventeen* magazine are explored. The second section includes studies centering on the way stories about schooling are covered in diverse mainstream informational media. These include the presentation of educational issues in *Reader's Digest* and the *New York Times* as well as the portrayal of dropouts in diverse magazines for the general public. The third section includes studies of schooling in the context of cinematic narratives set in educational settings. These include narratives about charismatic educators, elite prep schools, and persons struggling with disabling conditions. The fourth section includes studies suggesting the variety of popular modes, directed at diverse audiences, that feature an interplay of entertainment value and pointed, telling images regarding aspects of schooling. These include studies centered on schooling in mainstream comics and in cartoons aimed at a wide audience of educators as well as a study of what a week of television programming purporting to enhance schooling reveals about the relationship of schooling and television.

This set of studies in no way exhausts the possibilities for inquiry in this area. Indeed, our intent is quite the opposite. We hope here to open avenues of exploration and discussion at many levels. We believe that examining the portrayal of schooling in diverse popular-culture texts provides a way to extend conversation about the meanings and values embedded in school practices and experience. Critical examination of the content of popular culture promises to enrich the conversation by disclosing ways in which common understandings about the nature and direction of schooling are shaped, conveyed, and crystallized at different levels in and around schooling. Such conversation is, in the end, an antidote to complacency and the temptations of settled opinion. As Ariel Dorfman has commented, the need to examine deeply held views is easily overlooked:

> To get rid of old clothes, clothes that are comfortable, that wear well, that hold pleasant memories, is not easy. All too often our bodies have adopted to these clothes and taken on their form, their color, their smell. It is as if they had become our skin and we had been born with them.[21]

Many of the popular ideas about and images of life in schools, evident in diverse symbolic forms current in popular culture, are indeed comfortable. And they can be powerful as well, sometimes nourishing the imagination regarding what schooling is or might be and at other times affirming opinions that simplify, distort, or deny important dimensions of school experience. In any event, popular culture shapes the possibilities of what does and might take place in schools, by way of its impact on how we think about such things. For this reason alone, we would have to conclude that it is a good time to tune in.

NOTES

1. See, for example, Lawrence Grossberg, Cary Nelson, and Paula Treichler, eds., *Cultural Studies* (New York: Routledge, 1992); Frederic Jameson, *Postmodernism: Or the Cultural Contradictions of Late Capitalism* (Durham, NC: Duke University Press, 1991); and Henry Giroux, *Border Crossings: Cultural Workers and the Politics of Education* (New York: Routledge, 1992).
2. See, for example, Ben Agger, *A Critical Theory of Public Life: Knowledge, Discourse and Politics in an Age of Decline* (London: Falmer Press, 1991).
3. Arthur Danto, *Connections to the World* (New York: Harper & Row, 1989).
4. Amy Gutmann, *Democratic Education* (Princeton, NJ: Princeton University Press, 1987).
5. Robert Bellah et al., *The Good Society* (New York: Knopf, 1991), p. 3.
6. Jurgen Habermas, "The Public Sphere," in *Rethinking Popular Culture*, ed. C. Mukerji and M. Schudson (Berkeley: University of California Press, 1991), pp. 398–404.
7. Ibid., p. 398.

8. Ibid., p. 403.

9. See, for example, Martin Carnoy and Henry Levin, *Schooling and Work in the Democratic State* (Stanford, CA: Stanford University Press, 1985).

10. See Jameson, *Postmodernism.*

11. Jerome Bruner, *Acts of Meaning* (Cambridge: Harvard University Press, 1990), p. 35.

12. See Anthony Giddens, *Modernity and Self-Identity* (Stanford, CA: Stanford University Press, 1991).

13. John Thompson, *Ideology and Modern Culture* (Stanford, CA: Stanford University Press, 1990), p. 15.

14. Ibid., p. 25.

15. Ibid., pp. 3–4

16. See Paul Smith, "Pedagogy and the Popular Cultural Commodity Text," in *Popular Culture, Schooling and Everyday Life*, Henry Giroux and Roger Simon and contributors (New York: Bergin & Garvey, 1989), pp. 31–46. Also see Greil Marcus's model of "commodified culture-for-the-people" in his *Lipstick Traces: A Secret History of the Twentieth Century* (Cambridge: Harvard University Press, 1989).

17. See, for example, Theodor Adorno and Max Horkheimer, "The Culture Industry: Enlightenment as Mass Deception," in *Dialectic of Enlightenment* (New York: Seabury Press, 1972); related discussions in Jim Collins, *Uncommon Cultures: Popular Culture and Post-Modernism* (New York: Routledge, 1989); Giroux, *Border Crossings.*

18. John Fiske, *Reading the Popular* (Boston: Unwin Hyman, 1989), p. 6.

19. Collins, *Uncommon Cultures.*

20. Thompson, *Ideology and Modern Culture*, p. 15.

21. Ariel Dorfman, *The Empire's Old Clothes: What the Lone Ranger, Babar, and Other Innocent Heroes Do to Our Minds* (New York: Pantheon Books, 1983), p. ix.

adolescent protagonists and scenes set in school. Specifically, this study concerns the construction of images depicting adolescent autonomy and self-expression in relation to the spectacle of school experience. In chapter 2, "Education, Rock-and-Roll, and the Lyrics of Discontent," Gunilla Holm and Paul Farber examine mainstream musical expressions of views about schooling. The study analyzes the way rock-and-roll lyrics characterize school experience, as related to student longings for independence in a context of dependence. In chapter 3, "Learning in Style: The Portrayal of Schooling in *Seventeen* Magazine," Gunilla Holm examines the way images of and ideas about schooling enter into circulation by way of a popular magazine for female adolescents. In particular, this study centers on the relationship between the magazine's explicit educational messages, on the one hand, and its implicit messages about the greater importance of beauty, popularity, and style, on the other.

These chapters open topics for discussion and inquiry at many levels. At the level of schooling practices, there clearly arise the kinds of questions concerning meaning, power, and pedagogy that we have described in the Introduction. Consider, first, the process through which the formation of views about the meaning of school experience occurs. Such a process takes place over many years and is subject to diverse influences. Put most baldly, while many strive in schools to build relationships exemplifying constructive interdependence and trust, popular culture often constructs a world in which such efforts are absent or absurd. Teen heroes and models typically distance themselves from the school and most people in it. How does this vision of autonomy and distance from the goals, personnel, and practices of schooling influence the posture of the young with regard to their own standing in relation to the school? The question goes to the heart of issues concerning the conditions of cooperation and empowerment as well. How does the message of chic independence influence the building of relationships between teachers and students that extend beyond student complacency and grudging conformity? Teachers are sometimes empowering; schools do not always, or only, smother the interests of the young. But those who value and strive for the empowering possibilities must concern themselves with the conditions of trust and mutual respect that such learning requires. Popular culture is not neutral with respect to such conditions. This is why, finally, the pedagogical implications of this set of studies warrants consideration. A wide array of texts, including those examined in this section, provide educators with an avenue for opening topics of deep interest to students. As a source of alternative texts, forms of popular culture provide ways to engage the young in thoughtful reflection on texts that bear most directly on their experiences and desires. In addition, since many such texts construct an image of the world of schooling, they provide an especially powerful way to examine critically the process by which the social construction of meaning takes place. What would it mean for a genuinely concerned teacher to reflect with students on the way stereotypes about teachers and learners are formed and circulate? The range of implications that might extend from such inquiry is great.

In addition to in-school matters, this set of studies also has a bearing on the social context of schooling. Adolescent consumers of popular culture will not always be young (nor are all those consuming the texts in question now young). Attitudes and understandings formed about the nature and possibilities of schooling will be carried into future contexts concerning school issues. Much of what anyone thinks about schooling stems from personal experience, of course; but this does not dismiss the question of the interactive influence of popular culture. In particular, it is worth asking to what extent popular culture both stiffens dismissive attitudes about the culture of the school and opens avenues of potentially incisive critique. School culture may warrant the most negative of attitudes in some cases, but not always and not unequivocally. How does popular culture either limit or enable thoughtful attention to schools in a public that must support, and surely should monitor, them? The building of an audience for democratic deliberations about schools begins at an early age. Popular culture weighs in as it seeks and builds an audience in service to other, largely commercial ends.

The studies in this section suggest a range of questions and possibilities for further inquiry in and about schools. For one thing, inquiry is warranted regarding adjacent domains of popular culture geared to adolescent (or younger) audiences. It is an intriguing question, for example, whether and in what ways popular media directed toward younger children share characteristics of the materials examined in the studies presented here concerning teens. In addition, from the varieties of rap music to children's television there are multiple forms of popular culture constructing images and ideas about schooling. The scope of inquiry can thus be expanded along lines of the work presented here. Another avenue of potential inquiry involves a shift from the wide scope of this work to more narrowly focused, interpretive analyses of particular works of the kind we have surveyed. The studies included in this volume aim to explore a wide scope of works for interpretation, providing a context for more particularistic study. Hence, particular films, television programs, magazine articles, or music videos could be explored in detail, extending or challenging the analyses presented here. This kind of work is conducive to forms of inquiry concerning viewer/listener/reader responses to the content of popular-culture texts, and is especially pertinent to the exploration of pedagogical possibilities in this domain. This set of studies provides a context of issues and tendencies that will help to frame such ongoing critical inquiry.

1 Adolescent Freedom and the Cinematic High School

Paul Farber and Gunilla Holm

This chapter examines the relationship between personal autonomy and the school. This relationship is examined in two contexts. One of these is a theoretical analysis that raises questions and concerns about the troubled nature of the relationship between personal autonomy and schooling and suggests a difficult path forward. The other context is that provided by recent American films that construct narratives around images and ideas about the relationship of adolescent freedom and school experience. Examining this relationship in the two contexts provides a framework, then, for considering the interaction and significance of the two worlds of meaning.

FREEDOM AND THE CRISIS IN MODERN EDUCATION

Discussion about American education today includes a great diversity of views. Many of these, however, are myopic, polemical, or merely technical responses to socially and politically complex matters. Occasionally, however, more comprehensive and penetrating analyses surface. At such times, a fuller sense emerges of what is at stake and of the nature of the crisis we confront today in advancing human interests by way of the provision of education.

An example of the latter kind is found in a recent work of Robert Young. Addressing the crisis in modern education, Young notes, "[The] present struggle . . . is a struggle about the moral foundations of education, about its relation to the freedom of the individual and the purpose of the state."[1] Building upon the work of Habermas, Young finds this crisis embedded in the more widespread crisis tendencies found in advanced capitalist societies. Increasingly, members of society "look to governments and economic experts for explanations and solutions, only to recognize that both are relatively helpless. . . . The intrusion of governments, and their perceived failure to manage crime, poverty and the economy, leads to a crisis of motivation and meaning."[2] As the crisis deepens, Young continues, "fundamental assumptions of the democratic state, of the idea of the liberty of the individual, of the role of mass schooling in the education of an enlightened citizenry, and the like" are reexamined and placed in doubt.[3] In this context, Young's work provides a framework for examining these concerns and discussing the meaning and possibilities of emancipatory change.

The prospects for such change are not bright, however. As confidence in the progressive potential of institutions such as schooling deteriorates, important social trends gain momentum. The limits of democracy become evident. Paraphrasing Habermas, Young describes the social context in which change would have to occur:

> The mass franchise [is] a manipulated franchise, a product of the mass management of public opinion. The reigning personality type, which schools helped to shape, [is] one which [feels] at home in relationships of either domination or subordination, rather than mature autonomy and equality. The dominant mode of interaction in such societies [is] manipulation and the dominant character type [is] manipulative—literally proceeding as if people were things to be controlled by 'pressing the right buttons.'[4]

A particular kind of social science has been developed and put to use in this context as well.

> The appropriation of the findings of such a science by the advertising industry, by those who manage political campaigns and by an increasingly research-guided entertainment industry, was a bridge whereby [a] dwarfed vision of ethical and political reason entered the popular culture, providing social support for manipulative personal relations, thus completing the circle of limitation which has robbed advanced capitalism of its progressive possibilities.[5]

Still, Young does not despair in his analysis. Indeed, he suggests that society stands at the "threshold of a learning level characterized by the personal maturity of the decentered ego and by open, reflexive communication which fosters democratic participation and responsibility for all."[6] This claim is tied to the fragments of such learning that are already evident in contemporary society. The great problem is finding ways to further the development of such recognizably mature forms of learning and to institutionalize them. This would involve transforming institutional practices in keeping with the most progressive forms of learning.

This is a challenging task for educational institutions, since they are in the midst of what Young refers to as a "crisis of educational rationality." This stems from the fact that while education provides important examples of the kinds of learning that would take society forward, its history is also "a product of the one-sided development of our capacity for rational management of human affairs and rational problem solving."[7] As a result, the institution of mass schooling currently both contributes to the problem of society bent on managing lives and carries possibilities for fuller development as a vehicle for changes in the level of learning that society fosters.

But to develop its capacities as a vehicle of the latter, and critically needed, kind, the institution must solve the educational problem stemming from the fact that "as teachers have known for some time . . . [t]he school system is in the front line of loss of motivation and meaning." And it must solve that problem in spite of a larger sociohistorical situation in which modern democracies can be characterized in part by attacks centered on the very structures which "have already partly institutionalized greater social and personal maturity."[8] Readers familiar with current "school reform" struggles will recognize the truth of this claim with regard to the variety of efforts to limit or sidetrack progressive forms of learning that some reform programs contain.

Young's analysis provides a serious and comprehensive account within which to examine issues of individual freedom and the purposes of education. His perspective is, of course, subject to dispute on many fronts. Perhaps most contentious is his attempt to chart a course between the sentimental nostrums of neoconservative thought, with its empty pleas for a reestablishment of traditional values, and the varieties of postmodernist thinking that discount the very idea of progress as metanarrative excess. He asserts:

> The only way forward is through the present state of societal 'anomie' to a new, post-conventional maturity and a democratic reconstitution of popular culture as a culture of critical reconstruction.[9]

But what such a democratic reconstitution of popular culture entails and how it relates to currently prominent forms of popular culture are unclear. At the very least, Young's perspective suggests the significance of examining what those engaged in democratic processes of social change must contend with in the existing forms and content of mainstream popular culture. How, for good or ill, are the prospects for a "culture of critical reconstruction" affected by what presently circulates in and through mainstream American popular culture?

In order to examine this question in more detail, we will focus here on a relationship central to Young's analysis—namely, that concerning the role of schooling in the advancement of mature forms of individual freedom and autonomy. Young sees this relationship as highly problematic. This stems from the fact that schooling is constrained by an unavoidable double task:

> To resolve their own problems they must transcend their present incomplete and one-sided development, and they must also do this if they are to contribute to the solution to the problems of the society in which they are found. Conversely, their capacity to do this is limited by the immaturity of the society with which they are intermeshed and the corresponding limitations of the individuals which it has produced.[10]

The situation is therefore ambiguous and fluid. Developments in the institution of schooling can either contribute to or detract from possibilities for the realization of important forms of individual and collective human striving. From this perspective, what is at stake is the question of whether education will help individuals govern their own lives and, together, shape their own history. The participation of autonomous persons in a public process of this kind is what a culture of critical reconstruction is all about.

In contrast to this vision, we will explore the world of recent American films as they construct scenarios of individual freedom and its relationship to the school. By doing so, we can raise questions about and examine possibilities for the contribution recent films might make to the democratic reconstitution of popular culture of which Young speaks.

SCHOOLING AND THE IMAGE OF FREEDOM

The notion of "popular culture as a culture of critical reconstruction" is difficult to sustain in relation to recent films about school experience. During the 1980s American movies served up a host of images of adolescents. Youthful heroes on the screen accomplished many things, often in the shadow of the school. But perhaps reflecting wider social and political currents of an American society embracing the politics of Reaganism, their struggles and triumphs were depicted as a matter of individual zest and achievement. In films about (and presumably made for an audience of) adolescents, social institutions have no meaningful part to play in the lives of the central characters. They are, rather, a hindrance, spectacle, or mere backdrop to the important story of how individuals break away, express themselves, and get on with their independent plans.

An example of this is seen in John Hughes's film *Ferris Beuller's Day Off*, where one vivid and characteristic segment, spanning roughly three minutes, features the following: Ferris using his home computer to alter school records about his repeated absences while his nemesis, school disciplinarian Mr. Rooney, strives by phone to make clear to Ferris's mother how often he has skipped school; Ferris tootling playfully on a clarinet (saying he has never had a single lesson); a brilliant sketch of utter boredom as Ferris's stunned classmates sit in silence as their teacher drones on, answering his own questions as no one responds to his lame refrain, "Anyone?"; and, as we cut back to Ferris's home, Ferris joyfully dancing about to the theme of the old TV sitcom "Bewitched".

Ferris knows who he is, what he wants, and how to attain it. He is the very image of affluent elan, self-assured expressiveness, a free spirit. The contrast with the pathetic students who sit nearby his empty chair—let alone his superiority to the vindictive and petty Mr. Rooney and the stultifying and irrelevant teacher—could hardly be more plain. The movie is a celebration of Ferris's accomplishment in finding his own style and expressing himself; he speaks at times directly to the camera, allowing the audience to enjoy conspiring with him as he maneuvers to set his own course despite the fools who would keep him penned up.

Ferris exemplifies a common product, though an especially vibrant and widely pleasing one. He is youth on film, an adolescent defining and expressing himself, shaping his own life. This image captures aspects of diverse conceptions of freedom and personal autonomy. As Bergmann suggests,[11] the young (and anyone else who would be free) must grapple with the problem of gaining a sense of self, a sense of what thoughts, feelings, skills, and commitments, are most closely identified as one's own in order to experience freedom in their expression. Ferris is the essence of self-assuredness in this regard.

Freedom in this sense involves a secure grasp of what one's life is about and where it is headed. With this image in mind, consider the way Joseph Raz formulates the related notion of personal autonomy, saying that

> the root idea behind the ideal . . . is that people should make their own lives. The autonomous person is a (part) author of his own life. The ideal of personal autonomy is the vision of people controlling, to some degree, their own destiny, fashioning it through successive decisions throughout their lives.[12]

What is interesting with regard to this formulation is the extent to which Ferris overruns the qualifications that Raz carefully provides. Ferris is not *part* author but *the* author of his life, or so it would seem. He does not control *to some degree* his destiny, but controls it *thoroughly*, through the decisions he so effortlessly makes.

How typical is the image of Ferris Beuller in the cinematic construction of adolescent freedom and self-expression? We have examined this question with regard to mainstream American movies from the 1980s featuring scenes set in high schools, setting aside those that centered on an educator as the central character.[13] We sought first to understand how in the world of these films adolescent self-expression and freedom are constructed. What do adolescents express a longing for in recent American movies and what do they seek to do as authors of their own lives? In the following comments, we present an overview of what the central adolescent characters express and pursue as their goals, plans, and projects and how they express themselves and their interests in what they do.

First, when one considers who the adolescent protagonists are, the answer is readily apparent. They are mostly white, broadly middle-class males. More than half of all the films featuring adolescent protagonists focus on males, either as individuals or in groups. In only six of the forty-seven movies we studied were female protagonists featured prominently, while ten others featured couples or mixed-sex groups in roughly equal proportions. All protagonists were white. Interestingly, the lines are sharply drawn so that only rarely is it the case that males and females cooperate without coupling or romance, with *Pretty in Pink* and *The Breakfast Club* providing prominent exceptions.

Given this set of characters, then, what goals, desires, purposes, and commitments, do the youthful protagonists express? The students' goals, plans, and projects can be understood in terms of the following characteristics of the stories being told. First, a striking majority of the stories centered on goals, plans, and/or projects of one of two types. A large number of movies center on male characters looking for fun. *Bill and Ted's Excellent Adventure* exemplifies the spirit of many movies portraying the innocent escapades of adolescents. The *Porky's* series provides another example, one which focuses more on the possibilities of sexual adventure and good-natured ribaldry. Nearly as often, romance is the goal. Sometimes the stories involve both male and female protagonists exploring the problems and possibilities of romance, as in *Some Kind of Wonderful*. In other cases, movies center on either a male or female protagonist as he or she pursues romantic inclinations. *Lucas*, for example, portrays the romantic longings and struggles of an exceptionally bright and diminutive hero, and *Sixteen Candles* traces early romantic developments in the life of its young heroine.

A much smaller set of stories were about various struggles against particular obstacles or villains such as bullies, mean-spirited authority figures, and, in the case of *Mask*, the punishing effects of a physical condition. We would note also that stories constructed around struggles were not centered on conventional or formally organized games, contests, or sports for the most part, but were rather more idiosyncratic in nature. We will return later to this point. Where personal struggles are central to the story, a variety of plot devices are used. In some cases, the principal student-character or group is pitted in a struggle against other students. For example, *Three O'Clock High* features a mock shoot-out scenario tracing events leading to a monumental showdown between a good-natured, essentially ordinary kid and a bully of epic proportions. Poor or working-class students also struggle at times to gain an edge in a world dominated by conceited preppies. In *High School U.S.A.*, for example, the ordinary kid-hero has to win "his girl" from an obnoxious wealthy competitor. Likewise, in *Some Kind of Wonderful*, the mechanically inclined hero is enamored of Amanda, who for much of the story is focused on her own ties to the dapper rich boys in the school: she doesn't want a guy working in a garage. Similarly, in *Pretty in Pink*, the central character, a girl, struggles to overcome the social-class barriers separating her from the boy she desires.

Students also define themselves in terms of struggles with teachers, coaches, or the system itself. *The Breakfast Club*, for example, portrays the difficulties encountered by students who have been pigeonholed by the system in various ways and their struggle to gain a truer understanding of themselves. Less sophisticated struggles include Ferris Beuller's abovementioned battle with Rooney. In *All the Right Moves,* the star football player and his girlfriend negotiate the difficult terrain of overcoming a coach's unfair action concerning the player as it threatens their plan to escape the town they fear being trapped in, while in *Just One of the Guys*, the female protagonist uses an elaborate disguise to prove herself capable after having been a victim of a teacher's gender bias.

Finally, a few movies turn on the pursuit of self-discovery itself as protagonists seek to define who they are or express their unique perspective in some way; the challenge is to come to grips with who one really is. Both *Teenwitch* and *Teenwolf* work with the theme of trading away special powers in favor of being accepted as oneself and the struggle to get beyond superficial forms of success and popularity. Likewise, in *Heathers,* the ultimate challenge turns on the difficulty of shedding the false and destructive trappings of popularity and status in favor of more genuine attachments. There are, however, no stories about intellectual or academic pursuits (apart from the movies, not included in this survey, which center on the character of a charismatic educator). In movies centered on students, study is at most a peripheral affair.

In short, if one asks how the interests, motives, concerns, and commitments of the adolescent protagonists are constructed in these stories, the general picture is not hard to see. Across social-class categories, we watch young, white, mostly male characters seek sex, adventure, or victory over some temporary obstacle. They want to have fun, gain experience (especially sexual), pursue romance, party, overcome whatever it is that is hassling them. The projects tend to be spasmodic, transitory, opportunistic, idiosyncratic. This cinematic construction contains silences and absences as well, of course. Minorities are nearly absent while females are clearly underrepresented. Female friendship is strikingly absent: There are no portrayals of groups of female friends pursuing plans together, while there are numerous cases of all-male groups doing so, albeit in very loosely structured ways. There is also an absence of cooperative activity over time or of males and females or mixed-race groups interacting in supportive ways. Similarly, there are few examples of plans or projects that take substantial time and represent lasting accomplishment. Structured, socially integrated goals are rare: there are surprisingly few teams, and no other forms of collective work within a structured domain of activity. Groups wander and hang out; they do not train, discipline themselves in pursuit of goals, or compete.

Finally, no supporting role in the plans and projects of the young is played by teachers, administrators, or the skills and knowledge learned in school. The role played by schools and teachers is virtually never a matter of purposeful intent or good will in response to individuals. Rather, to the extent that schools or educators contribute something to the plans and pursuits of the young, they do so only indirectly. Being compulsory, schools set the stage for certain forms of interaction as some odd mix of characters is cast together in school settings mostly notable for the diversions they allow or cannot contain. And what is especially striking here is the virtual absence of exceptions, where something learned is worth learning or even helpful; where teachers are genuinely supportive; where schools help form what students draw upon in expressing , or in some way forming themselves. Genuine self-expression is seemingly independent of what is learned in school; at most it is something that happens there despite, or in opposition to, the obstacles schools present.

THE SPECTACLE OF LIFE IN SCHOOL

The interpretation above suggests how recent films construct a world of adolescence in which the school is insignificant to the freedom and self-expression of the young. This view of the nature of adolescent freedom and its relation to schooling stands in sharp contrast to the kind of vision evident in Young's analysis, wherein the social conditions for individual autonomy are bound up in the fabric of institutional life. In the world of teen-centered films, schools are at most a kind of plot device in which certain actions are framed or generated by the location in school of certain figures in the action or of other circumstantial occurrences. As the young strive to be "authors" of their own lives, school experience is not a meaningful part of the script—never interrogated, examined, enlightened. It would seem to be simply a given, and best forgotten.

But this picture is incomplete. Cinematic high schools are not simply portrayed as ineffectual and irrelevant. The vision of the school includes large numbers of characters and events that are presented as memorable in some way. Typically, what is memorable in schooling is the spectacle of people or events that present themselves as something to endure, ridicule, or mock. The formulas are unsurprising. The films under review generate a plethora of spectacles concerning school events, settings, and formal activities. They also provide a spectacle regarding types of characters encountered in school, including those who would try to teach in or govern the institution, as well as the variety of types of peers that the principal characters must contend with or suffer under. The cinematic construction of these two kinds of spectacles can be described briefly as follows.

Consider the way movies fashion scenes of school settings and events. First, most of the movies in question include scenes of classroom life. Occasionally these scenes involve images of students who appear to be engaged in learning. For example, in *My Bodyguard*, students attend carefully to a teacher reading from *Romeo and Juliet*, and in *Mask*, Rocky engages his fellow students with a spellbinding account of the Trojan War. Much more common, however, are scenes of classes in which strange, sexually charged, or comic events transpire to provide some kind of spectacle. In *Student Affairs*, for example, a sexy female art teacher succumbs to the advances of the gym teacher, disappearing for sexual intercourse behind a painting while students are told to work individually. Or consider the prank in *Porky's II* in which pegs are inserted into a frog being dissected to make it appear to have an erection, or the scene of masturbation in typing class contained in *All the Right Moves*.

A contrasting kind of spectacle is provided by classroom scenes of notable dullness or regimentation. The example described at the outset, of the droning bore in *Ferris Beuller's Day Off*, is paradigmatic. Another is found in *I Was a Teenage Zombie*, where an English teacher asks a question of a student who has just gone out the window, notes his absence, turns disaffectedly to the next student, and carries on. Mr. Hand's class in *Fast Times at Ridgemont High* exemplifies the characteristics of regimentation as he lays out the rules with the demeanor of a drill sergeant.

In short, within this set of movies, classrooms are either settings for spectacle, including spectacles of dreadful dullness, or hardly worth showing at all. Sometimes they are a backdrop for action completely unrelated to what the class is about, but more often, film makers find other school settings more suitable for that role. Hallways, locker rooms, and cafeterias are the most typical settings displayed in cinematic high schools. In hallways, students neck (*Class of Nuke 'Em High*, *All the Right Moves*), smoke pot (*Homework*), discuss romance and posture for the opposite sex (*Valley Girl*, *Pretty in Pink*), and fight (*Some Kind of Wonderful*). Locker rooms are especially useful for conflict and peeping: The football star confronts his coach's unfair criticism and is kicked off the team (*All the Right Moves*), bullies torture and harass weaker peers (*Just One of the Guys*, *Lucas*), boys find ways to peep into the girls' showers (*Porky's*, *Private School for Girls*), and girls apply their makeup (*Sixteen Candles*). Cafeterias likewise provide settings for a wide variety of activity, from social ranking (*Heathers*) to fights (*Just One of the Guys*). Libraries also appear on occasion in movies, often as a site for oddity: In *Screwballs*, the female librarian reads magazines featuring male pin-ups, while the library serves as a space for detention in *The Breakfast Club*. Study scenes set in libraries appear in *Some Kind of Wonderful* and *Zombie High* (in which zombielike students actually hit the books).

The spectacles of school experience—what films construct as worthy of attention apart from the private pursuits of their adolescent heroes—are rather predictable. Fights and other kinds of violence, sex-related activity, and games and dances predominate in the movies set in schools. Movies in our sample focused frequently upon scenes of violence. These include the murder sprees that dominate the set of horror pictures (*Student Bodies*, *Prom Night*), more purposeful killing (*Heathers*), power struggles within a school (*The Chocolate War*), and showdowns with bullies (*My Bodyguard*, *Three O'Clock High*). A number of rape scenes appear as well, including the one in *I Was a Teenage Zombie* in which, prior to being killed, the victim seems to enjoy being raped by a monster.

The spectacle of sex-related activity takes multiple forms as well, including school scenes of intercourse, necking, and voyeurism. In some cases, the movie as a whole is scarcely more than a showcase for such scenes, as is the case with *Private School for Girls* in which a class scene centers on intercourse and talk of penises, dorm interaction focuses on who can get the guy, a couple makes love in the principal's office, a boy dressed in drag sneaks into the girls' shower room, and so on. The other extreme is the kind of movie portraying school as the setting for innocent sexual awakening, such as *Sixteen Candles*.

Dances and proms are the most common single form of school activity portrayed. As sites for spectacle, these settings include contests for the prize girl (*Karate Kid*), scenes of horror (*Prom Night*), and social-class tensions and romance (*Pretty in Pink*, *High School U.S.A.*). Expressions of cultural differences are conveyed in prom scenes as well, as in the example of *Making the Grade* in which Eddie, an impostor in the prep school from the poor side of town, starts breakdancing among the stiff preppies. Dances and proms are also commonly constructed so as to offer a site for the objectification of girls. The attitude is captured in *Making the Grade* when, to prep the lads for the abovementioned dance, the coach tells them, "Nipples are like plastic tabs on chicken; they pop up when they are ready." As objects of attention at the prom, girls (especially prom queens) are often defrocked or defiled, as in *Zapped*, for example, when Barney uses his magical powers to expose the prom queen at the dance.

Spectacles of spectator sports never involve a focus on the game itself, but are staged so as to frame the activity of protagonists extending beyond the confines of the game (*All the Right Moves*, *Johnny Be Good*). In *Lucas*, the football game provides a setting for the undersized star to prove he is more than bright and charming. Basketball likewise provides a forum for a test of character in *Teen Wolf*, as the hero, having used his special powers to become a star, emerges even more heroic on court when he plays the final game in human form. Football and basketball emerge as the most common games. Girls' athletics, however, do not appear.

Within this set of stock images and scenarios, supporting characters are constructed in ways which likewise tend toward the stereotypical and offer spectacles of various kinds for the characters with whom one is supposed to identify. Most students portrayed in these movies fall into ready stereotypes. Jocks and cheerleaders are most common, followed by preppies, bullies, and nerds (half of whom are science whizzes). Academically inclined or seriously rebellious or independent-minded students are very rare.

We noted above the preponderance of males as central figures in the movies, those whose freedom, plans, and projects formed the core of the action. In this regard, it is worth noting further the place and treatment of girls in the set of movies. There are a few movies with female main characters or with girls who are not portrayed as being preoccupied with boys and sex. The exceptions include *Just One of the Guys* and *Pretty in Pink*, movies noted above in the discussion of protagonist concerns. Even in these cases, it is worth noting that romantic longings have a significant place in the story line. In other cases, girls play a significant supporting role connected to the male protagonist, as in *All the Right Moves* and *High School U.S.A.*

More often, girls are not portrayed as having—or at least expressing—a thought. They are objects of attention and sources of fantasy and challenge for the principal male characters. Being popular and beautiful is very important, and can sometimes be accomplished through simple remedies such as removing glasses and letting one's hair down (*Mischief*). In *Teenwitch*, it is apparent that witchcraft also can help, although the young woman who has gained style and popularity in this way still expresses the wish to be loved for who she really is.

Female bodies, if not characters, are often part of the spectacle. Scenes are often constructed so as to showcase breasts or buttocks (*Senior Week*, *Screwballs*). More comprehensively, girls are treated as property, owned, and sometimes traded by males. They are not allowed to be with people other than their boyfriends (*Restless*, *Teenwolf*). Girls are given as prizes, as when prostitutes are used as a graduation present in *My Tutor*, or portrayed as giving themselves as consolation to boys who are unhappy (*All the Right Moves*). In *Weird Science*, two boys want to trade their girlfriends for a "perfect" computer-generated woman. *License to Drive* captures the spirit with a reference to girls as dessert.

In short, the tendency for most of these films to build stories around male protagonists coincides with a common presence of girls as objects of interest and spectacle. Much the same can be said of teachers. Teachers, like students, are cast and played in terms of readily identifiable types. Some of the tendencies are as follows. First, more movies feature teacher-characters who are excessively lame and boring than those who are managing to be reasonably competent. We mentioned at the outset the paradigm of drudgery captured on screen in *Ferris Beuller's Day Off*. A shop teacher in *High School U.S.A.* is another, summing up his own day's work in one scene by saying, "I've lived through another class." A chemistry teacher in *I Was a Teenage Zombie* speaks in a monotone to a class preoccupied with other things, such as flirting and climbing out of the window. In the same movie, an English teacher reads a poem, without expression, to a totally disengaged class. In some instances, ineffective teachers face not boredom but utter chaos, as in *Rebel High* or *Class of Nuke 'Em High*.

Second, many movies offer examples of the teacher as manager or, when concern for order is taken to an extreme, drill sergeant. Consider, for example, the finicky Mr. Hand in *Fast Times at Ridgemont High*, as well as the battle-ax Beulah Balbricker in the *Porky's* series.

Balbricker becomes a "just" victim of student pranks, as does the "Fraulein" in *Princess Academy* who expresses her orientation by wearing a military uniform and boots and is eventually humiliated by way of a student-delivered aphrodisiac.

Third, numerous scenes are fashioned around images of the teacher as sexpot or sleazeball. Female teachers, especially if they teach French, quite often appear sporting a combination of features including tight-fitting clothes, pouting lips, and seductive voices. The French teacher in *Screwballs*, for example, becomes so aroused by the act of pronouncing the French words for "tongue" and "lips" that she must excuse herself from the class to regain her composure. Other teachers are overtaken by uncontrollable sex drives, as in *Porky's*, which features a female gym teacher who loses all control once she has sniffed the men's locker room. School movies sometimes provide opportunities to see women teachers exposed, as in *Private School for Girls* and *Senior Week*. Male teachers, like their female sexpot counterparts, sometimes are tormented with uncontrollable desires, as in *High School U.S.A.* when the male biology teacher and female school nurse have intercourse in the broom closet.

Another type portrays the teacher as deranged or demented. The English teacher in *Senior Week* is portrayed as a woman possessed, in this case by the desire to track down a student who has been dishonest about schoolwork and gone off on an escapade to Florida with his chums. She pursues him in a mad-dash obsessive cross-country hunt. Teacher oddness sometimes takes less pathological forms, as in the nerdish science teacher in *Monster High* toying with strange, unidentified experiments as students sleep through class. Numerous teachers are simply sick of or sarcastic about their work.

The abundance of such stereotypes stacks up against the small number of cases in which teachers appear capable of engaging students in a discussion or holding their attention with regard to something being learned, and a still smaller number who can be said to exemplify some degree of care and concern for students they encounter. These are teachers portrayed as somewhat engaging and likeable, not so much spectacles as decent human beings. Among the teachers who engage their students in some meaningful fashion is a prep-school English teacher in *Class* who manages to make several meaningful comments on student papers in class. The science teacher in *My Science Project* effectively encourages his students to "do something . . . something unique." He holds his students' attention because of his obvious fascination with their projects, including the strange machine found by the protagonist of the story. On rare occasions, more mundane successes of teachers effectively communicating with students is evident, as when the English teacher in *High School U.S.A.* endeavors to bring *Romeo and Juliet* to life for her students with a comment about the fated couple being hot for each other.

The portrayal of school administrators follows the lines of the comments above. The most common administrator stereotype involves weirdness or perversity. The aforementioned Mr. Rooney in *Ferris Beuller's Day Off*, for example, suggests the extent to which cinematic administrators sometimes go in pursuit of their particular obsessions. Sleazeballs appear as well, as in the case of the principal who is turned on by female students (*Screwballs*).

Another sizable group of administrators falls in the category containing lame and weak figures: the principal as wimp. In *The Class of Nuke 'Em High*, for example, an administrator confronting a gang of brutes mutters a threat to put a note in their permanent record, and withers at their ominous reply: "We'll be back—we're the youth of America." The remaining administrators include a number who seem reasonably decisive and competent and a smaller group who are portrayed as fundamentally authoritarian figures. Examples of the former include the administrators portrayed in *Class* and *Lucas* who play supporting roles reflecting a kind of competent normalcy. The stern disciplinarian of *Three O'Clock High* reflects the face of authoritarianism in schooling.

In short, when the movies in question create school scenes with peers and educators with whom the principal characters must contend, they do so in ways that make interaction unlikely, if not undesirable. The types encountered offer predictable spectacles of oddness, lust, or revulsion. The message constructed seems to be that schools are not sites for a wider array of meaningful relations, nor a community that respects the differences of its various members. Most of what takes place, like most of those encountered, is worth considering only to the degree that it stands out from the range of day-to-day experiences and provides some kind of spectacle or amusement.

FREEDOM AND THE SCHOOL

Recent cinematic constructions of youthful freedom and the spectacle of schooling are problematic when viewed in relation to Young's vision of a popular culture of "critical reconstruction." It is certainly true that some movies do suggest, or even powerfully illustrate, features of school experience that warrant critique and transformation—we can refer again to *Ferris Beuller's Day Off* and its wickedly funny portrait of teacher-centered boredom. But as we have shown, such elements are embedded in stories that turn on other more central matters. And in doing so, recent American films construct worlds of meaning that erode the very idea of institutional reconstruction. Rather, these films centering on student protagonists exploit a tendency to think in terms of a sharp dichotomy between the free expression of the young and the ugly, perverse, or merely comical world of the school.

To return to the example with which we began, Ferris Beuller gives the appearance of defining and fully expressing himself at every moment. He takes advantage of what the world provides without ever seeming to depend on anything or anyone within it: Nothing is so important to him that he must worry about how it is provided and by whom. Freedom itself is what matters. The power of his personality is located in the fact that he resolves perfectly the tensions normally experienced by people striving to identify and express a sure sense of self in a world of tangled and interdependent relationships. For a modern audience made up of persons, especially young adults, entangled in complex—perhaps oppressive—patterns of interaction, Ferris's freedom is a wonderful and pleasurable escape. When he looks into the camera and confides in us, we sense that we can take off on the flight of fancy with him. For Ferris, the resolution of the problem of oppressive entanglements in a social and institutional milieu comes from the fact that he can blithely dismiss anything problematic and ambiguous. Schools, like families and other social institutions, clearly embody patterns of activity and interaction that stifle individual expression and which can damage the conditions of personal autonomy. Ferris soars free of these. He exemplifies life without compromise and the uncertainties of interdependence.

Ferris is exceptional only in his style. His standing as a young protagonist who knows and expresses his heart's desire, sharply distinguished from normal affairs and other people, especially from caring adults, is typical of adolescent characters around whom movies are made. While everyone must, in fact, define and seek to express a self embedded in the complex conditions of social and cultural life, cinematic conventions simplify the matter. The normal affairs of ordinary experience and the function of institutions are set to one side or portrayed as obstacles of the pursuit of free expression. As a common narrative device, this serves to romanticize the plight of the admired and intriguing protagonists who must carry the hopes of genuine self-expression (and therefore freedom) against the collective forces of numbing compromise and empty conformity. Freedom means cutting your ties.

By constructing this dichotomy, these film narratives embody a romantic conception of adolescence in which the young must struggle to define and express themselves over and against an indifferent or even hostile and oppressive world. As adolescent heroes, the protagonists are depicted as being on their own, and for the most part, they are superior to those who are caught up in the everyday world—including the world of the school—that is fashioned so as to warrant the rejection, mockery, or mere indifference it elicits from the characters central to the story.

The romantic conception of adolescence as a struggle to identify and express freely what is true to oneself has roots in common experience. Young adults can scarcely avoid the need to locate themselves in relation to the patterns of activity and constraint in which their lives are embedded, including schooling. Individual identity formation takes place necessarily in a social context. If this process includes an important place for freedom and the genuine expression of self, the belief that it does is itself socially constructed within the modern sociohistorical context. The romantic conception of adolescence embraces the notion of free expression while denying the social roots of, and conditions for, individual freedom. If our interpretation is correct, this is precisely what the movies described above tend to do. They are made in ways that satisfy, exploit, and profit from a widespread desire to dissociate individual style, interest, and self-expression, on the part of the young, from the social conditions (including the commercial film industry itself) that foster them. Hence, while schools, along with family and other social institutions, are bound up in the way conceptions of self are formed and in the possibilities for freedom that derive from the sense of self, such tangled, often problematic, relationships are dismissed and denied.

The ideological consistency is evident, but what should we make of it? In light of the reflections with which we began, we should note the impact of these stories with regard to the problem of freedom as an educational good, and the possible role of schooling in advancing conditions supportive of the educational project of the kind Young describes. First, if one believes that the young, as citizens of a democratic society, are entitled to be as fully as possible the authors of their own lives, then as Raz suggests, those who work with the young are obliged to supply such conditions as are necessary to make some measure of personal autonomy possible. This duty clearly falls upon educators (among others). Teachers, administrators, and other school officials are obliged, then, to attend to the self-development of the young—a matter of considerable uncertainty, delicacy, and difficulty in the best circumstances—and to support efforts to repair the frayed social ecology with respect to conditions vital to the development of genuine autonomy, including tolerance and basic respect, nurturance, and support for diverse persons.

How these kinds of conditions can be advanced, and the responsibilities of educators to the young defined and fulfilled is a matter of ongoing concern, requiring careful deliberation and inquiry. At the very least, the fulfillment of such aims (however provisionally) depends on the quality of relationships in educational settings. Following Habermas, Young is again instructive with regard to the central importance of the kinds of communication that exist in schools. To foster the conditions of autonomy is to engage students in a process of uncertain growth, however subtly and inconspicuously. And related to this, stemming from the work of Nel Noddings, for example, is the helpful attention now being paid to the quality of caring that is or might be found in the context of schooling.[14] Ideas such as these suggest what direction reconstruction may take in schooling.

The ideological bent of recent teen movies, however, offers little to support such visions. Indeed, insofar as the project of reconstituting relationships in the school is concerned, they seem, rather, to poison the well. The project of building more open, mature, and caring relationships in schooling can only be hampered by the ideology of youthful freedom we have described, a kind of crude libertarianism. Popular films offer stories in which virtually all forms of adult or institutional action are empty or intrusive, denying the social conditions of personal autonomy and undermining the precarious fabric of decent and trusting relationships that many struggle to maintain in contemporary schooling. In commercial films, what matters is personal style and the idiosyncratic concerns of unique, detached individuals. This constitutes a message endorsing a lurch toward empty factionalism, what Gellner spoke of as "ironic cultures," in which individuals and groups divorce themselves from any sense of a shared system of beliefs and obligations and all efforts to judge their warrant.[15] Instead, the struggle to participate in public discourse gives way to the impulse to dismiss those we "cannot relate to" and pursue private, distinct horizons of freedom and satisfaction. There are, of course, exceptions to this rule, as in the case of *The Breakfast Club* in which diverse character "types" learn to communicate with each other, or in the way *Heathers* concludes with a scene of friendship emerging between girls portrayed as representing opposite ends of the spectrum of popularity and attractiveness. (It is worth noting that, in both cases, the evils and emptiness of "normal" school experience provides the context for these events.) Typically, however, adolescent-centered movies offer lessons in the importance of finding one's unique style and learning to distinguish between those characters with whom one can identify and the many who are not worth the time of day except as part of the spectacle.

This final observation should not be taken as a plea for film studies to "clean up their act" and produce more "uplifting" stories. Rather, we find the situation ripe for educationally constructive exchange. While the movies of this period construct a narrow range of images and ideas about the problems and possibilities of adolescent freedom and self-expression, this does not imply that the "reconstitution of popular culture" of which Young speaks must wait for Hollywood. In this context, we should note Fiske's suggestion that in thinking about popular culture, a distinction must be drawn between the variety of "texts" produced by the entertainment industry and the interpretations and uses of them that circulate widely.[16] In addressing the kinds of ideas circulating at this time in popular culture, the relationship of the crude libertarianism of popular films about young people to the problems and prospects in the institutions sustaining the life of the society is a vital topic for those embracing the educational challenge of our time to engage. As a starting place, educators could do worse than to examine the films of adolescence together with the young. They provide much to think about with regard to the pleasures they provide and what these suggest about the experience of adolescence and schooling. They also provide ways to address the impoverishment of their commercially driven vision and what is left out of the world they construct. If the very idea of public discussion regarding vital matters of public concern such as education is to be sustained, the cinematic construction of adolescence and schooling needs to be located in a conversation that is constructed so as to be more inclusive, and less harshly judgmental and divisive, than the story films have told. Ironically, the narrow world constructed in films opens avenues to a more encompassing, reconstituted conversation about the problems and purposes of schooling.

Such a conversation will not come easy. The movies we have studied construct a world of meaning which reflects the disdain for public responsibility, collective energy, and cooperative work for the public good that characterized American society in the 1980s. It has perhaps never been easier to dismiss the institutions of public life in favor of dreams of individual impulses and satisfaction. The struggle to achieve collective gains through the instruments of our public life, including schooling, is for many people today hardly an issue. As part of the social milieu in which the politics of education transpires, movies suggest indifference and cynical individualism, especially for the white, middle-class males whose fantasies of independence are most likely to be indulged.

For those working to advance some vision of the public good in schooling—working, that is, in the context of progressive and emancipatory ideas suggested by Young—one thing is clear. Mainstream forms of popular culture are not neutral with regard to such efforts. In the present case, a cinematic world of meaning is constructed which currently contains little space for the very idea of such a struggle and few terms with which to make sense of it. From an educational standpoint, what seems most clear is that the struggle to redefine and advance a conception of the good in education must address the deeper longings that commercial films play upon, and must find ways to satisfy them in the institutional settings of social life. It falls to schools to teach what these movies clearly do not: that finding one's voice need not imply standing alone.

NOTES

1. Robert Young, *A Critical Theory of Education* (New York: Teachers College Press, 1990), p. 3.
2. Ibid., p. 4.
3. Ibid., p. 7.
4. Ibid., p. 18.
5. Ibid., p. 20.
6. Ibid., p. 23.
7. Ibid.
8. Ibid., p. 23.
9. Ibid., p. 21.
10. Ibid., p. 23.
11. Fritjof Bergmann, *On Being Free* (Notre Dame: Notre Dame University Press, 1977); see also Maxine Greene's discussion in *The Dialectic of Freedom* (New York: Teachers College Press, 1988).
12. Joseph Raz, *The Morality of Freedom* (Oxford: Oxford University Press, 1986), p. 369.
13. The set of films studied were selected on the basis of their inclusion of scenes in secondary schools, and their availability on video within mainstream video markets. Sixty-two films in all were examined. This number excludes a set of ten movies which offer as their central protagonist a teacher or principal, a distinction that makes for a rather startling difference. For an account of these ten movies, see "A Brotherhood of Heroes," chapter 7.

With regard to the sixty-two remaining movies, forty-seven were found to feature adolescents both in school scenes and, critical for purposes of this analysis, as protagonists portrayed as being intent on doing or becoming something in the context of the film. In our analysis of what kinds of plans and projects were evident, we adopted a fairly charitable posture of interpretation in which a broad definition of what counts as a plan or project being expressed in the story was utilized: When the matter was in doubt we credited protagonists with intentions insofar as their cinematic activities were concerned.

14. Nel Noddings, *Caring* (Los Angeles: University of California Press, 1984).
15. Ernest Gellner, *Legitimation of Belief* (Cambridge: Cambridge University Press, 1974).
16. See John Fiske, *Reading the Popular* (Boston: Unwin Hyman, 1989).

2 Education, Rock-and-Roll, and the Lyrics of Discontent

Gunilla Holm and Paul Farber

> [A]s soon as I was old enough to emerge from the control of my teachers, I entirely abandoned my literary studies. Resolving to seek no knowledge other than that which could be found in myself or else in the great book of the world, I spent the rest of my youth traveling . . .
>
> —René Descartes

> We busted out of class,
> had to get away from those fools.
> We learned more from a three-minute record
> than we ever learned in school . . .
>
> —Bruce Springsteen

SCHOOL AND THE ROAD

Descartes expresses a view in his *Discourse on Method* that has found its way into popular song. It is a theme of modern times. While many now criticize the program of which his method was part,[1] the radical break with stultifying tradition reverberates across the centuries of modernity. For one who would seek the truth, the most important learning cannot be handed down in schools; traditional forms of learning are at best insufficient, and quite possibly an impairment. The goal is to see for yourself, make up your own mind. There is no substitute for firsthand experience and one's own wits. Where this combination leads will vary, of course. Descartes and Springsteen end up in different places, pursuing different ends. For one thing, Descartes returned to struggle with and help transform the institutions of learning of his time, though Springsteen (one supposes) has never looked back. But both suggest that one must break away from tradition-encrusted schooling to get on with what one must do as an autonomous being. Both speak a language of emancipatory, transformative experience beyond the authority of teachers.

This essay explores the theme of breaking away from the constraints of schooling as it finds expression in the lyrics of popular rock-and-roll songs addressing school experience. Our concern centers on the possibilities of emancipatory and transformative experience and how these relate to popular portrayals of contemporary schooling. In particular, we ask how prominent is the theme of breaking away and transcending school experience in popular songs about schooling. What other themes emerge? And how should we interpret the meaning of what songs say about schooling?

BACKGROUND: POPULAR MUSIC AND YOUTH CULTURE

This study centers on mainstream rock-and-roll songs from the late 1950s through the mid-1980s. Beginning in the 1950s, we can situate the study of popular songs in a context of youth culture. As Willis suggests,[2] early rock music has been regarded as the first sign of a distinctive youth culture. Rock music, in the view of some, has since become an international language for young people,[3] one that expresses opposition and rebellion to adult culture. Rock has also been seen as representing and focusing on a search for meaning in life[4] and as a way for teenagers to express and affirm their own culture.[5]

Another view of youth culture, encompassing a view of rock music within it, sees it as a response to deliberate marketing by the entertainment industry. However, even when seen in that way, the music is acknowledged to be a response to what the audience wants, as explored through marketing research.[6] There is a dialectic at work between the expressive force of youth culture and the manipulation and exploitation of youth by a rapidly growing entertainment and marketing industry. Responding to various parts of this process, observers of the nature and role of youth culture have engaged in a lengthy debate. In the eyes of some observers, the critical and rebellious perspectives of youth culture accelerate political change.[7] Others describe the way youth culture ultimately plays a role in recreating the status quo, even as it is critical of the status quo.[8] Further complicating interpretation of such issues is the observation that youth culture, as well as various other subcultural groups, exist within, and need to be analyzed in relation to, the dominant culture. Rock music is an expression of a subculture defined in part by its vigorous efforts to distance itself from the larger, constraining culture, a larger culture that also powerfully regulates the lives of those who consume and support the music. Major forms of youth culture, including rock music, are often generated, produced, and distributed under the direction of corporate sponsors and handlers. Important players in such industries have an interest in keeping wider societal norms and mores in place.[9] Hence, what we see in rock music is a popular and profitable attack on mainstream culture, though an attack that is not meant to achieve far-reaching change in society.[10] Instead, rock music is one avenue for youth to express resistance through personal or group style.[11] But even this resistance is, to some extent, dependent on the institutions that work to shape youth culture and group identity, and the audience of consuming individuals may not realize that they are reinforcing aspects of the social structure through the way they express themselves in everyday actions.[12] Nor is it apparent that the reasons for one's actions are not strictly a product of one's own thinking as a detached individual, but are themselves socially constructed.[13] These observations help explain how dependency of these kinds mutes the force of youth culture as a source of important critical understandings or transformative social ideals.

More recent work in cultural studies has sought to examine in more detail the meaning of the popular flow of images and ideas as they circulate among various individuals and groups within the culture.[14] A more fine-grained analysis of what is seen, heard, and understood by those engaging popular texts of various kinds promises revealing insights with regard to the significance of such texts in the lived experience of diverse persons. As work exploring the interactive processes of popular culture in the lived experience of the young proceeds, questions remain about the content circulated through forms of popular media such as the popular-music industry. As with other forms of widely distributed popular-culture products, songs provide a kind of raw material and provocation for meaning making on the part of listeners. Song lyrics make accessible a set of images and ideas about many things of interest to those who tune in. Some of these images and ideas involve school experience. This observation provides the basis for the analysis to follow. As a prelude to inquiry into the part popular songs play in the experience of listeners, we will explore what popular songs have placed into circulation over recent decades when they have taken up the topic of schooling. When lyrics turn to schooling, what patterns of commentary do they offer, and what meaning shall we make of the patterns we find? To these questions we can now turn.

ROCK LYRICS AND THE EXPERIENCE OF SCHOOLING

Despite its prominence in the daily lives of adolescents, schooling is not among the most common themes in the songs of youth culture. In an analysis of contemporary punk-rock songs, for example, Pomeray did not find that schooling was a prominent theme.[15] Rather, the four most common themes were political or social corruption, alienation, fear of nuclear war or military intervention, and personal responsibility, while the most common themes in popular songs were love, sex, rock-and-roll, and social issues. When schooling does arise in songs, schools are often portrayed as a background for the important social activities in their students' lives. Nonetheless, schooling has been an object of interest in numerous rock-and-roll songs over the years, and discernible patterns emerge with regard to its treatment in these songs.

In what ways have schools and teachers been portrayed in the lyrics of popular songs since the onset of rock-and-roll? Have there been shifts of perception over that time? Valuable work on these questions has been reported by Cooper.[16] For purposes of this analysis, we will follow and extend Butchart and Cooper's classification and discuss schooling in rock music in terms of "(1) images of teachers, (2) images of the formal content and processes of schooling, and (3) images of the school as a community and the center of youth activity."[17] In each area, we will describe the predominant themes that appear in a selection of forty-five songs—reviewed on the basis of their inclusion in previous discussions of these topics or their containing direct references to one of the three categories—and discuss the nature of discernible shifts in tone, content, or emphasis.

Images of Teachers

In most general terms, Cooper argues that teachers and principals "are neither admired nor respected" in the songs in question.[18] Student-centered songs portray teachers who do not understand what it is like to be young. They are described as being out of touch with the lives and problems of students. Teachers are often seen as mere rule-enforcers or, worse, preoccupied with efforts to undermine and ridicule students. Negativity is commonplace in comments ranging from early images of teachers as task masters to songs that convey far darker overtones regarding teachers as agents of a deadening socialization and conformity. The former image of teacher as boss is present, for example, in Chuck Berry's "School Day" (1957), in which the teacher is teaching "the Golden Rule, American history, and practical math," routinely enough. These efforts are not excoriated or mocked in the context of the song; rather, they are taken for granted and made less pleasant by the fact that "the teacher don't know how mean she looks." The shift toward more unsettling concerns about the very function of the teacher was evident in several songs. The Beatles, for example, sing in the voice of a person once victimized by teachers in "Getting Better" (1967):

> I used to get mad at my school.
> Teachers that taught me weren't cool,

> You're holding me down, turning me round,
> Filling me up with your rules.

Supertramp's "The Logical Song" (1979) expresses the complaint in terms of changes produced by teachers over the course and quality of a student's life. This song describes the moment when a child's sense of joy and wonder is superseded by being taught "how to be sensible, logical, responsible, practical," as he is molded for a "world where [he] could be so dependable, clinical, intellectual, cynical." Other songs simplify the matter to one of sheer hostility between teachers and students around the topic of rules, as in Alice Cooper's escape from school in "School's Out" (1972): "No more rulebooks, no more teacher's dirty looks." But whatever the role of the teacher is taken to be—taskmaster, socializing agent, or warden—the common sentiment, expressed forcefully in Pink Floyd's "Another Brick in the Wall" (1980), is an injunction: "Teacher, leave them kids alone."

While the comments above suggest the major theme in this area, there are occasions on which teachers are seen in a different light. One clear example, John Sebastian's "Welcome Back" (1976), stands out, in this regard, in its depiction of a likable person who answers the call to come back, as a teacher, to "where we need ya." It is exceptional, however, for as Butchart and Cooper point out, songs that convey positive images typically express admiration for teachers not because of how well they fulfill their educational obligations "but for their imagined erotic appeal."[19] This theme, too, has evolved somewhat over the years. Several early rock-and-roll songs expressed an innocent yearning for one's teacher. In "Mr. Lee" (1957), for example, the Bobbettes sing, "My heart is aching for you, Mr. Lee, 'cause I love you so and I'll never let you go." Similarly, in "Teacher, Teacher" (1958), Johnny Mathis voices a tender request: "Teacher, teacher, educate me with a caress." Such later songs as "To Sir with Love" (1967) continued this theme. More recently, instances of songs that carry a more overtly sexual appeal have emerged, as exemplified by Van Halen's "Hot for Teacher" (1984), a song which suggests an aggressively nontraditional reaction to the fact that "Teacher needs to see me after school." Teachers who are sex objects may be memorable, but they, like the teachers portrayed as harmful, are worth mentioning in songs increasingly for reasons having to do with their perversity.

Images of the Content and Processes of Schooling

As in the images of teachers, the descriptions of school content and the learning process have changed over time. Early rock-and-roll songs hardly feature a sustained tribute to the schools, but did sometimes indicate the value of what was learned in school. "Swingin' on a Star" (Big Dee Irwin 1963), for example, hints at the role of the school in terms of the possibilities of social mobility, noting that "if you hate to go to school, you may grow up to be a mule." And while Chuck Berry is not thrilled to be "working his fingers right down to the bone" in "School Day" (1957), he does express an attitude that suggests diligence with regard to school subjects: "Study 'em hard and hopin' to pass." Those songs that do sound a critical theme do so in ways that now seem tame, as when the Jamies exult in "no more dull geometry" in "Summertime, Summertime" (1958). Likewise, in Sam Cooke's "Wonderful World" (1960), the overarching sweetness of experienced feelings of love is set in contrast with what is not being learned in school:

> Don't know nothin' 'bout the Middle Ages—
> Look at the pictures and I turn the pages.
> Don't know nothin' 'bout no rise and fall.
> Don't know nothin' 'bout nothin' at all.

The lyric acknowledges the place of academic learning even as it declares the higher standing of romance as a focus of activity in school.

Such notions of the relative insignificance of school learning are supplanted in the early 1970s by a view that is harsher and decries the adverse effects of what is learned in school. A line from Paul Simon's "Kodachrome" (1973) captures the spirit of this kind of critique: "When I think back on all the crap I learned in high school, it's a wonder I can think at all." This orientation is developed by others in songs that range from those expressing a kind of reactive hostility to those that are more sophisticated and far-reaching in their critique. In the former category, outstanding examples of songs that harshly condemn and dismiss schooling include Alice Cooper's "School's Out" (1972), Brownsville Station's "Smokin' in the Boys' Room" (1974), and WASP's "School Daze" (1981), which summarizes the feeling this way:

> I'm here in a rage,
> A juvenile jail,
> and I'm here locked up in their cage.

More sophisticated criticisms can be found in such songs as Supertramp's "School" (1974). The lyric conveys the idea that students are locked in a struggle against those who seek to use school routines as a way to ensure the bleak conformity of "good boys." Those who give in are mocked:

> Teacher tells you stop your play and get on with your work
> And be like Johnnie—too good.
> Well, don't you know he never shirks.

The adversary who would enforce the school's regime is described as an ignorant agent of conformity:

> Don't do this and don't do that—
> What are they trying to do?
> Make a good boy of you,
> Do they know where it's at?

The perspective is echoed in Pink Floyd's anthem of profound discontent, "Another Brick in the Wall" (1979). The intent and nature of schooling is ugly and dehumanizing, a destructive factory of human conformity conducted by petty bullies in mean-spirited alliance with the machinery of the state. The lyric of resistance is widely known:

> We don't need no education,
> We don't need no thought control.
> No dark sarcasm in the classroom—
> Teacher, leave them kids alone!

A wide range of songs, then, disparages schooling as trivial and irrelevant at best or, what is worse, as a means for stifling what is best in students and instilling the worthless or deadening in its place. The point is not to learn in school but to survive it. The student does best to concentrate on what is truly of interest and look for the chance to get out of school and on with real life. Bruce Springsteen portrays the value of gaining release from school succinctly in the lines from "No Surrender" (1984) mentioned at the outset of this chapter:

School as a Setting for Youth Culture

Popular songs have expressed what surveys of student attitudes about schooling have long indicated,[20] namely, that students go to school to meet friends; teachers and classes are typically regarded as significant only by small numbers of students. School is the central meeting place for young people. The school provides the backdrop against which a variety of exciting activities takes place, a sense typified by Paul Simon's "Me and Julio down by the Schoolyard" (1972).

As a social setting in earlier rock-and-roll songs, the school has a somewhat innocent and carefree air. The antics of "Charlie Brown" (The Coasters 1959) take place in school, as do a number of more traditional activities. Songs celebrate a variety of activities including "Graduation Day" (The Arbors 1967), the culmination of a week's work in class with the Friday night dance in "High School U.S.A." (1959) by Tommy Facenda, and the pleasure that follows when you "let your colors fly," as the Beach Boys put it in "Be True to Your School" (1963). In the latter song, the Beach Boys express the value of having a school in which one can be involved and share pride, happily remarking: "What's the matter, buddy, ain't you heard of my school? It's number one in the state." Such songs credited schools with a role in providing a kind of local identity, a theme that has not been sustained.

The school and the classroom also form the background for the romantic relationships on which many songs center, as in "The Leader of the Pack" (1964). Dating is more important than being a good student and doing homework ("Hey, Schoolgirl" 1958). Indeed, the school is used as a backdrop for real living, as in the Jamies' remark in "Summertime, Summertime" (1958) that with the school year's end "it's time to live and have some thrills." Likewise, in "School Is Out" (1967), Cat Stevens addresses the possibilities of life that open at the moment school is left behind:

> We're coming out of school today
> And we're so happy to be alive.
> It's gonna be the best day,
> The best day of our lives.

By the early 1970s, the tone changes, as exemplified in Alice Cooper's lyric about the last day of schooling: "School has been blown to pieces" and is out forever ("School's Out" 1972). The climate no longer has the innocence of the earlier tunes, and a darker, angrier sense pervades many songs that describe the social side of schooling. The Ramones, for example, in "Rock 'N' Roll High School" (1979) "just want to have some kicks . . . just want to get the chicks." School is unfair and much depends on your family background, as in Supertramp's "Bloody Well Right" (1974). A good deal of what takes place in school is a social response to the burdensome rules and regulations ("Smokin' in the Boys' Room" 1974; "School's Out" 1972). And the sense of being trapped and confined like prisoners is unambiguously expressed in "School Daze" (1981):

> School Daze, I'm here doing time.
> School daze, my age is my crime.

The futility and the hopelessness described above in relation to "Another Brick in the Wall" (1979) colors all aspects of school experience. Schooling is too menacing, too destructive, too confining to be portrayed as the kind of neutral site of pranks and romance, let alone collective school pride, that it had been seen to offer before. The setting is more charged with dark and threatening characteristics. Hostility is on the rise, and the very idea that there might be some kind of beneficent purposes and possibilities within the institution has vanished from popular songs of school experience. Schooling seems not to lead anywhere and offers little that is memorable or worthwhile in its own right. It increasingly sounds like something rotten to be endured and forgotten.

BREAKING AWAY WITH RENÉ

What significance should we attribute to this survey of lyric portrayals of schooling? Specifically, we are inclined to ask how the tide of criticism and condemnation connects to the theme of emancipatory activity Descartes (and later, Springsteen) expresses in describing the need to seek and learn beyond the confines of a school. Descartes was no hermit, no wanderer. The breaking away he describes is part of his effort to transform the institutions of learning of his day. Perhaps the message of rock music contributes to similar struggles today, helping some to articulate and recognize the need to set one's schooling in perspective in establishing an autonomous perspective. The lyrics of discontent and resistance might in this way offer materials for thought and response and set the stage for new learning and the reconstruction of institutions. Descartes's method, calling forth individuals to develop their powers of critical reasoning and thereby to transcend the prevailing limitations of the institutions of their day, may find a surprising ally in the themes of popular song. But we should not rush to this conclusion.

Several points can be offered as to the meaning and significance of the lyrics of discontent with regard to schooling. In inquiring as to the significance of what we hear in songs about schooling and teachers, we find evidence that young people sense, receive, and, in turn, express through popular songs a very critical view of the educational system. Rock-and-roll songs consistently express profound distress with teachers and the content of their schooling. They mirror many of the deeper concerns that some school reformers have voiced for many years: Schools are devoid of meaningful content; students are disengaged from learning in classes they consider irrelevant at best; schools are bureaucratic quagmires, full of rules that serve no worthwhile purpose; genuine interest and significant learning and experience have little place in school. Students feel that they are simply doing time, fulfilling a duty by being in school. Overall, it is a pointless chore.

Why then put up with it? As a generation of students reared on increasingly sharp versions of these themes come into maturity, the critical messages embedded in their music may lend impetus to their desire to free themselves from an institution that they have found constraining, perhaps helping to build the consensus needed to transform it. A revolution in school reform may already be grounded in the shared sense of profound discontent evident in songs about schools.

While there are many reasons to wish this were so, such a sanguine interpretation raises many questions. In the following remarks, we propose an alternative interpretation and suggest what implications follow from it.

Rejections of Authority in Schooling

The kinds of doubt and dismay popular songs voice about schools are hardly unique; similar sentiments are expressed about other institutions, and by persons other than the young. Across society, widespread disaffection is expressed with the way institutions are managed. A crisis in confidence concerning the professions, government, and public and private institutions is frequently noted.[21] This raises a fundamental question as to why established relations of authority endure despite the deep sense of their dubious legitimacy. How are bonds of authority preserved in traditional patterns of activity when such activity is widely and publicly scorned?

Richard Sennett examines this issue in detail in *Authority*.[22] Here he discusses ways in which bonds of authority are preserved and extended beneath a surface of rejections. One pattern of rejection centers on what he dubs "fantasies of disappearance," a notion that is especially pertinent to our subject. As Sennett puts it, a fantasy of disappearance involves the belief that, in some setting that is unsatisfactory, "everything would be all right if only the people in charge would disappear."[23] Expressed in various ways, the fantasy of disappearance allows those who voice it to account for any and all deficiencies in the activity of which they are part. But more than this, it also makes it possible to carry on in a dependent role in forms of activity that are experienced as unsatisfactory or illegitimate. That is, the fantasy of disappearance is a kind of rejection of authority that simultaneously reinforces existing bonds of authority. Those who are in charge can maintain their control over, and typically without serious challenge from, those wishing them away.

But why would rejection of authority remain at the level of a fantasy and not erupt into actual challenges to authority in more cases? To understand this, we need to consider, in particular instances, why those who are subject to forms of authority that they privately doubt nonetheless depend on maintenance of the authority relation in question. In the case of schools, it is widely, and perhaps increasingly, evident that schools play a critical gate-keeping and springboard role in modern societies. For most students in school, it seems uncontestably the case that the school is a critical link to their future prospects in life—prospects, moreover, that in recent years are becoming increasingly tenuous and uncertain. Students know that their chances in life are bound up in a system with particular characteristics and standards of judgment. The exercise of authority in such a system is critical to them; it matters very much that one can satisfy the demands of authority in terms of conduct and learning. Authority figures are recognized as being in a position to pass judgment on how well students measure up to the standards that they maintain. Ultimately, students know that they are dependent on the continuance of existing patterns of authority if those patterns of authority to which they submit are to pay off as expected.

Given this scenario, it matters little that the authority to which one is subject is legitimate, so long as it is reasonably consistent and predictable in providing the conditions that allow one to take care of perceived needs. The school may consist of dubious rules and requirements, and it may demand a preoccupation with what seems trivial or irrelevant. Authority figures may be seen as essentially ridiculous in their demands and concerns. But they nonetheless provide a semblance of necessary order tied to the social and economic roles of the school. And so the structure and exercise of authority are given their due. Exceptions emerge, of course—indeed, large numbers of students reject the authority of school figures and drop out at some point. What many find in doing so, however, only serves to remind those who remain in school of the difficulty and danger they hope to avoid by staying in the game and doing what the school requires. Large numbers of students in American schools take this route, many of them in a state of perpetual disengagement from all but what is minimally required in school.[24]

For reasons having to do with getting on in the world, therefore, many students comply with school authorities. But the sense that the bonds of authority are not legitimate does matter at a deeper level. Our needs are not centered only on what we can achieve for ourselves in society. Relationships with teachers are not only exchanges of student compliance and work for teacher approval and recommendations (typically in the form of grades)—or rather, we would wish for them not to be only that. For, as Sennett suggests, human beings help construct authority relations because of a sensed need for strength and guidance. And where we are engaged in authority relations in which this need is not fulfilled, a reaction is predictable. In the case of authority relations in schools, like those in various social institutions, confidence in the strength and guidance of those in charge has eroded. But while the bonds of authority have weakened, the institutional fabric of sanctions and payoffs based on the judgment of authority figures remains in place.

The result is a situation in which students are inclined to preserve the system on which they are dependent, while simultaneously expressing the dismay they sense that those they depend on have not the strength or vision to take care of them. The fantasy of disappearance expresses this dilemma. Wishing away the authority of those who run the schools, students passively comply with a system of regulations and requirements that they do not respect. Rejecting authority, they learn to submit.

The songs we have reviewed provide one vehicle for the fantasy of disappearance. They typically express the sentiment that what is needed is to be left alone, that the best situation for learning is one in which no authority figure is present to stifle genuine experience itself with those like oneself.

Teachers in Authority Disappearing

The extent to which the fantasy of disappearance is present in the thinking of young people in and around schools and how it may interact with other dimensions of school experience are open questions. One suggestive piece of evidence regarding the appeal of such an orientation to authority in education surfaced in a set of interviews conducted by the authors with prospective teachers.[25] The interviews featured extensive consideration of the nature and sources of teacher authority in schools as these are perceived by preservice teachers. Two considerations dominated the discussion, and bear on the current subject. First, as reflected in the songs of popular music, teachers in schools, insofar as they are authority figures, are seen to be preoccupied with maintaining control, seemingly for its own sake. There were few comments about knowledge or positive values of learning and meaningful activity. Rather, to attain a standing as a teacher is to put on the mantle of control, to become what the songs often decry.

But while acknowledging this role as a grim necessity, the preservice teachers voiced yet more strongly a second theme. In their view of the matter, by far the most important source of one's standing as a teacher is one's ability to engage in lively, open, mutually respectful forms of interpersonal interaction. Nothing counts so much as one's personality, flair, humor, and the like. That is, these young people saw themselves as entering a position in which the key to their authority was, in effect, to appear not to have any. They seemed to see themselves operating in a very personal milieu, drawing from and representing little outside of their own interpersonal skills. In this they present, as their response to the institutional requirement they sense with regard to being in control, an expression of the fantasy of disappearance; they will exert control—because they must—but they will do it without appearing in the image of authority.

This example strikes us as indicative of the seductiveness of the fantasy of disappearance. In this case, the would-be teachers were, if anything, more tolerant than most regarding the schools, since they had all decided to return to them as teachers. Furthermore, they have all been engaged in the process of professional socialization into the roles and responsibilities they will soon assume in schools. That they are able nonetheless to harbor and express both the thought that authority in school is mostly about control and that they can exercise such control on the basis of personality and human relations suggests the nature of the problem of which rock songs are part. The lyrics of popular songs about schools and teachers contribute to a deeply escapist tendency of thought. They articulate the desire to dismiss, ridicule, or wish away authority figures whose controlling activity is accepted as a given in life. What this phenomenon does not include—and may even subvert—are the ideas that "the given" is a social construction that can be criticized and transformed and that critical distinctions can be drawn with regard to the way authority is exercised in actual practice.

SIMULATIONS OF REBELLION

The interpretation we have sketched above suggests that it is a mistake to assume that widespread, popular criticism of schooling either leads to individual emancipation or contributes to a climate of imminent change. Individual dependence on institutions and institutional resiliency are not so easily overcome. Indeed, according to this analysis, songs that capture the spirit of the fantasy of disappearance may actually contribute to institutional resiliency and make meaningful transformations more difficult to achieve. A pair of reasons can be offered in support of this claim. First, popularly shared fantasies of disappearance serve to deflect attention away from the reasons many people are dissatisfied with the arrangements that current patterns of school authority and power maintain. Such an orientation diverts critical attention from the root causes of discontent. Secondly, as evident in the preservice teachers' views, fantasies of disappearance undermine the transformative possibilities of personal and professional growth by encouraging an unrealistic view of what is given and possible. Genuine transformation in schools must build on what is best in our traditions of practice and on questioning the "given-ness" of every aspect of practice in order to preserve what we truly value in education.

It follows that, to the extent that the songs are correct in the force of their criticism and that something must be done to better the conditions for meaningful learning in school, the songs themselves—and other elements of youth culture, no doubt—must become an object of critical study. This is so because transformative inquiry and commitment cannot thrive in the atmosphere of fantasies of disappearance. The first step is to expose the appeal of such fantasies. For those involved in education, this activity has the benefit of providing a way to study how it happens that so much that is decried by so many for so long is nonetheless accepted as a given. A hard look at the fantasy of disappearance would open inquiry into the dynamics of this phenomenon.

As the climate of escape is confronted, both the elements of truth carried in the lyrics of popular music as well as their patent nonsense with regard to the critical issues in education can be explored. For those who teach, it is especially vital that they learn that, despite the tenor of popular appeals for authority to disappear, they must renew their standing as figures of strength and guidance; they must stand for something. The alternative, which the fantasy of disappearance helps preserve, is the kind of institutional patterns of authority which the teachers we interviewed hoped to master: no one seems to be in charge, but control still "happens" as we all passively submit to the pull of institutional life, humming songs of discontent along the way.

LIST OF SONGS REVIEWED

"Abigail Teacher" (Warner Brothers 5409)
by Freddy Cannon (1964)

"Alma Mater" (Warner Brothers BS 2623)
by Alice Cooper

"Another Brick in the Wall (Columbia 11187)
by Pink Floyd (1980)

"At Seventeen" (Columbia 10154)
by Janis Ian (1975)

"Be True To Your School" (Capitol 5069)
by The Beach Boys (1963)

"Bird Dog" (Cadence 1350)
by The Beach Boys (1963)

"Bloody Well Right" (A & M 3647)
by Supertramp (1974)

"Charlie Brown" (Atco 6132)
by The Coasters (1959)

"Don't Stand So Close to Me" (A & M 2301)
by The Police (1980)

"Everybody's Talkin'" (RCA 0161)
by Harry Nilsson (1969)

"Getting Better" (Capitol SMAS 2653)
by The Beatles (1967)
"Graduation Day" (Date 1561)
by The Arbors (1967)
"Harper Valley P.T.A." (Plantation 3)
by Jeannie C. Riley (1968)
"He's a Rebel" (Philles 106)
by The Crystals (1962)
"Hey Schoolgirl" (Big 613)
by Tom and Jerry (1958)
"High School U.S.A." (Atlantic 51-78)
by Tommy Facenda (1959)
"I'm Hot for Teacher (Warner Brothers)
by Van Halen (1984)
"Kodachrome" (Columbia 45859)
by Paul Simon (1973)
"Leader Of The Pack" (Red Bird 014)
by The Shangri-Las (1964)
"The Logical Song" (A & M 2128)
by Supertramp (1979)
"Me And Julio down by the Schoolyard" (Columbia 45585)
by Paul Simon (1972)
"Mr. Lee" (Atlantic 1144)
by The Bobbettes (1957)
"My Generation" (Decca 31877)
by The Who (1966)
"No Surrender" (Columbia 38653)
by Bruce Springsteen (1984)
"Rock 'N' Roll High School" (Sire 6070)
by The Ramones (1979)
"School" (A & M 3647)
by Supertramp (1974)
"School Day" (Chess 1653)
by Chuck Berry (1957)
"School Daze" (Magic 93000)
by WASP (1981)
"School Is Out" (Deram 18005)
by Cat Stevens (1967)
"School's Out" (Warner Brothers 7596)
by Alice Cooper (1972)

"Smokin' in the Boys' Room" (Big Tree 16011)
by Brownsville Station (1974)
"Society's Child (Baby I've Been Thinking)" (Verve 5027)
by Janis Ian (1967)
"Summertime, Summertime" (Epic 9281)
by The Jamies (1958)
"Swinging on a Star" (Dimension 1010)
by Big Dee Irwin (1963)
"Teacher, Teacher" (Columbia 41152)
by Johnny Mathis (1958)
"Teach Me Tonight" (Abbott 3001)
by DeCastro Sisters (1954)
"Teach Your Children" (Atlantic 2735)
by Crosby, Stills, Nash, and Young (1970)
"Terminal Preppy" (Alternative Tentacles 27)
by Dead Kennedys
"The 'In' Crowd" (Charger 105)
by Dobie Gray (1965)
"To Sir with Love" (Epic 10187)
by Lulu (1967)
"Wake up Little Susie" (Cadence 1337)
by The Everly Brothers (1957)
"Welcome Back" (Reprise 1349)
by John Sebastian (1976)
"Wonderful World" (Kleen 2112)
by Sam Cooke (1960)

NOTES

1. See, for example, Stephen Toulmin, *Cosmopolis: The Hidden Agenda of Modernity* (New York: The Free Press, 1990).
2. Paul E. Willis, *Profane Culture* (Boston: Routledge, 1978).
3. G. Mungham and G. Pearson, *Working Class Youth Culture* (Boston: Routledge, 1976).
4. Willis, *Profane Culture*.
5. J. Clarke, et al., "Subcultures, Cultures and Class," in *Resistance Through Rituals: Youth Subcultures in Post-War Britain*, ed. S. Hall and T. Jefferson (New York: Holmes & Meier, 1975), pp. 9–74.

6. M. Brake, *The Sociology of Youth Culture and Youth Subcultures: Sex and Drugs and Rock 'n' Roll* (Boston: Routledge, 1980).

7. L. M. Seagull, *Youth and Change in American Politics* (New York: Franklin Watts, 1977).

8. See P. E. Willis, *Learning to Labor* (New York: Columbia University Press, 1977).

9. Clarke, et al., "Subcultures, Cultures and Class."

10. Brake.

11. D. Hebdige, *Subculture: The Meaning of Style* (New York: Methuen, 1979).

12. A. Giddens, *Central Problems in Social Theory* (London: Macmillan, 1979).

13. R. S. Sigel and M. B. Hoskin, *The Political Involvement of Adolescents* (New Brunswick, NJ: Rutgers University Press, 1981).

14. P. Willis, *Common Cultures* (San Francisco: Westview Press, 1990).

15. R. P. Pomeray, "An Ethnographic Study of Punk Rock in Western Michigan: Identity in a Youth Subculture" (Master's thesis, Western Michigan University, 1986).

16. B. L. Cooper, "It's a Wonder I Can Think at All: Vinyl Images of American Public Education, 1950–1980," *Popular Music and Society* 9 (1984).

17. R. E. Butchart and B. L. Cooper, "Perceptions of Education in the Lyrics of American Popular Music, 1950–1980." *American Music*, (Fall 1987), p. 273.

18. Cooper "Vinyl Images of Education," p. 53.

19. Butchart and Cooper, "Education in Popular Music," p. 273.

20. See John I. Goodlad, *A Place Called School* (New York: McGraw-Hill, 1984).

21. See, for example, R. Young, *A Critical Theory of Education* (New York: Teachers College Press, 1990).

22. Richard Sennett, *Authority* (New York: Vintage Books, 1980).

23. Ibid., p. 39.

24. See Michael W. Sedlak, et al., *Selling Students Short* (New York: Teachers College Press, 1986).

25. Paul Farber and Gunilla Holm, "Preservice Teacher Perceptions of Teacher Authority in Practice" (Paper presented at the Annual Meeting of the American Educational Studies Association, Chicago, 1989).

3 Learning in Style: The Portrayal of Schooling in *Seventeen* Magazine

Gunilla Holm

The purpose of this chapter is to explore how schooling is portrayed in the magazine *Seventeen*. The magazine is widely read among young women and teenage girls. It has a long track record of giving advice and framing concerns regarding personal growth, career choices, and other issues related to schooling and female adolescent identity formation. This essay explores the nature of these messages and how they have changed between the years 1966 and 1989.

Little research has been done on magazines for teenagers nor on how teenagers read these magazines. Some aspects of women's magazines, occasionally including *Seventeen*, have been researched. Examples include studies centered on the type and quality of fiction[1] and on advertisement[2] in magazines. The portrayal of schooling has, however, never been the focus of a study of women's magazines or, more restrictively, teen-age magazines. More widely, in a survey of women's magazines from 1949 to 1980, Ferguson found that they had changed very little over the years. She argues that they continually support a cult of femininity, encouraging a focus on oneself and one's physical appearance with the ultimate goal of attracting a man.[3] While physical appearance is seen as important for occupational success, the most significant achievement is still finding the right man.[4] This focus on winning a man was also found to be common in a study of sports coverage in women's magazines, including *Seventeen*.[5]

In terms of their explicit content, the articles pertaining to educational topics that *Seventeen* published have tended to emphasize different sets of topics and concerns during different periods of time. The articles from the 1960s can be characterized as being infused with a spirit of activism. The articles of this time portrayed students as being involved actively, often with a critical perspective, in shaping their own lives and schooling experiences, as well as being active in relation to larger societal issues. This activism focused on such issues as racial integration, the creation of alternative high schools, and the building of schools in poor countries. Articles from the mid- and late 1970s are characterized by the influence of feminism. Articles proliferated that dealt with feminism and discrimination in educational institutions and with young women's educational and career opportunities. The 1980s might well be dubbed the time of narcissism. The focus is on the individual and how she can succeed in school with as little effort as possible. Absent from schooling is the concern for equity, diverse others, and societal issues.

Despite the shift in focus evident in the articles, however, *Seventeen* nevertheless presents a fairly stable general orientation for girls regarding education. And importantly, it is an orientation that starkly contrasts with mainstream rhetoric regarding the purposes of public education. The standard narrative account of schooling emphasizes its role, or at least its potential, in providing girls and young women with more equal opportunity, paths to work and careers, and conditions for serious engagement in learning that leads to personal fulfillment. Regardless of the changes in explicit content of articles concerning education over the years, *Seventeen* has been constructing a remarkably consistent counternarrative regarding the education of girls. *Seventeen* constructs a narrative in which "learning in style" is essential, and this means not only being fashionably dressed and stylishly beautiful but also learning to stay within the parameters laid out for the female adolescent. Conforming both with regard to looks and behavior is the key to success as defined by *Seventeen*. Being connected to a male is essential for success even in education and careers. Since leisure activities, such as reading *Seventeen*, may be as important as formal schooling for young women searching for their identity and educational prospects, it is important to examine what specific messages are given to female adolescents through the magazine. The counternarrative in *Seventeen*, through its focus on the cult of femininity, undercuts discussion about and encouragement of girls developing into independent and self-supporting women with careers. Hence, while the magazine deals quite extensively with schooling, its influence on girls' thinking about how education can contribute to who they are and what they might become is deeply problematic. In light of this, this chapter provides a detailed account of *Seventeen*'s counternarrative regarding the meaning of education in the lives of its readers.

READING *SEVENTEEN*

Seventeen is aimed primarily at white girls and young women roughly between the ages of thirteen and twenty-four years. The heaviest readership is drawn from girls in the lower grades in high school. In a study of 147 teen-age girls, Evans[6] found that *Seventeen* was the magazine read most frequently. He also found that a high proportion of the readers were subscribers. The more frequent readers tended to have lower academic status. The popularity of the magazine seems to be related to the clear focus of the magazine. The specific target group and the high proportion of subscribers might give the readers a sense of belonging to a group with which they can identify.

Like other teen magazines (or "teenzines," as they are sometimes called), *Seventeen* considers its focus to be on personal growth and self-improvement. However, Evans found the teenzines to be dominated by fashion topics, "feature articles, beauty care, entertainment features, and special recurring columns."[7] Evans also found that, of the magazines studied, *Seventeen* gave the most space to advertisement, almost 57 percent of the magazine's total space. Of the topics the teen-agers found most interesting, career and education features ranked twelfth, indicating that these topics were of marginal interest to them. The four most popular topics were sports, fashion clothing, horoscope, and dating and friendship. It seems that one reason that the magazines do not focus more on education is that it is not a topic that sells. It may not be an appealing topic for advertisers either. In the mid-1970s, when the number of articles focusing on educational and career issues for young women was the highest, the total number of pages in the magazine was at its lowest for the twenty-four-year survey period, due in large measure to the presence of fewer advertisements.

The magazine has been published since 1944, when the name was changed from *Stardom*. This analysis is based on the years 1966–89. The circulation figure was 1,384,357 in 1967–68, and had increased to 1,859,840 in 1989–90.[8] Every issue of *Seventeen* from 1966 to 1989 was scanned for titles indicating some connection to schooling. Such connections to schooling included articles dealing with schools, teachers, students, administrators, teaching, learning, subject matter, extracurricular activities, college and career planning. The articles on these topics were then read and coded according to the principal emerging topics. The five major classification categories that emerged included general schooling, interpersonal relationships, gender, looks, and consumption. Each of the major categories had a set of subcategories. For example, the subcategories for general schooling topics were how to succeed, practical issues in how to apply to college and finance a college education, majors and career choices, teachers, subject matter, student-centered concerns (such as school uniforms), and extracurricular activities. Most of the features and advertisements related to schooling appeared in the yearly back-to-school issue in the fall. There were, however, occasional features at other times of the year, such as prom articles and school-related advertisements in the spring.

SCHOOLING AS PORTRAYED IN *SEVENTEEN*

In articles specifically addressed to aspects of schooling in *Seventeen*, what topics and trends appear? Over the years, numerous articles have appeared raising questions about or criticizing various school practices and tendencies. First, numerous articles have conveyed and reinforced the impression that students are in school simply because they have to be, and that school work is not where real learning takes place. As one girl explained, for example, "Being a cheerleader gives me a reason for going to school" ("Cram Course for Cheerleaders," Sept. 1973, p. 115). An article against year-round schooling notes simply that "summer vacation can be the most creative period in a student's year" ("Year-around School? No Way," Sept. 1988, p. 161). In most articles over the years, the sense is conveyed, whether in a lighthearted or serious manner, that something is wrong with schooling. One implied reason for the dissatisfaction is that students have no say in their own schooling. One article suggests, for example, that an alternative system with minicourses has been proven successful "because everyone takes the courses seriously. Because students choose subjects they're interested in, lectures often produce spirited discussion" ("Is Your School Ready for Mini-Courses?," Aug. 1973, p. 46). As early as 1971, both students and teachers were criticized for negotiating about and being too focused on grades, especially since the grades do not seem to matter in the long run. This piece challenges students to work for personal satisfaction, not grades ("Are Grades Really Necessary?," May 1971). Another article, centered on graduation, raises questions posed by an 18-year-old student. Instead of having an empty graduation ceremony, she suggests that graduation is a time to evaluate school experiences or at least listen to the most interesting students speak and not necessarily to the class president or the class valedictorian ("Graduation Ceremonies Are Archaic," May 1971). A principal from Pennsylvania outlined in 1969 what is wrong with public education and how it could be changed. Among other things, public schools are seen as stifling individual creativity and intellectual growth. Schools are segregated and stratified, and follow an outdated curriculum ("A Little Bit of Rebellion Is Good for the Soul . . .

and the School," Sept. 1969). Finally, alongside, and in some cases evident in, the range of articles critical of schooling, the intrinsic worth of schooling was sometimes affirmed in the early years under review. During the late 1960s, for example, articles appeared discussing curriculum reforms and innovative, alternative high school and college programs—issues that were rarely entertained in later years.

This kind of relatively serious discussion of problems with public schools coincides with numerous frivolous counterparts. The trend towards articles conveying a more lighthearted or self-centered perspective on education has become markedly more prominent in the 1980s. Even though there is at least one article almost every year on how to succeed in high school or college, get good grades, or do well on tests, the number of these types of articles increased in the 1980s. A similar increase is noticeable regarding practical issues about applying to college. Such articles include stories on financial aid, college interviews, and college visits. This contrasts with and supersedes the discussion in the 1960s focused on issues concerned with making careful college choices in accordance with one's educational goals. This kind of deliberation included, for example, questions about private versus public institutions and about the nature of junior colleges. The more recent focus is on the importance of obtaining a college degree rather than on issues concerning a college education. This is further evident in articles on teachers. Before 1980 there was only a handful of articles on teachers, but since then articles on how to take advantage of teachers, how to "convince teachers you are smart" (1983), how to "fool a teacher" (1986), or how to "plot your way to an A" (1986) have become more numerous. In these articles we find, for example, that in order to look smart, a student should wear glasses and carry a newspaper and a dense book; to act smart a student should, among other things, "use big words" and cultivate an obscure interest and be very "obsessive about it—obsession is very intellectual" ("How to Act Smart," Aug. 1983, p. 223). In order to get an *A*, students should read the star guide (horoscope) about teachers in order to know how to satisfy them. For example, Gemini teachers love to talk and explain. To "thrill them: keep asking 'why'?" ("Teacher Feature," Sept. 1986, p. 156). The issue here is not learning or teaching, but a self-centered concern of the students, namely how they can be "successful" without learning. Another typology of teachers characterizes them as (1) Just one of the kids, (2) The dictator, (3) The professional substitute, (4) The nerd, and (5) The mom ("You Know the Type," Sept. 1986, p. 107). Such a typology plays on the possibilities students have to identify their own teachers as cartoonlike figures while taking no account of relationships with teachers whose work they might respect. Criticism of teachers and teaching is, however, not entirely a phenomenon of the 1980s. Already in the 1960s an article suggested that teaching is not something that is valued among students. In the article, presented as a discussion between six students, some of the comments about teaching were:

> "I do want to teach, but I don't want to become a teacher."
>
> "I would rather dig ditches because at least you can dig a different ditch every day."
>
> "I want to teach in college. I wouldn't like the day-to-day teaching grind of a high school teacher."
>
> ("What Makes a Good Teacher," Aug. 1966, p. 430)

These same students were asked if there were differences between male and female teachers. Only one student wholeheartedly thought they were equally capable. Other comments included:

> "Men teachers are more self-assured and they discuss things more freely. They are less inhibited than women. Our English department is made up mostly of unmarried women and some of them won't even read a poem about love in class."
>
> "A man cares most about success in his work, and a woman about success in her home."
>
> "I think a man tends to have more control of the class."
>
> ("What Makes a Good Teacher," Aug. 1966, p. 427)

In short, being a teacher is problematic, and being a female teacher is even worse.

One last category involves the nature of school knowledge. In one instance, knowledge attained in school is described as bits and pieces of more or less trivial information to remember. Examples of bits of information to remember, described in an article titled "Things Every High School Graduate Should Know," include three famous feminists (Margaret Sanger, Sojourner Truth, Betty Friedan) and three "smart cookies." These cookies are "Freud, Marx, and Einstein: All had beards, spoke German, and espoused unorthodox ideas about what's going on here and who's in charge" (June 1981).

In summary, articles in *Seventeen* have addressed education topics directly over the years, sometimes describing dissatisfaction with teaching and learning, while more often treating playfully, if not in fact trivializing, such matters. A theme underlying the discussion about schooling across the years is a sense of chic detachment. Occasionally this theme operates in articles calling attention to serious flaws in the way schools function, and sketches of alternative possibilities. More frequent is the approach that suggests that since one has to go to school, one might as well find ways to have fun and get good grades in the process. These comments from students, framed as "school year resolutions," capture the spirit of the predominant disposition.

> "I'm going to have more fun this year"
>
> "I want to gain weight."
>
> "I want to try harder to get along with my friends. . . . Also I don't want to get so mad at my teachers when they do stupid things."
>
> "I want to stop putting so much pressure on myself about schoolwork."
>
> (Aug. 1988, p. 201)

This orientation toward self-enhancement, commonly expressed in discussions of how readers can succeed in manipulating teachers for good grades, has become more prominent in recent years.

PERSONAL PROBLEMS AND INTERPERSONAL RELATIONS

Reading two and a half decades of *Seventeen*, it seems that personal problems and interpersonal relations have become more complicated and more numerous. Before 1977 there were occasional articles about how to survive freshman year and cafeteria food in college. In more recent years, nonacademic survival guides and advice have proliferated. For example, there have been articles on dorm-room decorating, a topic not mentioned earlier. How to get along with roommates is a frequently occurring topic. Current trends, such as co-ed dorms, are reflected in these articles. Interpersonal relationships with teachers were not discussed before the 1980s; but in this decade, articles appeared on such topics as having a crush on a teacher and sexual harassment by teachers.

While current research shows that relationships and feeling connected to others are very important to adolescent females, the interpersonal features in *Seventeen* rarely deal with relationships and friendships in-depth. Instead they seem to be aimed at assuring young women that they will be able to get along with their roommates and that eventually everybody will have dates, especially if certain forms of advice are followed.

Romance and dating are considered an integral part of school life. Girls are, for example, given advice by college men on what they like in girls. In an interview with Harvard freshmen, one student comments:

> I like to feel that I know more than the girl does about what's going on in the world. . . . I don't like to feel that I have to be talking about anything especially intellectual or discussing the war in Vietnam. I just want to be comfortable and easy with a girl. ("Five Freshmen at Harvard," May 1966, p. 155)

For this Harvard freshman, girls are recreational and preferably not too smart. Another freshman stated explicitly that "I want to be the boss" (p.270). Some years later, in 1977, a student gives advice to other girls that being too smart will create problems with friends and especially with dating ("Don't Call Me an Egghead," Sept. 1977). The parameters are laid out for girls if they want to fit in. There is no room in *Seventeen* for the kind of alternative female behavior that Roman, for example, describes in her study of punks.[9] And without dates and males, female students seemingly do not have an identity. In the 1980s there were also two dating articles dealing with a more serious issue—abusive and violent dates.

A second aspect of the romance theme is the prom, which was introduced in 1973 with the article "Prom Fever Is Back in Some Places." *Seventeen* contributed to bringing back the prom. Since 1973, sixteen articles have been published on the prom. Most of them are related to material pursuits such as what to do with prom dates and prom-dress contests, topics reflecting the commercial perspective of *Seventeen*. There are, however, a pair of articles questioning current practices regarding the prom. A prom drop-out describes her feelings when she realized she was not going to the prom because she had no date. Girls are also encouraged to break the traditional pattern by asking a boy to the prom.

A third aspect of the romance-in-school theme centers on sororities, which have been discussed occasionally across the years. In 1966 discrimination against Jews, blacks, and Catholics was discussed along with dating and friendship in sororities ("Sororities: Do They Still Swing?," Aug. 1966). In 1974 an article announced that sororities had made a comeback. In a survey of who was accepted in thirty-seven chapters,

> twenty said appearance counted. . . . If a girl has a really bad complexion and hasn't tried to do anything about it . . . that might prevent her from getting a bid. . . . [T]he rebel, 'the Jane Fonda type' . . . may find it harder to get into a sorority than one with more moderate views. ("Sororities: Is Sisterhood for You?," April 1974, p. 192)

The emphasis on relationships with men in school and college in *Seventeen* contributes to the magazine's marginalization of education for female adolescents. Such articles have tended to focus attention on matters that make serious learning, independence, and female friendships peripheral concerns.

SCHOOLING—A SPECIAL CONCERN FOR FEMALE STUDENTS?

The number of articles related to women's issues increases slowly in the 1960s and early 1970s, reaching a peak in the late 1970s, then nearly disappearing in the 1980s. The pattern here seems to reflect changes in the women's movement. When the women's movement entered the mainstream, it also entered *Seventeen*; and when the women's movement lost some of its momentum, the number of articles focusing on women's issues declined in *Seventeen*. Here I will discuss only those articles directly related to schooling, specifically articles addressing the kinds of problems girls might encounter in school. Are teachers and schools biased against girls? Are girls discriminated against? These are questions that had not been raised before in *Seventeen*. Many of the articles dealing with feminism in high school and college are among the most critical and detailed articles related to schooling. In "How Is Women's Liberation Doing in the High Schools?" (April 1971), a survey is given regarding the meaning of women's liberation, recent lawsuits by young women against schools, and forms of sexism in the schools. This article states that the reason that boys do better academically is due to the fact that girls are socialized to avoid being smarter than boys, since if they are smarter, boys will not like them. Tracking by sex is discussed, as is the omission of women from history textbooks. Sexism by teachers is also condemned. "High school feminists are opposed to 1) girls being *required* to take anything *because* they are girls, 2) girls being *prevented* from taking anything because they are girls, and 3) equal but separate classes " (p.180). (Yet even this article takes pains to point out that "most women's liberationists . . . have boy friends" (p.183).)

The subtle and overt discrimination a girl might encounter in choosing a career in law, for example, was discussed by Martin Margulias (So you want to study law, 1971). Letty Cottin Progrebin's 1975 article "So You Want to Be a Doctor!" explains the type of discrimination women will experience if they choose a medical career. She begins by discussing the societal pressure on girls to become nurses instead of medical doctors and moves on to explain the discrimination young women will face in medical school with almost exclusively male professors and biased textbooks. She also warns that this prejudice will still exist when they move on to hospitals and patients. A few quotes by 17-year-old girls illustrate both the prejudice and the determination of these girls to overcome the hurdles:

> When I was interviewed to get into the biomedical program, they asked me if marriage was going to stand in my way. Do they ask that of boys?
>
> I'm prepared to get discrimination both ways—as a woman and as a black. Especially in the field of neurosurgery, where there are few women or minority doctors.
>
> There aren't enough women in surgery. I'm going to prove that you don't need masculine muscles to be a good surgeon.
>
> (p. 110)

The debate about feminism and discrimination was carried out in various articles throughout the 1970s. A girl who has decided on a medical career emphatically states, "I've never played the role of a 'dumb female'. I value my femininity, but nobody is going to keep me from doing what I want just because I'm a woman" ("Paging Dr. Kathleen Makielski," Sept. 1974, p. 126). Other articles portray girls who are not concerned at all with these issues, however. The following comments from an article on "The Senior Mood" exemplify this tendency:

> I don't see myself as part of the feminist movement. . . . If something happened that was really unjust to me personally, that might get me into the movement. But nothing ever has. I believe in equality between all people, but I don't think the way to do it is by raising the women's power or raising the blacks' power. I just believe in being nice. (Jan. 1975, p. 104)
>
> I plan to go to college for at least four years. After that I'll probably end up being a housewife like my mother. I don't see myself in a career until my kids are out of school and don't need me anymore. I don't like working mothers. I'm not a women's libber. (Jan. 1975, p. 105)

Occasionally there are interviews with males, or comments from males writing in the "In My Opinion" column about these issues. Their views span the whole spectrum from statements to the effect that they want their wives to work because that was what they grew up with ("The Senior Mood," 1975), to "the liberated girl might best be treated as a gentleman might treat a pregnant lady: i.e, with great care and compassion, remembering that because of her condition she might be prey to strange cravings and odd desires" ("Liberated Girls Need Tender Loving Care!," Dec. 1971, p. 160).

Gender issues, such as the tension between traditional and nontraditional roles, are particularly common in articles on going to college and choosing a career.

GOING TO COLLEGE?

In 1966 (the first year of the review), readers received mixed messages on the question of whether to go to college. In the article "Do I Really Have to Go to College?" (Feb. 1966) reasons were given why it might be just as well for a girl not to go to college immediately after high school:

> Girls, unlike boys, have all sorts of opportunities for college education later in life—between marriage and motherhood or after the children are beyond infancy. . . . And women, unlike men, can change careers, once or several times, later on in life. They can learn to be librarians or social workers or editors or teachers in their mid-thirties. (pp. 36–37)

Finding a job—even if it is a dead-end job is pictured as a better choice than being unhappy about going to college.

> Doing a top-notch job as a library assistant or a dental technician or a receptionist or a sales clerk may give you, and other people, much more satisfaction than spending four years building an undistinguished record at an undistinguished college. . . . It is so easy to argue that these are "dead end" jobs—but they don't have to be. In fact, your success at such a job may convince you that you're "not so dumb after all." . . . [Is] a job a "dead end" if you really love it? ("Do I Really Have to Go to College?," Feb. 1966, p. 37)

This ambiguous stand in support of education for girls is reinforced as late as 1982—presented in the context of a debate on feminism—in comments by the conservative political activist Phyllis Schlaffly:

> I believe that of all the career choices a woman can make being a wife and mother offers the most love and fulfillment, the most long-range satisfaction, and the greatest potential for a lifetime of happiness. . . . I also meet other young women who have decided to have a baby or two but have decided not to take care of their babies. . . . Young women should prepare themselves with an education and a skill so that they will be able to support themselves if necessary. ("What Women Really Want: Two Contrasting Views on Feminism," May 1982, p. 190)

Hence, education is portrayed by some even in the 1980s as a back-up strategy or at least as optional for women.

If a girl decides to go to college, which type of college should she choose? Coeducation and women's colleges have been discussed over the years. In 1969, for example, an article presented important aspects to consider in choosing a co-ed college, including the observations that you have to look attractive all the time and there is an unlimited number of attractive men to date ("Coeducation: The Walls Are Tumbling Down!," June 1969).

The opinion on women's colleges changed across the years. A 1967 article pointed out that women's colleges may not provide you with the best education. It is difficult for women's colleges to lure "good teachers away from the more exciting atmosphere of the big universities. . . . [A]n all-girl class, though it is usually polite, obedient and receptive, is less interesting and challenging to teach than a coeducational class" ("The Women's College," Aug. 1967, p. 212). Articles focusing on the positive aspects of going to an all-female college began to appear in 1974 ("A Women's College Can Do More for You!," Oct. 1974). Among the reasons for going to a women's college were: (1) you don't have to look good and deal with men all the time, (2) students' academic performance is higher, (3) there are more women's studies courses, (4) the colleges are smaller, and (5) female students are in charge of clubs and student government ("Why All-Women's Colleges Are Better," Aug. 1975). The large number of women on the faculty serving as role models for students in women's colleges is also presented as a major reason for the increasing popularity of the colleges ("Why Women's Colleges Are Coming Back," April 1979).

Even though there are numerous articles on how to apply to a college, how to survive the first year and new roommates, and similar topics, there has not been consistently strong support for girls going to college. The support has increased over the years, but *Seventeen* has been careful to present an alternative view for those who do not want to further their education. Similar vacillation is found with regard to views of what type of career adolescent girls are encouraged to choose.

CHOOSING A CAREER—FOR WHAT PURPOSE?

There were numerous profiles of women in various jobs and articles on advantages and disadvantages of a variety of careers in the 1960s and 1970s. The career emphasis—and, indirectly the, emphasis on going to college to be educated for a career—is totally absent in the 1980s. This is especially remarkable given the backdrop of what was becoming known about the aspirations and plans of young women. Tittle, for example, found in the late 1970s that sixteen- to seventeen-year-old girls had sincere educational and career plans, and discovered that, while there were no gender differences in educational aspirations, girls were still more likely to choose traditional—and lower-paid—occupations such as service and nursing. In addition, 79 percent of the girls planned to work while their children were between three and twelve years old.[10] Indeed, by the 1980s, for most girls there was no question whether they should get an education and work,[11] but many girls remained uninformed regarding their choices and, in particular, the consequences of choosing most forms of traditionally sex-segregated work. Consideration of such topics fell out of sight in *Seventeen* in the 1980s even as the issues intensified for most girls.

This avoidance in the 1980s of the topic of women working was also found by Christian-Smith in a study of romance novels. She argues that few women could afford to live the life portrayed in the novels. In her study, the novels of the 1970s were most influenced by the feminist movement. The 1980s represented a shift back to the tendencies evident in the 1960s.[12] A similar pattern is found in *Seventeen.*

The careers discussed in the 1960s focused on traditional options and career paths: secretary, nun, airline stewardess, librarian, nurse, and teacher. In articles addressing the topic of women in careers, the value of the career is often presented in terms of the way it supports motherhood. For example, an article mentioning college teaching points out that a female professor can schedule her "teaching so it doesn't seriously interfere with" being a wife and mother.

> Perhaps more important, college teachers can move from one school to another much more easily than elementary or high school teachers. This means that if your husband's job forces you to move to another city, your own professional life isn't likely to be seriously disorganized. No matter where you move to, you're likely to find yourself within comfortable distance of a college that can offer you a full- or part-time teaching position. Not many career choices offer this kind of flexibility. ("What about College Teaching," Feb. 1967, p. 259)

In this way, even careers that are somewhat nontraditional are dealt with from a traditional point of view. A female mail carrier was unusual in the 1960s, but the discussion of that occupation moves again to relationships with men rather than the advantages of the job. One young girl stated in an interview that the job has "male as well as mail benefits" ("Face to Face with a Female Mail Carrier," Nov. 1969, p. 38). This way of discussing occupations and careers is probably quite appealing to young women, because, as Roman points out, in reality the private and public spheres in the lives of women tend to blend.[13] An article on nursing, for example, points out that nurses can take time off (for example, twelve years) to marry and raise a family, but, because the job is so interesting, they typically return to work ("The Career Where the Action Is," March 1968, p. 238). And while the piece states that marriage opportunities are not the main reason for choosing nursing, it points out that "nurses have the highest marriage rate of any profession" (p.238). This emphasis on women as homemakers, mothers, and wives has also been found in a study of fiction in women's magazines from 1940 to 1970.[14] Again in an article on secretarial work ("The State of the Secretary," March 1966), we learn a lot about how secretarial work and marriage fit together. There are places, such as hospitals, where the chances for finding a man are better because "very few secretaries marry their bosses" (p.229). Bosses, who are assumed to be male, want a secretary who is satisfied to stay on the job for a while, who is not looking for opportunities for upward mobility. After a woman has seen how a company works, "you may decide you'd much rather be a secretary than a designer" (p.229). Career advancement is actively discouraged here, it seems, because "after you've reared your children," you will be able "to 'go back to work' more easily than the woman whose specialized skills have either become obsolete or been taken over by automated machinery" (p.229). And what qualifications does a secretary need?

> Perhaps the two most important secretarial qualifications . . . are the ones that can't be learned in courses off by yourself: sensitivity to other people and a mature personality. The ideal secretary not only knows what is on her boss's mind at the same time that he does but knows also exactly how to behave in relation to him—that is, she knows the often subtle difference between reminding him about something and nagging him, between a helpful suggestion and butting into something that's none of her business, between an easy-going informality and uncomfortable intimacy. It is these qualifications as much as "efficiency" that makes for a long and happy relationship between the secretary and her boss. ("The State of the Secretary," March 1966, p. 230)

The tone changes in the early 1970s when marriage and motherhood are questioned as the main career choices for women ("Marriage and Motherhood Aren't for Everyone," July 1971). The societal pressure to follow this route is acknowledged though. Role models are provided in several articles. This follows a similar trend in women's magazines.[15] From 1975 to 1977 there is a significant push to encourage young women to go into nontraditional careers: the military (three articles), law enforcement (two), medical school (two), sports (three), radio and TV (two). Discussions about salaries and the differences between men and women are absent from articles both about traditional and nontraditional occupations and careers. The fact that women earn less than men, independent of education, job level, years of experience, number of years not employed (because of family responsibilities), or marital status,[16] was a topic that even the seemingly more progressive editors in the mid-1970s did not want to deal with. Similarly, discrimination in the job market was ignored as a topic. Even in the serious attempt in the 1970s to push nontraditional careers, many writers reverted to traditional modes of thinking, as in, for example, "New Careers for You in Law Enforcement" (March 1975).

> Because law enforcement today is detailed, technical and scientific, young women can work in police laboratories, fingerprinting divisions, identification, community relations, communication, juvenile bureaus—the list is varied. Women can now choose the kind of police work for which they are best suited. (p.76)

The basic message for girls is to go into law enforcement but stay off the dangerous work on the street. This is at odds with the picture, in the same article, of a policewoman on a bike. Similarly, in "New Military Careers for Women" (March 1973), there is no serious discussion of what it means to join the Navy. Instead, being in the Navy means going to Hawaii or traveling abroad and seeing the world. They go dancing, swimming, and shopping. During the day they work as secretaries. Marie, used as an example, "prepares papers and helps arrange appointments for the commander in chief of the U.S. Pacific Fleet" (p.126). Indeed, many of the nontraditional careers are portrayed as not noticeably different from traditional careers, such as those consisting of secretarial and clerical work.

It is in this area that we see the most change over the twenty-four-year period. In the 1960s, choosing a career that made it possible for a young woman to keep up with her responsibilities as wife and mother was acceptable. Finding a husband was very important. A woman's career had to be flexible. In the 1970s, the focus on marriage decreased in importance. Girls were encouraged to fight for what they wanted, to choose the career they really wanted, which might mean, for example, becoming a doctor instead of a nurse. But, even here, in many articles on nontraditional careers, the more traditional and frivolous aspects of a career were often emphasized. The absence of a career emphasis in the 1980s is surprising. The assumption seems to be that girls are free to choose what they want—career or no career—even though, as recent research suggests, such an assumption is not credible.[17]

CONSUMPTION

Seventeen has always emphasized consumption, but this emphasis has become more prominent in the 1980s. In taking advantage of the vast teen-age market, advertisers often focus on perceived needs related to schooling. The number of advertisements that used school themes and settings for selling products was the lowest in 1970–74. After that the trend picked up. Even though the number of school-related advertisements increased from twelve in the period 1970–74 to fifty in 1980–84, the greatest increase was in the number of pages on which advertisements were placed. In 1970–74, schooling advertisements appeared on up to sixteen pages per year. The number of pages on which such advertisements appeared had increased up to 194 per year in 1985–89 as more advertisers placed multiple-page advertisements in the 1980s. These advertisements, most of which appeared in each year's back-to-school issue, were analyzed with regard to how aspects of schooling were employed in selling products. The use of schoolbooks was interpreted to signify the presence of a school somewhere in the background. Sometimes this school was visible in the background (outdoors) or implied through a laboratory or library. The text usually signified that the product was useful for going back to school.

Not surprisingly, the advertisements discount education and suggest that for girls school is a place where looking good and impressing others with your style is what counts.

> "This fall's required reading: fashion footnotes" (Aug. 1976)

> "Lesson number one . . . study these smart new collegiate corduroys" (Aug. 1977)

> "Majoring in bottoms" (Aug. 1977)

> "Multiple choice knits. Just add, and attract. Zwicker plus you equals a second glance from guys" (Aug. 1978)

> "Go to the head of the class in smart looking shoes from Thom McAnn" (Aug. 1982)
>
> "If I can't go back to school in Adidas I won't go back at all. Face it . . . going back to school may not thrill you, but Adidas has something that will" (Aug. 1982)
>
> "Zwicker creative studies—the never dull fashion curriculum. Bonus for a clever girl—your highest marks—knits by Zwicker" (Aug. 1975)
>
> "Back to school bargains from BIC. A good lesson in arithmetic" (Aug. 1975)

In other words the school itself is of no real concern and all subjects are peripheral to the focus on looks and accessories.

> "Your back to school face kit" (Aug. 1982)
>
> "The subject is . . . face, eyes, nails/lips" (Aug. 1989)

These two advertisements emphasize the face, but most focus on clothes and shoes.

The advertisers' message is reinforced by fashion spreads and articles focusing on clothes and other things "needed" for going to school. Before 1978, there were only a few articles on clothes and such things as bags or school accessories. But starting in 1978, there were up to ten articles or fashion spreads per year on clothes, shoes, bags, and a variety of other things supposedly needed for going to school.

The emphasis on looking good is not limited to having stylish clothes and shoes. Makeup and hair care and styles have become more important in the 1980s. There is also more emphasis on managing your weight. Make-overs are quite common, because, as Smith argues, women's bodies are always pictured as being in need of improvement.[18] Adolescents are certainly socialized into this way of thinking at an early age, and *Seventeen* makes its contribution. Stereotypical images of women like these have been documented elsewhere[19] and proven resistant to change.[20] Intellectual pursuits and intelligence are often coupled with looking good. This is evident in stories such as those concerning what kind of clothes you would wear if you go to college ("Next Month, Leda Natkin, 18, Starts College—at Harvard University," Aug. 1980); the idea that being skinny is more important than intelligence ("Why Are Girls Obsessed with Their Weight?" Nov. 1989); "looking smart" ("School Spirit," Aug. 1983); and the importance of looking one's best "all day" ("My name: Julie Ann—Age:16—Occupation: Student—My Assignment: To Look My Best All Day," Aug. 1984).

Lewis argues that the department store and, later, the mall were conceived of as the great escape for middle-class housewives.[21] *Seventeen* helps to maintain this notion by grooming young girls to become primary consumers. Schooling becomes related to a product that is advertised and then consumed. There are no links to the intrinsic values of schooling. People buy a product because they assume it "will signify a certain social class, status, lifestyle,"[22] or some other desirable characteristic. As Lesko points out, beautification and consumption are very important in the formation of feminine identities.[23] *Seventeen* trades in images of solidly middle- to upper-middle-class style and status. The clothing style is upscale, with schools in the background looking like Ivy League or prep schools—high-status backdrops to successful consumption and appearance. For most of the girls reading *Seventeen* such images are part of what Pressdee refers to as "proletarian shopping"—the consumption of images rather than commodities.[24] It is very likely that most of the girls reading *Seventeen* are semiproletarian shoppers in the sense that they rarely, if ever, buy the expensive products, and instead often buy cheaper versions of the advertised products. It may even be the case, as Fiske argues, that such shopping can be a somewhat empowering and liberating activity, enabling girls to try out various identities by flipping through the pages of advertisements. When paired with actual shopping, the girls not only play into the interests of the advertisers but also control the images others, including certain important males, have of them. In this way, they gain partial control of themselves at an age when control is being slowly wrested from their parents. Similar expressions of independence through fashion have been documented elsewhere.[25]

Be that as it may, such images and patterns of consumption clearly distance the imperatives of style from the demands and possible benefits of education and intellectual effort. The emphasis on school fashion and looks strengthens the perception of schooling and success as products to be obtained through merchandise and grades; there is never a suggestion that one need be much concerned with learning about anything else.

CONCLUSION

While there are three discernible trends—activism, feminism, and narcissism—in the articles published between 1966 and 1989, the most compelling aspect of *Seventeen*, from an educational perspective, is the counternarrative implicitly running across the years. *Seventeen* explicitly focuses on style and fashion, but offers also a consistent pattern of messages which trivializes education and its ideal of full human development and wide opportunities for girls. Together these two characteristics are problematic with regard to how female adolescents are socialized into their adult roles. Importantly, while the feminist movement had an influence on the articles published in the late 1970s, it had no long-term impact on this counternarrative. Achieving the desired appearance and being successful at attracting males are more important than anything that can be achieved through learning and the nonsocial aspects of going to college.

The counternarrative also places an emphasis on relationships of particular kinds. Relationships are very important for female adolescents in their identity formation and even in their process of becoming independent.[26] *Seventeen* emphasizes relationships, but on a very superficial level centered on helping adolescents to fashion identities that will help them get along with roommates and dates. Strong friendships in school are not discussed. Even though primary attachments have been shown to be important to adolescents,[27] there is no discussion about the role of parents in adolescents' struggle with school or choice of careers. The educational interests and concerns of parents have no part in discussions of schooling.

Finally, the underlying orientation of *Seventeen*—that adolescent females should think of themselves and their future in ways closely tied to their relationships with males—sharply contrasts with the most recent research on female adolescents. As Mendelsohn has shown, for example, girls in an all-girl school experienced a clear sense of independence and freedom from the need to seek approval from boys.[28] Not harboring fantasies about a romance that would sweep them off their feet, the girls very much wanted to be independent and in charge of their own affairs. Such accounts represent well the progressive narrative of what schooling ought to provide for all students. *Seventeen* is encouraging quite the opposite with its ambiguous messages conveyed to girls concerning their relations to men as girls consider high school, college, and careers. Overall, female adolescents are provided a story of how to learn to become adult women within the confines of traditional, mainstream female roles, and this, in the end, is what a *Seventeen* education in "learning in style" is all about.

NOTES

1. E. Jensen, "Women's Fiction Today: It's a Fast Track; Writing for Women's Periodicals," *Writer's Digest* 56 (August 1976).

2. E. Goffman, *Gender Advertisements* (New York: Harper & Row, 1979).

3. M. Ferguson, *Forever Feminine: Women's Magazines and the Cult of Femininity* (London: Heinemann, 1983).

4. S. A. Basow, *Gender Stereotypes* (Pacific Grove, CA: Brooks/Cole, 1986).

5. J. Leavy, "Sports Chic," *Womensports* 4 (March 1977).

6. E. Evans, "Adolescent Females' Utilization and Perception of Contemporary Teen Magazines" (Paper presented at the Biennial Meeting of the Society for Research on Adolescence, Atlanta, 1990).

7. E. Evans, et al., "Content Analysis of Contemporary Teen Magazines for Adolescent Females" (Paper presented at the Annual Meeting of the American Educational Research Association, Boston, 1990), p. 8.

8. *Ulrich's International Periodicals Directory*, The Bowker International Serials Database (New York: Bowker, 1990).

9. L. G. Roman, "Intimacy, Labor, and Class: Ideologies of Feminine Sexuality in the Punk Slam Dance," in *Becoming Feminine*, ed. L. G. Roman, L. K. Christian-Smith with E. Ellsworth (New York: Falmer Press, 1988).

10. C. K. Tittle, *Careers and Family: Sex Roles and Adolescent Life Plans* (Beverly Hills, CA: Sage, 1981).

11. L. Weis, *Working Class without Work* (New York: Routledge, 1990); J. Mendelsohn, "The View from Step Number 16," in *Making Connections*, ed. C. Gilligan, N. P. Lyons, and T. J. Hanmer (Cambridge: Harvard University Press, 1990).

12. L. K. Christian-Smith, "Romancing the Girl: Adolescent Romance Novels and the Construction of Femininity," in *Becoming Feminine. The Politics of Popular Culture*, ed. L.G. Roman, L. K. Christian-Smith with E. Ellsworth (New York: Falmer Press, 1988).

13. Ibid.

14. H. H. Franzwa, "Female Roles in Women's Magazine Fiction, 1950–1970," in *Women: Dependent and Independent Variable*, ed. R. Unger and F. Denmark (New York: Psychological Dimensions, 1975).

15. J. A. Ruggiero and L. C. Weston, "Work Options for Women in Women's Magazines: The Medium and the Message," *Sex Roles* 12 (1985); L. A. Geise, "The Female Role in Middle Class Women's Magazines from 1955 to 1976: A Content Analysis of Nonfiction Selections," *Sex Roles* 5 (1979).

16. J. M. Nielsen, *Sex and Gender in Society* (Prospect Heights, IL: Waveland Press, 1990).

17. The AAUW Report, *How the Schools Shortchange Girls*. (AAUW Educational Foundation and National Education Association, 1992).

18. D. E. Smith, "Femininty as Discourse," in *Becoming Feminine*, ed. L. G. Roman, L. K. Christian-Smith with E. Ellsworth (New York: Falmer Press, 1988).

19. Goffman, *Gender Advertisements*, Center for Research on Women, Wellesley College, Wellesley, MA.

20. A. E. Courtney and T. W. Whipple, *Sex Stereotyping in Advertising* (Lexington, MA: Lexington Books, 1983).

21. L. A. Lewis, "Consumer Girl Culture: How Music Video Appeals to Girls," in *Television and Women's Culture*, ed. M. E. Brown (Newbury Park, CA: Sage, 1990).

22. A. A. Berger, *Media Analysis Techniques* (Newbury Park, CA: Sage, 1989), p. 21.

23. N. Lesko, "The Curriculum of the Body: Lessons from a Catholic High School," in *Becoming Feminine: The Politics of Popular Culture*, ed. L. G. Roman, L. K. Christian-Smith with E. Ellsworth (New York: Falmer Press, 1988).

24. M. Pressdee as quoted in John Fiske, *Reading the Popular* (Boston: Unwin Hyman, 1989) p. 16.

25. Angela McRobbie, "Working Class Girls and the Culture of Femininity" in *Women Take Issue*, ed. Women's Studies Group, Centre for Contemporary, Cultural Studies (London: Hutchinson, 1978).

26. L. Stern, "Conceptions of Separation and Connection in Female Adolescents," in *Making Connections*, C. Gilligan, N. P. Lyons, and T. J. Hanmer (Cambridge, MA: Harvard University Press, 1990) pp. 73–87.

27. J. P. Salzman, "Save the World, Save Myself," in *Making Connections*, C. Gilligan, N. P. Lyons, and T. J. Hanmer (Cambridge, MA: Harvard University Press, 1990).

28. J. Mendelsohn, "Step Number 16."

II FRAMING THE STORY

Representations of Schooling for the General Public

The nature and direction of schooling concerns all citizens to some degree and many people greatly. How such concerns are shaped and understood, however, is not obvious in most cases. While some citizens concentrate their attention on educational concerns close at hand—as a parent or a practitioner—most do not. Rather, as citizens, we keep in touch with and talk about what takes place in schools by way of various media. In some cases the medium is someone else with firsthand exposure to schooling practices, but often it is the various media of public information that provide a sense of what is taking place in schools. As is widely recognized, the channels of information that provide a sense of being in touch are not simple conduits of raw data but strong filters and shapers of what is news. Who, for example, is not aware of the "crisis" in American education today as a result of listening to the news or reading the newspaper? The actual conditions of teaching and learning may be hazy for most people, and yet few would deny having a fairly settled opinion on the general state of affairs.

In this section, we turn to studies of popular sources of information about aspects of American schooling. In particular, these studies examine print media that are widely presumed to be informative about, among other things, the state of affairs in schooling. The media in question provide works that seek to satisfy the desire to grasp what is taking place in schools. As the studies in this section suggest, numerous questions might well be aired with regard to the way informational accounts of schooling work to construct certain possibilities for public discourse and understanding about schooling. Questions arise as well concerning how such mediated understandings interact with other factors affecting persons, policies, and events in and around schooling. Practitioners and policymakers have a clear stake in how educational matters are treated in popular informational media, and, as these chapters suggest, so do others interested in public deliberation about schooling practices.

Three case studies are included in this section. In chapter 4, "Reader's Digest and the Mythology of Schooling," Eugene F. Provenzo, Jr., and Andrea Ewart examine the way that *Reader's Digest* represents school issues and teachers in articles appearing over the years. The analysis centers on the presentation of educational topics in terms of a narrowly defined ideology—one that deflects much of the responsibility for problems found within the schools from the culture at large and places it on the shoulders of teachers. Chapter 5, "The Image of the High School Dropout in the Twentieth-Century Popular Press," by Jeanne Ellsworth and Robert B. Stevenson examines how a wide array of popular magazines have characterized the phenomenon and framed consideration of both the problems involved and the young people themselves. Chapter 6, "*New York Times*'s Coverage of Educational Reform: The 1950s and 1980s Compared," by Ohkee Lee and Michael Salwen, examines the way in which the *New York Times* covered stories involving educational issues in two distinct periods of educational ferment. The clustering and characteristics of news coverage during periods of "crisis" are presented in this study.

Why does it matter that all concerned parties must rely on popular media for much of what they know about schooling? Consider, first, the significance of that observation from the perspective of the school itself. Popular coverage of schooling bears directly on the politics of education, particularly with regard to the central tension of school governance. This tension centers on the fact that schooling evokes and requires both some degree of professional judgment and control, on the one hand, and public—including parental—involvement on the other. The locus of control is always somewhere between these poles of interest and engagement. Because of this, it is important to recognize how popular sources of information frame issues and even provide a language for diverse participants to engage in the ongoing politics of schooling. The quality of deliberations regarding particular issues is conditioned by how such issues are posed and understood. In addition, the diverse parties to school governance also operate in the context of wider understandings about what takes place in schools, their range of general problems, and educational possibilities. Practitioners and the public alike rely on popular sources for a general orientation to school affairs. If there is a crisis or teachers are failing or the bureaucracy of schooling is contributing to mediocrity—or whatever else comes to be widely believed—such awareness provides a context for any issues of a more particular kind that might be addressed. Finally, and most broadly, popular forms of coverage of school topics reflect, and, in turn, generate anew, important attitudes and beliefs about the purpose of schooling and the characteristics of those involved. Public conceptions of what teachers are like, why students drop out, what schools are failing to do, and so on are crystallized in and reinforced by the process that socially constructs such matters in the popular informational media.

The studies in this section provide a starting place and suggest lines for further inquiry into such matters. One topic that comes into view involves consideration of issues of voice and access in popular-media accounts of schooling. Whose accounts are heard? What interests and points of view are less well represented or not represented at all in the kinds of stories examined in these chapters? In addition, further inquiry is called for that extends aspects of the analyses presented here into other informational media, including nonprint media such as television documentaries or short news spots. Finally, a range of intriguing pedagogical possibilities opens up with regard to critical study of how stories about schooling are constructed in various popular media, and what their content, as well as their silences and omissions, reveal about the social construction of meaning. Teachers and students share a world of practice that is represented in diverse forms of popular informational media. The nature of such representations and their role in framing, enabling, and limiting democratic deliberation about schooling can stand as object lessons in how public perceptions are formed and modified over time.

4 *Reader's Digest* and the Mythology of Schooling

Eugene F. Provenzo, Jr., and Andrea Ewart

The Chilean writer Ariel Dorfman, in *The Empire's Old Clothes*, has examined in detail the role that "industrially produced fiction" (comic books, mass-produced and -consumed children's literature, and popular magazines such as *Reader's Digest*) have played in shaping contemporary consciousness.[1] According to Dorfman, these works are by no means neutral:

> They constantly give us a secret education. We are not only taught certain styles of violence, the latest fashions and sex roles by TV, movies, magazines, and comic strips; we are also taught how to succeed, how to love, how to buy, how to conquer, how to forget the past and suppress the future. We are taught, more than anything else, how not to rebel.[2]

Dorfman maintains that by looking critically at our culture's popular literature, we are forced to look at ourselves in new ways. Making reference to the fairy tale *The Emperor's New Clothes*, Dorfman challenges his readers "to look at their own selves and their own society with eyes newer than their clothing."[3]

Dorfman devotes an entire chapter in *The Empire's Old Clothes* to the examination of the *Reader's Digest* as a social and cultural document. Although he reviews a wide range of subjects (foreign policy, colonialism, and so forth), he does not look specifically at how education, teaching, and schooling are depicted in the *Digest*. In the following essay, an attempt is made, using Dorfman's model, to examine how the magazine presents these subjects.

As Dorfman suggests, it is important to understand the way in which publications like the *Digest* function—"to strip them of their mystery, or lay bare their secret structures."[4] In doing so, alternative models of culture and education are revealed.[5] As a mass-circulation publication—one that not only reflects the culture that has created it but also shapes the attitudes of millions of readers—the impact of the *Digest* on the general public may be much greater than one may at first assume. The magazine provides its readers with what it describes as "the best of current reading." It gives the reader the impression that it has searched the world over to select articles that provide the right answers to contemporary issues. The *Digest* constantly makes reference to its objectivity and implies over and over again that it supplies its readers "what they need to know." As Dorfman explains:

> The *Digest* achieves what society cannot achieve in reality. . . . For one bubbling, fantastic instant, each person is transmuted into a know-it-all, without having to be modified by that knowledge, without conduct or practices being affected by its use.[6]

There is no recognition on the part of its readership that the information that the *Digest* presents may reflect a very specific and circumscribed point of view—a specific ideology—or that the content of the magazine may fulfill certain hegemonic functions.[7]

The *Digest* first began publication in 1923 and is the most widely circulated monthly magazine in the free world, with a total English-language circulation in 1984 of over 17 million copies.[8] It is circulated in numerous foreign editions and is translated into sixteen languages, as well as being available in large-type and braille editions.[9]

For the purposes of this study, we examined all of the issues of the *Digest* published during the postwar era (1945–1987). Our approach was straightforward. After having assembled the table of contents for every issue of the magazine from January 1945 to December 1987, we then selected any articles that dealt with schooling, elementary and secondary education, and teaching. In the case of regular features that appeared in the *Digest* (such as "My Most Unforgettable Character") each was separately reviewed to make sure that an article about some aspect of schooling or teaching was not overlooked.

On the average, two articles relating to some aspect of teaching or elementary and secondary schooling were included each year in the *Digest*. Some years saw a clustering of the publication of articles on education, while other years saw no articles on education published in the magazine.[10] What stands out about these articles is how remarkably consistent they were in their format and message over the course of the forty-two years of publication reviewed by the researchers. In reading the articles, unless they are identified by some specific individual or historical incident, it is often impossible to determine when they were written and published.

In this context, the message put forward by the *Digest*, as well as its function, is particularly worth noting. The *Digest* may play a much more consistent role as a vehicle of popular education and culture than has been recognized up until this time. This role, which extends over time and diverse geographical settings, is all the more powerful when one considers that the *Digest* is not a magazine that people are forced to read but one they seek out and read for themselves. It is a magazine whose format and content is spontaneously consented to by tens of millions of readers. In this context, it can be argued that the *Digest* reflects what are powerful hegemonic forces within the culture.[11]

Understanding the role of the *Digest* as an instrument of cultural hegemony is critical to the argument of this study. Like Raymond Williams, we assume that publications such as the *Digest* act as instrument of a hegemony that "saturates" our consciousness. In doing so, it encompasses

> a whole body of practices and expectations; our assignments of energy, our ordinary understanding of man and his world. It is a set of meaning and values which as they are experienced as practices appear as reciprocally confirming. It thus constitutes a sense of reality for most people in the society, a sense of absolute.[12]

Williams explains that

> hegemony supposes the existence of something which is truly total, which is not merely secondary or superstructural, like the weak sense of ideology, but which is lived at such a depth, which saturates the culture to such an extent, and which, as Gramsci put it, even constitutes the limit of commonsense for most people under its sway.[13]

According to Williams, one can understand a dominant culture only if one understands the social process on which it depends—that is, "the process of incorporation."[14]

This process of incorporation is inherent in the structure and organization of the *Digest* and its articles. In the following section, we look specifically at the content of the articles included in the *Digest* that deal with education.

EDUCATION AND THE *DIGEST*: 1945–1987

In considering the forty-two-year time frame covered by this research, we concluded that the *Digest* focused on two main themes related to education. The first may be called "What's Wrong with the Schools?" and the second, "Innovations and Reforms that Promise to Transform the Schools."

Under "What's Wrong with the Schools?" the *Digest* presents in various articles a picture in which the schools are failing to fulfill their duty. If students can't read or compete academically with foreign students, then we must blame teachers who can't teach or "bad" schools and their administrators who don't get the necessary job done.

"Innovations and Reforms that Promise to Transform the Schools" involves the presentation of ready-made solutions to the problems that face the schools and the teaching profession. This theme appears in articles about miracle-working educators and innovative and startling reforms that will revolutionize and transform the American educational system overnight.

The *Digest*'s division of its articles into these two themes and related subthemes allows it to fulfill the social functions noted by Dorfman:

> The reader who buys the *Digest* does it, among other reasons, to escape intellectual analyses. . . . He wants the world comfortably transmitted without previously having had to question it.[15]

In our reading of education-related articles published in the *Digest* during 1945–1987, there were no articles that examined the typical school and almost none that identified the school system in America as a highly complex social institution with both successes and failures. In the two following sections, we proceed to examine the main themes that the *Digest* did systematically present in its discussion of education, teaching, and schooling.

What's Wrong with the Schools?

An example of how the *Digest* presents the theme of "What's Wrong with the Schools?" is found in a 1947 article entitled "What Is Your Education Worth?" According to the article,

> the educational system of the United States has disappointed the world. . . . The reason, of course, lies in ourselves. . . . In the 19th century, the American red schoolhouse had a fundamental and uncomplicated purpose: to teach freedom.[16]

The essay continues:

> The century of the red schoolhouse was one in which knowledge and wisdom were esteemed and education was regarded as the greatest prize. . . . Thus the first failure of our schools is our growing inarticulateness. . . . Since our school system has failed in its most fundamental purpose, the teaching of articulation, it has altogether failed.[17]

The article concludes with the following advice:

> Let us, then, liberate our schools. Let us find, and pay for, teachers whom we can respect; and let us respect them—so that our educational system may cease producing self-infatuated, junk-loving child-adults.[18]

Despite its attempt to appear to be addressing the issue, the article really does nothing more than set the stage for blaming teachers for the alleged failure of the public schools. It is able to do this by first isolating one feature: the ideological content of education, which it deems to be inculcation of respect for the ideas of liberty. The "red schoolhouse," because of its loyalty to those ideals, produced

> men like Adams, Jefferson and Lincoln, who understood the philosophy of our Constitution, were able to enunciate it in words which cut into the very walls of time.[19]

There is no recognition of the fact that different historical epochs make different demands of its "heroes." According to the article, the schools have failed because they no longer produce Jeffersons and Adamses. By implication, this is because teachers today no longer respect and teach the old values of the Constitution.

A 1963 article, "Why Johnny Can't Get a Job?" states emphatically, "It is time to ask ourselves: What is public education for?" The article concludes:

> The lopsided picture of jobs begging for men while men beg for jobs suggests that something must be done to bring the two together. That something must be a new kind of schooling for today's needs.[20]

Somehow the lack of jobs, the failure to match men with work that fills their skills and what business needs, is a problem created by the schools and, in turn, the teachers and administrators who work in them.

This type of approach is repeated again in a 1971 article "Schools for Failure," whose author, Lester Velie, assesses the work of inner-city schools in Kansas City, Los Angeles, Chicago, Washington, and Philadelphia. He concludes that

> all [ghetto schools] are pushing out or graduating unprepared, lost youngsters. Failure is their most important product.[21]

No attempt is to made to analyze the failure of these inner-city schools in the context of the larger society. Everything is minimally analyzed and then only at the level of the schools themselves.

This characteristic use of minimal analysis on the part of the *Digest* permits the parcelling of issues into small and manageable units of knowledge. According to Dorfman:

> After opening the booklet we find on its title page a jumble of themes on the most diverse topics. It replicates a fragmented reality, reproduces the world's division in separate little parcels identical to those the reader is used to finding in his daily experience. Every area is clearly delineated and set apart from the others, separated from any possible global cohesion.[22]

This type of simplistic approach to the problems faced by the schools is repeated again and again in the *Digest*. A 1955 article entitled "Are Our Children Learning to Read?" isolates teaching methods as the cause of failure in our schools, ignoring such factors as home environment, racial prejudice, learning disabilities, and so on. It begins:

> At a PTA meeting in Boston recently a worried mother said: "I'm a college graduate. My husband is a lawyer. Yet our fifth-grade son can't pick up a simple book and read it out loud! What's the matter?"[23]

The child's failure to be able to read is seen as the school's fault. Its inability to teach the child to read is attributed to which method of teaching reading is used with its students—either the old-fashioned phonics method or the new sight method of instruction. The authors conclude that most "good" public schools use both methods.[24] After a discussion of how both methods can be integrated, a simple nostrum is presented to the reader by the authors: Follow the technical approach outlined in this article (i.e., use both methods together) and children will be able to learn to read without difficulty. As a result, the schools will become good again.

Another simplistic approach by the *Digest* included in a 1966 article on student level assignments announces that the failure of the schools is the result of misplacement.

> If you have a child in school today, the chances are about 50-50 that he is at least a grade ahead of the one he should be in. More, the consequences of this misplacement may follow him through his entire school career, even in college.[25]

The authors argue that many of the "problem children" who visited their clinic had

> only one major problem: they were adjusting badly to school. And in almost every case we found that the child had been started in school too soon.[26]

The authors continue their argument, maintaining that schools use chronological age or IQ to determine placement, ignoring what they consider to be the most significant measure needed, that of maturity. A simple solution or treatment takes a complex problem and solves it without any difficulty.

In the 1976 article "Why Johnny Can't Write," the failure of students to learn how to write is attributed to causes that range from inadequate grounding in the basics to the fact that the school curriculum no longer requires a wide range of reading. Television is cited as a contributing factor as well. The *Digest*, however, finally concludes that the primary problems lies ultimately with the teaching profession:

> Even the effects of television might be countered if students were required to learn the written language in the classroom. There, however, overcrowding and increased workloads have led many teachers to give up assigning essays and to rely, instead, on short-answer exercises that are easier to mark.[27]

Despite efforts to appear broad-minded, it is the teacher who is isolated as the scapegoat by the *Digest* for the problems found within the schools. The article criticizes teachers who insist on emphasizing creativity; "another group of villains" are the teachers who misuse the principles of structural linguistics and so believe that there is no need for their students to study formal language rules, etc." So,

> despite the laudable efforts of some individual teachers . . . very little improvement in the writing skills of American students is likely unless the entire educational establishment recaptures the earlier conviction that the written language is important.[28]

Throughout the forty-two years of articles that we examined, the *Digest* consistently maintained that American public schools were in serious trouble. In a 1981 article entitled "Help! Teacher Can't Teach!" the teacher, as usual, is targeted. The *Digest* explains:

> Increasingly, too, parents have begun to blame the shortcomings of the schools on the lone and very visible figure at the front of the classroom.[29]

The tradition of blaming the teacher for the problems of American education can be found throughout the articles we examined. The problems faced by teachers in their work are consistently their problems, rather than those of the larger society. According to the logic of the *Digest*, if teachers are dissatisfied with their work, it is their own fault rather than society's problem to correct. A 1949 article by Wilma Morrison, for example, entitled "Teachers at the Wailing Wall," argued that

> teachers, day by day, by careless word and by deliberate misstatement, are selling their profession so short that they are driving young students away from teaching.[30]

According to Morrison, the shortage of teachers in the classrooms had resulted from the teachers' own complaints, or 'wailing,' about problems in the schools and their profession. No recognition was made of the low social status assigned to teachers or of their poor salaries and working conditions. The article explained that

> as a matter of fact, there is nothing downtrodden or ignored about today's teachers—except in the minds of some of them.[31]

Presumably, teachers have only to stop their "wailing" and recognize that "they hold a magic key into the hearts and homes of their town or neighborhood," and their problems will be solved.[32]

What begins to emerge from this part of our analysis of the *Digest*'s articles is that, despite the seeming variety of topics and issues addressed by the articles, the main problems found within the American educational system are a result of the failure of teachers who can't or won't teach, or who do not have the intelligence and wisdom to adopt obvious technical solutions that are available to them (i.e., those suggested by the *Digest*).

In laying blame on the teaching profession for the problems in the schools, the *Digest* does not hesitate to propose solutions. In this context, we examine the second major theme that dominates the articles that we read in the *Digest*.

Innovations and Reforms that Promise to Transform the Schools

The *Digest* assumes that the reform of schools is indeed possible, provided that there are people working within the schools who are sufficiently dedicated to carry out the sort of changes necessary. The *Digest* is convinced that schools that have been "bad" can be made "good." Typically, this can be accomplished by an individual who, through a combination of extraordinary effort and ability, can overcome seemingly impossible conditions. Often these individuals are successful in their efforts because they employ some obvious method or technique, the importance of which eluded the average educator. To demonstrate this point, the *Digest* highlights some particularly dedicated and effective teacher or administrator who acts as a "miracle worker."

An example of this can be found in the 1985 article "High Marks for Big D's Schools," which describes the poor quality of education provided by the Dallas schools: "At that time the schools were led by superintendent Nolan Estes, a flamboyant 'progressive' educator." Unfortunately, most of the programs implemented by Estes did not work. Finally, as the *Digest* reports, Estes left his position and was replaced by Linus Wright. According to the *Digest*, the contrast between the two men and their philosophies could not have been more profound. Wright is portrayed as an educational wonder worker who transformed the schools.

> "School is a place to learn important things," [Wright] said. "That means English, math, science, history and foreign languages. Just about everything else is irrelevant."[33]

This miracle-worker and his philosophy of basic education produced what the *Digest* describes as a turnaround throughout the Dallas school system. As presented, the evidence is clear that Wright's reforms have produced marked results—standardized test scores being cited to support this statement.

Similar types of articles included in the *Digest* emphasize the difference that an individual can make. In many respects, the *Digest*'s approach is highly romantic. This is particularly evident in the magazine's portrayal of teachers. If teachers collectively are bad, according to the *Digest*, then, despite this fact, it is still possible to find dedicated and self-sacrificing individuals who epitomize all that a teacher should be, as defined by the magazine. One such teacher/miracle worker was Bill Lane, a science teacher in a poorly equipped rural school in the state of Washington.

According to a 1955 article, Lane's students, over a seven-year period, won a total of $70,000 in scholarships in open competitions against the nation's most gifted students—students who attended fully equipped schools. Even though his school lacked proper laboratory facilities, the *Digest* explains that Lane's students were able to triumph because of his exceptional efforts as a teacher. Quoting Lane, the *Digest* explains that "what bright youngsters need most . . . is somebody to help guide the course upward."[34] Basic equipment and administrative and parental support are not necessary if a teacher can be found who is sufficently dedicated to achieve the task.

The *Digest*'s belief that good teachers and administrators will find ways to overcome seemingly insurmountable odds is emphasized again and again. In a 1952 article entitled "She Fought for the Children," Ione Swan, the principal of Wilshire-Crest School in Los Angeles, is described as a lone woman "armed only with her righteous wrath [who] licked the whole Los Angeles School Board."[35] According to the story, Swan fought—despite temporarily losing her job—for improved playgrounds and services for her students. Revealing the corruption of the Los Angeles school board, she played a key role in their defeat in the county elections. Fired, without any money, she contracted to spend $628 to go on television and radio to convince voters not to reelect the board:

> The night before the election she broadcast her story, with no mention of money. "There was too much else, far more important, to tell," she explains. But hundreds of citizens sensed her need and mailed her one and five dollar bills—totaling $623.[36]

In the universe of the *Digest,* those with a just cause never suffer for having taken a risk to pursue their beliefs. Mrs. Swan gets back her job and the money she spent on advertisements criticizing the school board.

The *Digest*'s solutions are always simple and straightforward. Problems are never multidimensional or complex. Changes are always produced by a miracle-working administrator or teacher who recognizes a single factor that is responsible for the failure of an educational program or school. By implementing one—typically simple and straightforward—reform, the problems faced by the schools can be solved. Such efforts can often lead, according to the *Digest*, to extraordinary results. In a 1966 article entitled "Dropouts Anonymous," Mary Stewart is presented as the moving force behind an unusual school aimed at eliminating student dropouts. A dropout herself, she overcame impossible odds to achieve her own education. Disturbed by the large number of dropouts, she decided to do something on her own to help reduce their growing number. Through her efforts with her organization Dropouts Anonymous,

> dropouts and youngsters still in school improve their reading to the point where they are able to do class work with some assurance of continuing success.[37]

The article describes how four similar centers using Stewart's model were set up elsewhere in California. It concludes with the assertion that Stewart's program will spread further and prove an important means of solving the dropout problem.

Miraculous work on the part of dedicated teachers and administrators not only solves major educational problems, but also saves money and time. For example, a 1958 article describes a reading program used in the elementary schools of Joplin, Missouri. The program eliminates traditional grading, and groups students according to their reading level rather than their age, thus creating a situation in which

> nobody is frustrated by being behind the rest of the class, and nobody is bored by being ahead. Everybody's a success. . . . At the end of the semester . . . results showed that their reading had progressed about twice as fast as usual: they had done a year's work in one semester.[38]

The success of the program is a result of the work of one or two inspired individuals. In the case of the Joplin reading program, it was initiated by Superintendent of Schools Roi S. Wood and implemented by a particularly talented principal by the name of Cecil Floyd. No reference is made to research concerning the study habits of students, problems related to learning disabilities, or similar issues. Instead, a determined superintendent and one of his principals just make things happen.

One can, of course, be highly cynical while reading this article, which was published in January 1958, and ask why the program, if it was so successful, is not still in use today? This question can be asked consistently in reference to the curricular reforms touted in the *Digest*.

For example, a 1970 article entitled "They'll Never Stop Learning" describes a new type of school in North Dakota in which

> the teacher is no longer concerned with instructing an entire class. . . . Instead the teacher fosters truly individualized learning developing from each child's particular interest.[39]

The article goes on to describe a classroom built using open construction, with moveable walls and partitions, that allows the teacher to divide the classroom into a number of different "interest centers." If the *Digest* was so correct in its analysis of the benefits of open construction classrooms, why aren't we still building these types of schools today? While interest centers are still included in many schools, open construction is as dead as the dinosaurs.

This question must also be asked about another article, published in 1970, entitled "Bold New Directions for U.S. High Schools," which focused on innovative programs being used in various schools across the country that encouraged student participation in curriculum planning and organization. Test material is cited in the article which shows the superior academic and social performance of students in such programs.[40] These programs, touted by the *Digest* as revolutionizing education, do not survive today.

One final example is provided by a 1985 piece entitled "The Teacher Who Took on the Establishment." The article cites the innovative work of John Saxon, a math teacher, and describes how he dramatically contributed to the improved performance of students in three separate math programs. According to the article, Saxon developed innovative new ways of teaching mathematics which were consistently opposed by the educational establishment. The article implies that his innovative methods are laying the foundation for a renaissance in mathematics education.[41] Does he have any followers?

As demonstrated in the examples cited above, change and innovation in the schools described in the pages of the *Digest* result largely from the efforts of an individual rather than of a group of people. In the entire period in which we reviewed articles for this research, there were almost no articles about groups of educators working together to bring about some sort of innovation or reform. Collective action did not seem to be considered a realistic or desired option.

CONCLUSIONS

Many more examples could be cited to demonstrate the two major themes ("What's Wrong with the Schools?" and "Innovations and Reforms that Promise to Transform the Schools") empasized by the *Digest* in the education articles it published between 1945 and 1987. Only rarely does the *Digest* rise above the rhetoric of its ideology and worldview to address education in a wider context.

What is evident throughout the forty-two years of articles we examined is that when any major educational or social problem involving the schools occurs, the solution to the problem will ultimately come from the initiative of some particularly determined or innovative individual. The ultimate cause of these problems are only rarely examined in a larger social, cultural, and political context. Bill Lane produces outstanding science students without equipment in an isolated rural location. Ione Swan loses her job and defends her students against a corrupt school board. Mary Stewart fights the dropout problem by arguing that students drop out simply because they have trouble reading. Nowhere is the issue addressed that the dropout problem might be a result of a series of larger social dysfunctions. John Saxon solves the problems of students having difficulty in math by developing an innovative curriculum. The idea is never even addressed that the problems that students have in mathematics may also derive from other causes (broken homes, drug abuse, and so on). In the universe constructed by the *Digest*, there are few connections between events that occur in the schools and conditions in the society—only a vague and extremely nebulous understanding of cause and effect exists.

This is consistent with Dorfman's broader analysis of the *Digest*, in which he argues that "the social is reduced to the individual, and the individual to individualism." Collective action for the purposes of social change is almost never discussed.[42] Ironically, according to Dorfman, the *Digest*'s

> feverish individualism does not imply variety. On the contrary, such a solution can only work because the publication has reduced each person to a recipe made up of the usual ingredients. Before he or she can appear in the pages of *Reader's Digest*, each human being must pass through an implacable process of selection, editing, condensation, and remodeling, just as if he were on an assembly line of the intellect, until the final product conforms to the specifications of a common human denominator—the "average man" who supposedly lurks deep inside of every one of us.[43]

On the surface, one can argue that the *Digest* is a relatively harmless popular magazine. As an artifact of popular culture, it provides helpful information and entertainment to tens of millions of readers. In fact, as demonstrated by Dorfman, and more specifically in the case of the education-related articles examined in this study, the information it does provide is highly circumscribed and potentially misleading. By reducing issues to simplistic but manageable units, it leads to what Dorfman refers to as the infantalization of the adult reader. Complex issues involving schools and teachers become simple. No problem is without a solution. All that is needed are dedicated people with good ideas and the necessary dedication to act.

Unfortunately, the world may not be as simple or as rational a place as the editors of the *Digest* would like us to believe. The *Digest* is neither neutral or harmless. It provides the reader with knowledge that does not fit the reality it purports to demonstrate. In addition, by focusing on a narrow range of topics and making them appear to be the main source of our society's educational problems, it leads the reader away from addressing what are in fact the real issues that must be dealt with if the genuine reform of our educational system is to be undertaken. In distracting its readers from the real issues that must be dealt with, it is functioning more as a vehicle of ideology than of critical thought, more as an instrument of hegemony than of enlightenment.

NOTES

1. Ariel Dorfman, *The Empire's Old Clothes: What the Lone Ranger, Babar, and Other Innocent Heroes Do to Our Minds* (New York: Pantheon Books, 1983); of related interest, see Ariel Dorfman and Armand Mattelart, *How to Read Donald Duck: Imperialist Ideology in the Disney Comic* (London: International General, 1975).
2. *Empire's Old Clothes*, p. ix.
3. Ibid., p. x.
4. Ibid., pp. 6–7.
5. Ibid., p. 7.
6. Ibid., p. 150.
7. The examination of the *Digest* in light of its ideological perspective is critical to this study. Like Nicholas Burbules, we feel that both Marxist and neopositivist conceptions of ideology "have often suffered from the premise that ideologies are demonstrably 'false' and propagandistic." Instead, he argues that: "we should understand ideology on the model of a literary text; as a portrayal of social and political life that is suggestive, poetic and nonliteral; as telling *a* truth if not *the* truth." For Burbules, "the process of ideology analysis and ideology-critique is akin to literary criticism; it includes an attempt to hold a portrayal accountable to social reality while recognizing that ideologies that capture the popular imagination, however partial or biased, must be granted a degree of coherence and plausibility." See Nicholas C. Burbules, "Tootle: A Parable of Schooling and Destiny," *Harvard Educational Review* 56 (3): 239–40.
8. *Magazine Industry Market Place* (New York: R. R. Bowker, 1985), p. 277.
9. Bill Katz and Linda Sternberg Katz, *Magazines for Libraries* (New York: R. R. Bowker, 1986), p. 485.
10. Our criteria for the selection of articles from the *Digest* for inclusion in this study was based on whether or not their primary focus was on some aspect of elementary or secondary schooling or the profession of teaching. We did not include articles that would fall under the category of humorous stories, interesting vignettes, and so forth. Selection was in some instances difficult when an article talked about the experience of an individual in school. For example, a 1956 article by Dorothy Canfield Fisher about some of Booker T. Washington's experiences as a student at Hampton Institute, entitled "The Washed Window," might have been included in the study. These and other pieces, such as the 1959 article "An Open

Letter to America's Students" by President Dwight D. Eisenhower, were excluded. Our focus was essentially on articles that talked about the condition of schools, the reform of education, the work of teachers, educational innovations, and the like. A list of the titles of the articles included in the study, in chronological order of their publication, is as follows: "The Little Professor of Piney Woods," "Is This the School of Tomorrow?" (1945); "How Georgia Teachers Got a Raise," "Teach Them How to Live," "Shall Our Public Schools Give Sex Instruction?" "What Is Your Education Worth?" "Chicago's Schools Throw off Their Shackles," "Our Schools Need More than Money" (1947); "Shall the Churches Invade the Schools?" "What Do We Want from Our Schools?" (1948); "Teachers at the Wailing Wall" (1949); "Denver Schools Connect Learning with Life," "Our Schools Have Kept Us Free," "Who Owns Your Child's Mind?" (1951); "She Fought for the Children," "Every Child Has a Gift" (1952); "Our Children's Debt to John Dewey" (1953); "In North Carolina the Students Drive Their Own School Buses," "The Court's Decision and the South" (1954); "Bill Lane's Students Win the Prizes," "Are Our Children Learning to Read?" "A New Way to Pay Teachers" (1955); "Are European Children Smarter than Ours?" "Bay City Beats the Teacher Shortage," "The Little Professor of Piney Woods," "Are U.S. School Children Being Cheated?" (1956); "Three R's and an S for Service" (1957); "Johnny Can Read in Joplin," "Three Cheers for George Washington High!" (1958); "Why Not 'Year-Round' School?" "Education for All the Children of All the People" (1959); "The Day I Quit Teaching School" (1960); "Why I Object to Federal Aid to Education," "The Church, the Government and the Schools" (1961); "Has the Supreme Court Outlawed Religious Observance in the Schools?" (1962); "Why Johnny Can't Get a Job" (1963); "How Children Can Learn the Economic Facts of Life" (1964); "Is Religion Banned from Our Schools?" (1965); "Your Child May Be in the Wrong Grade in School," "Dropouts Anonymous," "Should Teachers Strike?" "The Case for Year-Round Schools" (1966); "The Case for Enlightened Sex Education," "Can Negro Children Make the Grade," "An Experiment in Sex Education" (1967); "Dan Fader's 'Help-Yourself' Textbooks," "Sex Education: Blunt Answers for Tough Questions," "The Big Push for Teacher Power" (1968); "Is Your Child's School Safe from Fire?" "Can We Stand Strikes by Teachers, Police, Garbage Men, Etc.?" "Sex Education: Powder Keg in Our Schools" (1969); "Should Parochial Schools Get Public Funds?" "Hunger in the Classroom," "I. Integration—A Tragic Failure," "They'll Never Stop Learning," "Bold New Directions for U.S. High Schools," "The Case of the Pregnant Schoolgirl" (1970); "Schools for Failure" (1971); "Should Your Child Go to School?" (1972); "The Furor over School Textbooks," "Teachers on the March," "What Do Your Child's Test Scores Tell You?" "Why Johnny Can't Write" (1976); "The Coming Battles over School-Finance Reform" (1977); "Teach Values, Not Guilt," "Schools That Work" (1978); "Should Prayer Be Restored to Our Public Schools?" (1979); "Inner-City Schools that Work," "A Little School against the Big Bureaucracy" (1980);

"What Ever Happened to Sex Education?" (1981); "Self-Appointed Censors: Threat to Our Schools," "The School that Went Straight," "More 'Buy' for Your School Bucks" (1982); "How to Save Our Public Schools" (1983); "The School that Teaches Real Life," "Guess Who Spells Disaster for Education," "I. Our Public Schools: Up from C Minus" (1984); "The Teacher Who Took on the Establishment," "The Seven Kinds of Smart," "Why Our Children Aren't Reading," "High Marks for Big D's Schools" (1985); "Should Schools Offer Sex Education," "What We Must Teach Our Children," "Politics and 'Peace Education,'" "We're Teaching Our Kids to Use Drugs" (1987).

11. For background on hegemony and its implications for education, see Michael Apple, *Ideology and Curriculum* (London: Routledge, 1979); Michael Apple (ed.) *Cultural and Economic Reproduction in Education: Essays on Class, Ideology and the State* (London: Routledge & Kegan Paul, 1982); Michael W. Apple, *Education and Power* (Boston: Routledge, 1983); and Michael W. Apple and Lois Weis (eds.), *Ideology and Practice in Schooling* (Philadelphia: Temple University Press, 1983).

12. Raymond Williams, "Base and Superstructure in Marxist Cultural Theory," in *Schooling and Capitalism: A Sociological Reader*, ed. ____ (London: Routledge, 1976), p. 205.

13. Ibid., pp. 204–205.

14. Ibid., p. 205.

15. Dorfman, *Empire's Old Clothes,* p. 137.

16. Philip Wylie, "What Is Your Education Worth?" *Reader's Digest* (September 1947), pp. 23–24

17. Ibid., p. 24.

18. Ibid., pp. 24–25.

19. Ibid., p. 24.

20. Lester Velie, "Why Johnny Can't Get a Job," *Reader's Digest* (January 1963), pp. 152, 154.

21. Lester Velie, "Schools for Failure," *Reader's Digest* (July 1971), p. 147

22. Dorfman, *Empire's Old Clothes,* p. 138.

23. Jhan and June Robbins, "Are Our Children Learning to Read?" *Reader's Digest* (September 1955), p. 169

24. Ibid., p. 171.

25. Frances L. Ilg and Louise Bates Ames, "Your Child May Be in the Wrong Grade at School," *Reader's Digest* (August 1966), p. 56.

26. Ibid., p. 56.

27. Merrill Sheils, "Why Johnny Can't Write," *Reader's Digest* (April 1976), pp. 74–75.

28. Ibid., p. 77.

29. "Teacher Can't Teach," *Reader's Digest* (January 1981), p. 88.

30. Wilma Morrison, "Teachers at the Wailing Wall," *Reader's Digest* (August 1949), p. 83

31. Ibid., p. 83.

32. *Ibid.*

33. Trevor Armbrister, "High Marks for Big D's Schools," *Reader's Digest* (December 1985), p. 58

34. Frances V. Rummell, "Bill Lane's Students Win the Prizes," *Reader's Digest* (January 1955), p. 29.

35. Albert Q. Maisel, "She Fought for the Children," *Reader's Digest* (March 1952), p. 49.

36. Ibid., p. 52.

37. Don Weldon, "Dropouts Anonymous," *Reader's Digest* (August 1966), p. 17.

38. Roul Tunley, "Johnny Can Read in Joplin," *Reader's Digest* (January 1958), p. 42.

39. Arlene Silberman, "They'll Never Stop Learning: Excitement in North Dakota," *Reader's Digest* (July 1970), pp. 210, 215.

40. Arlene Silberman, "Bold New Directions for U.S. High Schools," *Reader's Digest* (August 1970), p. 91.

41. Trevor Armbrister, "The Teacher Who Took on the Establishment," *Reader's Digest* (March 1985), pp. 23–24, 25–28.

42. A limited number of articles about teachers' unions are included in the *Digest*. Consistently, teachers' unions are criticized and seen as putting the welfare of teachers before those of the children and public whom they serve. See, for example, Paul Friggens, "Should Teachers Strike?" *Reader's Digest* (November 1966), pp. 95–99; Paul Friggens, "The Big Push for 'Teacher Power'," *Reader's Digest* (September 1968), pp. 70–75; Paul Friggens, "Teachers on the March," *Reader's Digest* (February 1976), pp. 112–15; Eugene Methvin, "Guess Who Spells Disaster for Education?" *Reader's Digest* (May 1984), pp. 89–94.

43. Dorfman, *Empire's Old Clothes,* pp. 143–44.

5 The Image of the High School Dropout in the Twentieth-Century Popular Press

Jeanne Ellsworth and Robert B. Stevenson

> Drop, dropouts out of school,
> Proud of the will to fail.
> You won't find us in the school hall—
> Look in the pool hall
> Or in jail.
>
> Ignoramus, there you are,
> Sitting in your hopped-up car,
> And your brains ain't up to par,
> And your ears stick out too far.[1]

This parody from a 1964 issue of *Time* magazine caricatures the dropout in terms of failure, idleness, ignorance, nonconformity, even criminal behavior and immorality, and encapsulates some of the feelings American society has come to have toward the high school dropout. Society has constructed images of who drops out of school, why they do so, and how their dropping out constitutes a public problem. These images are part of the social reality in which approximately one-quarter of all students do not complete high school,[2] and, as such, are worth scrutiny.

Furthermore, the public image of the dropout, at least as much as the view of the professional educator, is an important part of the social context in which educational decisions are made about policies and programs that address dropping out. This public image is shaped by the media's portrayal of school dropouts and the biographical, historical, economic, and sociopolitical factors that surround the problem. Efforts, therefore, to understand educational policies and practices that affect the retention of students in school until graduation need to consider media messages as part of the context in which the general public forms its conceptions of dropouts and its beliefs about why people do or do not succeed in school.

By and large, the general public is most likely to form dispositions, develop perspectives, and make decisions about schools and the individuals who drop out of them through the information and views proffered by the popular press, as well as through their own experiences and those of their families and friends. While it is difficult to determine the messages mediated by individual experiences and transmitted through personal contacts, representations of educational issues in the popular press are readily available for analysis.

In this essay, we examine the images of the high school dropout which have appeared in the popular press since the turn of the century. In particular, we analyze how the press has defined three aspects of the dropout issue: the nature of dropping out as a social and individual problem, the characteristics of dropouts, and the ways in which dropping out might be prevented. The qualitative data base for the study is comprised of articles in popular magazines of the twentieth century. In addition, a count was made of articles pertaining to high school dropouts in *The New York Times Index* in order to corroborate historical trends in the attention given to the topic (as measured by the number of articles published at different times during the period in question). Each of the magazine articles was indexed in *The Readers' Guide to Periodical Literature* under a heading pertaining to dropouts or withdrawal from school. The *Readers' Guide* indexes "English language journals of general interest,"[3] including virtually every major popular magazine published in North America. Therefore, articles identified through this index provide sources of insight into many aspects of popular culture.

From the original *Readers' Guide* listings, several subsets of articles were eliminated from consideration. First, articles in magazines intended for professional readership, such as *Phi Delta Kappan*, *American Education*, and *Monthly Labor Review*, were omitted. Second, as we were concerned only with high school dropouts, articles focusing on student withdrawal from college were eliminated. The resulting set of ninety-seven articles was drawn from thirty-seven different publications representing a broad range of periodicals, including national magazines intended for general adult readership (such as *Reader's Digest*, *Look*, *Life*, and *Parents*), but also some targeted to more specific populations (such as *Ebony* and *Woman's Home Companion*).[4] While there are some relatively expensive and primarily subscription magazines in the sample, there are also a great many sold routinely on newsstands and in drug stores or supermarkets.

The public's perspective on the issue of students dropping out of school is likely to be affected by how the press: *(a)* define the nature of the problem, *(b)* characterize dropouts as individuals and as a group, and *(c)* portray solutions to the problem. Therefore, a set of focus questions corresponding to each of these areas of concern was developed for analyzing the content of the articles that were identified. The first question we asked in reading each article was, Why has dropping out been seen to be a problem? Stated another way, What have been advanced as the consequences of dropping out? Next we asked, Who are the dropouts? Or more specifically, What characteristics have been attributed to individuals identified as dropouts? Finally, we posed these questions: (1) How has it been suggested that the problem should be addressed? and (2) What kinds of strategies have been presented? These questions provided the initial framework for identifying recurrent themes across the articles and for relating such themes to different time periods (and, hence, different social and historical circumstances).

We read the articles independently and coded each article in relation to the above questions. Our separate analyses were then compared and discussed. Given that most of the articles were relatively straightforward in their presentation of the issue, it was not surprising that there was little disagreement between us about the messages being conveyed. It should be noted that few articles actually addressed all three sets of questions, but every article focused on at least one set of our focus questions.

Our attention was drawn first to the periodic fluctuations in the numbers of articles about dropping out which have appeared during different times during the study period; the first section of this chapter describes those fluctuations in historical and educational context. Next, we consider the prominent themes in the articles' presentation of the nature of the problems that dropping out of high school creates for individuals and society and the apparent connections of these themes to types of programs intended to address the problems. In the subsequent section, we examine themes in the portrayal of who drops out of school and why they do so, particularly as reflected in and reflective of efforts to reduce the dropout rate or to help those who have dropped out. We conclude by considering how images of the problem, of dropouts themselves, and of programs are interrelated and in what ways they have broader implications for students and educators.

DROPOUTS ON THE EDUCATIONAL AGENDA

The popular press's treatment of the dropout issue (or any social issue) is related to the formation of public attitudes toward the issue. This relationship is neither simple nor unidirectional; the public does not passively accept and act on media messages and media content is shaped by its perception of public values. Nevertheless, the media are collectively an important agent in agenda setting. As a factor in the setting of agendas, the press tends to influence and/or reflect the prioritization of certain issues in public discussion and official action. That is, there are "data showing a correspondence between the order of importance given in the media to 'issues' and the order of significance attached to the same issues by the public and politicians."[5] While media research is directed toward sorting out the dynamics of this relationship, the correspondence itself suffices for the purposes of this paper. In other words, to what degree the press reflects and shapes public concern about dropouts does not affect our arguments; rather, we consider the image of the dropout as portrayed in the popular press as one factor that helps frame questions and answers about the phenomenon. It is the dropout as an issue of priority that we consider here by examining the waves of concern about the dropout as a social and educational problem during this century.

Before World War II, the topic of high school dropouts received very little attention in the popular press, and school leaving referred primarily to truancy—in other words, to leaving school before, and not at, the legal age, as we have come to define it. A total of nine articles on school leaving were indexed in *Readers' Guide* between 1900 and 1945; five of these appeared in a single magazine, *Survey*, which was associated with the anti–child labor campaign. These articles denounce school leaving only in the context of reformers' perspectives on the unacceptability of child labor and the hardships of laboring life.

This limited attention to high school completion is not surprising considering that, during the early decades of this century, attending high school at all was something of an accomplishment—only about one in ten young people of high school age even attended high school, and among those, only about 10 percent attained the diploma.[6] While the numbers of high school enrollees and graduates increased steadily during this period, there remained questions about whether high school was indeed right for *all* young people, and, if so, whether it should try to keep *all* until graduation.[7] Many young people found that life without a high school education was satisfactory and secure. The labor-intensive nature of the economy meant that jobs for those who left high school or never attended were plentiful, and there seems to have been little social stigma attached to quitting school after age fourteen or so.

High schools continued to enroll an increasing proportion of eligible young people during the 1920s and 1930s. A temporary decline in enrollments, attributable to young people engaging in military service and war-related employment during World War II,[8] was succeeded by further expansion, until in the 1950s about 86 percent of young people were enrolled in high school and about half graduated.[9] The first half of the century, then, was a period of expanding high school enrollment but limited concerns about completion. As LeCompte states, "When a society is still trying to serve the 'never-ins' educationally, the 'dropout' is not a problem."[10]

As early as 1946, however, incipient concerns about students who failed to finish high school surfaced as evidenced by eighteen articles on the subject which were published in popular journals between 1946 and 1959. Two factors might be related to this increased attention. First, with over half of high school students remaining until graduation, the high school dropout had become part of a minority, and, as such, it has been argued, dropouts came to be perceived as deviant.[11] As a minority that did not conform to the new norm of completing high school, dropouts conceivably attracted the attention of the media. Second, returning veterans and the recession of the early 1950s brought youth unemployment to a rate double that of the overall national rate.[12] The spectre of large numbers of unemployed out-of-school young people on the streets, articles of the period suggest, also attracted public and media notice.

Attention to the problems of dropouts escalated from the 1960s through the early 1970s; sixty-seven articles appeared from 1960 to 1974. During this period, the phenomenon of leaving high school before attaining the diploma became commonly known as "dropping out," and the individuals, as "dropouts." Not only had articles begun during this period to consistently use these terms, but in 1964, *The New York Times Index* initiated the subject heading "Dropout Problems," and in 1965, *The Readers' Guide* adopted the heading "Dropouts."

Efforts to investigate poverty included the allocation of funds for research into issues of youth, employment, and schooling. This research provided statistics and perspectives from which the popular press could frame stories of dropouts, as evidenced by the fact that virtually every article from 1962–1964 quoted the figure of the 7.5 million young people soon to enter the labor force. As part of government initiatives aimed at the elimination of poverty, social programs were developed for the unemployed, including large numbers of high school dropouts, and those programs provided newsworthy subjects for press coverage.

Several years of comparatively little press attention to the problem of high school dropouts were reflected in the publication of only ten articles on the topic from 1975 to 1983. A decline in the country's economic competitiveness with other industrialized countries reordered government priorities to reflect a conservative political agenda. Competency testing and other accountability measures, rather than issues of social and economic equity, became the focus of educational policy initiatives at both national and state levels. A preoccupation with the role of education in both the nation's economic decline and its desired resurgence removed concerns about dropouts and other "at-risk" individuals from the educational agenda and hence from the topics of interest to the popular press.

By 1984, the popular press had once again picked up the issue of the high school dropout, spurred, presumably, by the alarms about U.S. education raised in the "excellence reports" of the mid-1980s; from 1984 to 1989, twenty-six articles relating to dropouts were published. Publicity surrounding declines in standardized test scores—especially as compared to other industrialized nations in direct economic competition with the U.S.—and the publication of reports that recommended tougher standards for high school graduation drew attention to measures of school performance. In keeping with the drive for accountability, the dropout rates of individual schools, districts, and states, as well as the rates for different racial, ethnic, and social-class groups, were publicized. Dropout rates came to be one indicator of school success or failure and, therefore, of the health of the nation's education system.

The ebb and flow of attention given to dropouts in the popular press reflect changing economic and political priorities rather than changes in the status and problems of dropouts. That is, the degree to which the issues surrounding dropping out are apparently newsworthy has fluctuated more in response to concerns about national competitiveness than to actual rates or conditions of dropping out. Hence, while the general trend of this century has been toward increasing the number of students who complete high school, the group of young people who fail or choose to quit has been periodically identified by the popular press as a public "problem."

THE NATURE OF THE PROBLEM

In addition to influencing the establishment of public problems, the press also provides information and views that define and elucidate for readers the nature of the problem. Consequently, media images and definitions indirectly enter the context in which decisions are made regarding how to handle those problems, on both individual and institutional levels. In the case of the high school dropout, interpretations of why dropping out constitutes a social problem have been central to popular media considerations of the problem. In particular, during the 1950s and early 1960s, when dropping out of high school was first considered a problem of substantial proportion, more than three-quarters of the articles devoted paragraphs or pages to explaining just *why* the public ought to be concerned, outraged, and/or spurred to action. The articles under consideration focus less on definitions of the nature of the problem after the mid-1960s; less than half of the 1965–89 articles deal with such definitions. By that time, it would seem, the nature of the problem had become obvious and so needed less emphasis; in the words of a 1989 article, "While educators remain deeply divided over the best way to get kids to stay in school, there is no dispute over the urgency of the problem nationwide."[13]

The most prominent themes among those articles that define the nature of the problems are that dropouts constitute an economic liability to the nation, that dropouts are a threat to social stability, and that dropouts suffer personal losses. We analyze each of these themes in terms of the messages contained about dropouts and the relationship of these messages to the measures offered or recommended in response.

The Dropout as Economic Liability

High school dropouts, it has consistently been emphasized in the popular press, constitute a serious national economic problem, chiefly because they are far more likely to be unemployed, underemployed, or unemployable than are graduates. A 1965 article asserts:

> Regardless of who he is, the drop-out, in general, faces a bleak job future compared to that of the high-school graduate. A 1960 report by the Bureau of Labor Statistics stated: 'It takes longer for (dropouts) to get their first job. The jobs they get initially aren't nearly as good, especially for girls, either in level of skill or earnings. This disparity increases even over a comparatively short span of years. The amount of unemployment . . . is much greater, and the rate of unemployment, at a given time, is unquestionably higher.'[14]

Not only has the employability aspect of the dropout situation been consistently part of the popular image, it has often been presented as the central issue of concern in the articles under consideration. Explanations of the personal or national economic consequences of leaving school before graduation appeared in three-quarters of the articles that included explanations of the nature of the problem. In addition, placement of this issue in the introduction or conclusion of articles further suggests that the dropout as an economic liabilty has been presented as a first and/or ultimate concern.

The increasing importance of the high school diploma to an individual's job prospects has been explained in several ways. First, and most obviously, basic literacy and numeracy, as represented by the high school diploma, have been portrayed as essential for young people entering the job market. Second, a number of articles emphasize that, with increasing numbers of job applicants for each position, employers began to use the high school diploma as an initial screening device. An analysis of youth and the job market described the 1962 situation, for example, as "a buyer's market. . . . In a labor market where high school graduates are plentiful, why settle for less?"[15]

In a third way, the diploma has come to take on not only an increased economic importance but also a further and deeper social value. As LeCompte persuasively argues, "The diploma came to represent not so much acquisition of cognitive skills but a 'conformity certificate', attesting to the fact that the holder had learned how to survive in an institution long enough to assure good behavior in similar organizations such as factories, offices, and other workplaces."[16] This value of the diploma is reflected in the popular image of the problem, as exemplified in a 1962 article in which an employer states that "it isn't just that these kids lack education. The complications are psychological and social. The youngster who quits high school tends to be very defensive and not as easy to work with as other people."[17]

As un- or underemployed or unemployable, dropouts have been portrayed as a substantial impediment to the national economic well-being in several ways. First, the dropout has been perceived as failing to make contributions to the national economy by not adding to the gross national product and by paying little or no taxes. Since unemployed dropouts (rarely are employed dropouts mentioned) also have little or no income, they cannot be consumers of material goods and services, and therefore they further fail to contribute to the economic prosperity of the nation. In the words of a dropout program worker quoted in a 1963 article, "Today's dropouts are tomorrow's consumers. If they cannot be productive, their purchasing power is severely curtailed."[18]

In addition, high school dropouts are cited for their failure to add to the labor pool. A 1957 article exhorts the reader to

> consider what a loss a million half-educated children can represent for our nation! . . . [H]ow many potential engineers and trained technicians are being lost in industry this very fall? How many of these dropouts might be scientists who could contribute to the development of a rich future for our country?[19]

And more than thirty years later, the concern persists in the fact that "businesses say they find it increasingly difficult to find employes [*sic*] who have the necessary skills, even among applicants who have a high-school diploma."[20]

Many articles also emphasize that dropouts, besides failing to contribute, create a drain on the national economy. Portrayed as collectors of unemployment insurance and welfare payments, as fillers of prisons, as less healthy, safe, and/or reliable workers, high school dropouts are considered a potential or actual drain on national economic resources, because they "end up on the relief rolls or in the jail," and thus "cost us more money."[21] In some cases, just how much "more money" has been estimated, as the following excerpt from a 1965 article illustrates:

> Today's dropout is an economic and social liability in our culture. The economic loss can be measured in reduced lifetime earnings (estimated variously between $68,000 and $97,000), smaller tax payments ($17,000 to $24,000), welfare and unemployment benefits paid ($10,000 to $20,000), increased delinquency ($6,000 to $10,000), increased illness (twice the average), and reduced purchasing power.[22]

Our purpose here is neither to argue with the accuracy of these facts and figures nor to suggest that economic life without a high school diploma is unproblematic. Rather, we consider the image of the dropout which this emphasis suggests. First, the popular press tends to use the word "dropout" to stand for "unemployed dropout" or simply "unemployed young person," as is evident in the quotation above. Not all dropouts, it is occasionally mentioned, fail to find jobs or even build careers. Conversely, not all un- or underemployed, delinquent, or welfare-receiving young people are dropouts. But a consistent use of the word *dropout* in connection with statistics about and discussions of unemployed youth tangles images of economic liability with dropouts, and helps to create an image of dropouts as economically dependent.

Second, the dropout is portrayed as having made a choice to become such a liability to himself and society. In the words of several articles, dropouts commit "economic suicide."[23] In this respect, the dropout has often been characterized as being economically and/or socially naive, even stupid. Young people who are considering quitting school, for whatever reason, "seem to have no idea of how bad things are."[24] These young people "are in trouble," reports *Parents Magazine*—"deep trouble, even though they may not know it."[25] Too late, the refrain goes, young people learn that joblessness is a reality of dropping out or that life in entry-level positions is difficult, more difficult than school, and "the dream of 'I'm going to get a job and stand on my own' is shattered."[26]

Notably, not all dropouts are naive about their employment prospects, as revealed by a few articles in which minority dropouts can be seen to be at least somewhat aware that completing high school means little in the face of racism. A 1961 article in *Ebony,* for instance, includes the possibility that for some African-American students, an understanding of the futility of trying to "escape from the ghetto" actually adds to the likelihood of dropping out.[27] Similarly, an article about Native American dropouts published in 1969 argues that the belief that education leads to the good life "for many sectors of North American society . . . flies in the face of observable facts."[28] These observations, however, appear in magazines with limited audiences, not in those with broad majority readership and large circulation.

In other cases, however, minority youths' own voices in journals with wide readership speak clearly of these themes, but their messages are largely ignored. In a 1951 article, for example, dropout Mike, the child of immigrant parents, looks toward to his job prospects with this simple but powerful critique: "It's not what you know in this world—it's *who* you know that counts." However, the article stresses his "problem parents" and "an oversensitive Syrian temperament" in relation to his decision to quit.[29] "Dark sixteen-year-old Harold" reveals a similar lack of naivete about his life chances: "I've never had a really good job. Even during the war I had only dirty jobs. . . . Sometimes I see them taking white boys. It has always been that way for colored people."[30] The author, however, in the succeeding paragraph and throughout the article, continues to wonder why the prospects of unemployment are not "making the youngsters flock back to school."[31] While individual dropouts and members of minorities appear to realize that there are larger sociocultural reasons for their unemployment, the articles in our sample almost unamimously maintain that the primary, if not the only, employment obstacle is young peoples' failure to complete high school.

The Dropout as Menace to Society

As some of the excerpts which illustrate themes in the previous section suggest, the dropout has also been portrayed as a menace to society. Several articles state that both in the act of leaving school and through their negative experiences after dropping out, dropouts are likely to reject not only education and its institutions but also society more generally. Un- and underemployment, it is argued, lead to the kinds of "dead ends" that produce "dangerously alienated drifters who not only have dropped out of education but have very nearly dropped out of society itself."[32] This rejection has been portrayed as a potential threat to traditional societal values and institutions. For example, consider this 1949 appraisal of the dangers of dropouts:

> The disgruntled masses of youngsters who have been let down by the schools are a force in public opinion and their opinion of school is low. No one supports what he does not like and their grudge against schools could block many a community effort. It could wear down our educa-

> tional ideals to the point of their disappearance, and certainly no one who feels a sense of responsibility for the future of our democracy wants to see that happen![33]

Less explicitly, the dangers of the high school dropout are suggested in this 1962 *Look* article which describes dropout Chuck and his peers:

> All of the other boys I saw, in Toledo and in other cities, pretty generally shared Chuck's barren existence and his attitude of futility. They felt and talked and acted like castoffs, abandoned by themselves and by society. Three of these had already had brushes with the law—one for stealing hubcaps, a source of easy money; another, for breaking into a house. "To tell you the truth," one said, "I don't give a damn about anything. My parents feel the same way."[34]

Furthermore, as suggested in the excerpt above, this rejection has been construed as leading to criminal behavior. Idleness, restlessness, and the need for money are sometimes pointed to as the precipitators; in other instances, the movement toward crime among dropouts is suggested as having chiefly psychosocial origins. The dropout has been seen as "delinquency fodder,"[35] and the public has been warned that, "unable to find a better life in the streets, a large number of young people turn to crime."[36] Beyond ideas about dropouts being drawn to specific individual criminal activities (such as stealing hubcaps), there have been concerns that broader uprisings were brewing among young urban dropouts. The term "social dynamite," popularized by the writings of James Conant in the early 1960s and quoted in several articles in our sample,[37] gave a vivid name to ill-defined fears of criminal and/or antisocial "explosions." More recently, although couched in the less strident terms of the mid-1980s, the Education Commission of the States reported that

> at-risk young people also constitute a threat to our political stability. A society in which two-thirds to three-fourths of the population become steadily more affluent while the remainder—including a disproportionate share of minorities—spirals downward, simply will not work.[38]

Personal Loss

The problems associated with dropping out of high school have not all been framed in broad societal terms; the individual's personal losses have also received wide and consistent attention in the popular press, particularly during the 1960s. Dropouts, magazine articles have pointed out, suffer regret, rejection, self-doubt, discouragement, failure, humiliation, and personal anguish. They are defeated and "woebegone,"[39] "permanently behind the eight-ball,"[40] individuals about whom "nobody cares."[41] Dropouts' difficulties and lack of self-esteem are treated, for the most part, with some sensitivity and sympathy. Scars inflicted by poverty, schooling, and racism, while not deeply explored, are presented as real and poignant results of the experiences that led to and followed from dropping out of school.

Ultimately, however, virtually all of the sadness, discouragement, and failure is linked to the "headache of finding and keeping a job."[42] President Johnson's comments, quoted in a 1965 *Parents Magazine* article, are representative:

> The young man or woman who grows up without a decent education . . . is often trapped in a life of poverty. He does not have the skills demanded by a complex society. He does not know how to acquire those skills. He faces a mounting sense of despair which drains initiative and ambition and energy.[43]

If the dropout finds employment, it is likely to be "in bottom-rung, low paid drudgery,"[44] which is better than no job, perhaps, but results only in further loss of self-esteem and frustration. "These [dropouts] are the ones," a 1957 article warns readers, "who will come to feel deep regret. Their prime of life will be spent bewailing what they might have done, what they could have been."[45]

The primary nature of the problems both for individuals and for society, then, has been defined as being located in dropouts' loss of employability. This conception has been reflected in some of the ways in which schools and society have chosen to deal with the problems associated with dropping out. Particularly from the 1950s through the early 1970s, programs designed to help young people readjust to life after they have dropped out were the prevalent type featured in the popular press. Finding jobs and preparing students for them have been the major aims of these programs, as they have sought primarily to provide training and employment counseling. As the headline of a 1963 article made clear about a dropout program, "JOBS! At Trade-Tech everything else is secondary."[46]

Dozens of programs emerged from the concerns about dropouts' employability—"job upgrading," "school-work" programs, "continuation schools," "job training centers," Job Corps, and "Career Study Centers," to name a few. Basic literacy and numeracy have often been elements of these programs, but primary emphasis has been on manual skills, as exemplified by the mid-1960s Job Corps program in which "trainees will learn their trades with the minimum of class work" and instructors aimed to "get them working with their hands and with tools as fast as we can."[47] Typically, these programs stressed not only trades and skills but also the development of attitudes and habits appropriate to the workplace, such as punctuality, proper dress and grooming, and such principles of the workplace as "Minutes Are Pennies."[48]

Increasingly, the notion that dropouts' personal perspectives and interpersonal skills were as much to blame for their employment difficulties as their skills has implied that programs should include efforts to improve self-esteem and build positive attitudes among dropouts. As early as 1952, the need to help young people discover "how to understand themselves and others" was recognized and addressed in dropout programs.[49] Dropouts, a number of articles emphasize, need to raise their sights and revise their low expectations and goals. "The task," as one article puts it, "is to get them to see that life presents more opportunites for them—not just the luckier people—than they dreamed of."[50]

WHO DROPS OUT AND WHY

More recently, with the notion that dropping out is indeed a problem more firmly established, popular magazine articles have devoted increasing space to issues of who drops out and why they do so. The public attention, presumably, shifted to include examination of and programs for students before they become dropouts. Since the mid-1980s, this shift in emphasis is evident in the increasing use of the term "at-risk," which signifies the need to identify and help problem youngsters long before the issue of dropping out arises.

As questions of who drops out and why began to occupy increasing portions of articles, it was regularly mentioned or implied in the articles under consideration that the reasons for dropping out of school are complex and multiple. However, two clusters of factors which appear consistently since the late 1940s are readily identifiable. Each of these clusters—characteristics of dropouts themselves and characteristics of their relationships with schooling—include various individual "reasons" for dropping out.[51] Furthermore, as is the case with definitions of the problem, each cluster of dropout characteristics helps to create and sustain images of the dropout and of what measures are appropriate in dealing with the problem.

Characteristics of Dropouts Themselves

Within this cluster of characteristics, dropouts' personal problems—related to home and family, personality and temperament, and culture and/or neighborhood—are portrayed as important influences on their success or failure in school. These factors are believed to reside within dropouts themselves, and are frequently presented as impediments that students bring to school and that interfere with the ability of the schools to interest or educate them. In the words of a school board member quoted in a recent article, "You can have the most state-of-the-art school in the world, but if a student is bringing a lot of baggage to school, he's not going to learn."[52]

Family patterns that have been considered deviant from the norm are a pervasively portrayed element of dropouts' characteristics. Being "fatherless" (defined as not living, for any reason, with one's biological father), coming from a "broken home," being raised by a working mother, or living in foster care, for example, have been suggested as frequently-seen and influential factors in dropouts' difficulties. In addition, dysfunctional relationships and communications within families have been cited in students' school failures. Family situations have been portrayed as interfering with education in a number of ways, as the following excerpts suggest:

> Often he [the dropout] is being raised by only one parent, who must work for a living and cannot give him or his education the attention needed.[53]

> They come from homes where the interpersonal relationships are virtually nil, where the lines of communication between the parent and child are primitive and in no way serve to develop the child as a total personality. The cultural patterns of these people are shoddy and superficial and even in a state of what you could call a breakdown.[54]

> A major part of the blame for today's high dropout rate is being placed on the nation's rising divorce rate and the resulting breakup of families. Dropouts typically are from broken homes, [a high school administrator says], where baby-sitting and financial needs conflict with the child's going to school.[55]

The generalizations of the preceding article excerpts are supported by large numbers of personal profiles of individual dropouts in which their home and family lives typically receive much attention. The following excerpts are representative:

> For a number of reasons—the slum he lived in, the father he never knew, the mother who worked nights—he had never been able to concentrate on his schoolwork and was always near the bottom of the class.[56]

> Fatherless since childhood, Pat Davis, 18, moved in with foster "aunt" when her mother died. Behind in school, too shy to get help, she felt she should earn her own way.[57]

> Take Peter Brown of Elwood, N.J., who did well in school—until his mother blurted out that he was adopted. Peter became a chronic runaway, staying up all night in amusement parks on the Jersey shore before finding his way to [an adolescent shelter].[58]

> My parents split, and they got so involved in their own lives that they really didn't care what I did. What difference did school make?[59]

> Billy has a score of problems. He is one of several children. He has been physically and emotionally abused by a father who has left home. He prays nightly that his father won't return. His mother puts in long hours at a local shop for minimum wage. He's responsible for the younger children when she's not there.[60]

Dropouts' personalities, temperaments, and/or abilities are also regularly portrayed as factors that interfere with the attempts of schools to educate them. Difficulties with motivation are among the specifics cited in this regard—students may be characterized as lacking motivation or as misplacing their motivation on some endeavor other than schooling, such as when students are more interested in "earning a fast adult buck,"[61] working on cars, selling drugs, or, in the case of girls, attaining "the only degree *she* wants . . . MRS—and soon."[62] Dropouts have also been characterized as rebellious, belligerent, or basically incapable of the work demanded of them in high school.

The cultural background of the dropout is regularly cited as influential in the failure to finish high school, but the nature of this influence varies. Dropouts' cultural or ethnic group, it has been suggested, may devalue education;[63] difficulties with the English language may be at issue;[64] the "scars of racism" may have discouraged young people;[65] or poverty and life in the slums may make going to school and/or staying in school difficult, if not impossible.[66] In general, the personal, family, or ethnic factors implicated by articles in the failure of dropouts to stay in school are portrayed as having negative effects on students' ability to deal with the academic life of school. Academic achievement so hampered is slow or nonexistent, and students, the story goes, lose hope and determination and subsequently drop out. Students' personal lives and circumstances are portrayed as standing substantially alone and apart from their school lives, except to the degree that difficulties outside of school become impediments to schoolwork.

From this simplistic cause-and-effect portrayal of dropping out of high school comes the implication that, primarily, counseling and support are needed to help students remain in school. In articles that provide parental advice, overwhelmingly that advice includes, or is restricted to, the suggestion that parents seek counseling for the student or the family:

> To avert this downward progression, parents of a failing child should certainly start by consulting his teacher or school supervisor. But this is often only a first step. A child in grave difficulty will need counseling of a sort that the school is generally not equipped to give. Such counseling may very well involve the parents, too.[67]

Schools and special programs described in articles since the 1960s have increasingly considered and used counseling and/or therapy-based approaches to deal with potential dropouts, presumably helping young people through their personal or family difficulties and so making it more likely that they will not leave school. For example, one program that deals with urban youth

> targets these kids headed for trouble and surrounds them with a coordinated network of caring adults. For every 10 to 15 kids there is a counselor who visits in their homes, gets to know their friends, investigates family trouble and helps them find the resources they need to cope with problems.[68]

Another direction in which stay-in-school programs have gone, particularly in the past decade, speaks to the image of the dropout as unmotivated. Programs have used extrinsic motivational approaches that reward and/or withhold rewards on the basis of school attendance and/or achievement. Monetary or material prizes[69] or punishments, such as retracting or withholding dropouts' drivers' licenses[70] appear to have both emanated from and added to the notion that students simply lack the tenacity or personal fortitude to stick with education and their schools.

Characteristics of Dropouts' Relationships with Schooling

This second cluster of factors implicated in the phenomenon of school leaving has been part of articles since the late 1940s, but has received relatively little attention when compared with factors related to dropouts themselves. While about half of the reasons coded for this study were related, at least peripherally, to students' school experiences, these reasons were included in just about one-third of the articles, as opposed to personal characteristics, which were mentioned in more than three-quarters of the articles. The school-related cluster of reasons for dropping out included, chiefly, the notions that students were bored with and uninterested in school and that various school processes had been hurtful enough to individuals to lead to isolation, alienation, and, ultimately, dropping out.

The most frequently mentioned aspect of school-related problems is that students simply dislike school, often because they are bored. Throughout the time period we examined, the notion that students are uninterested in what schools have to offer them academically is pervasive. As a 1949 article put it, "It's not that there's a strong pull to leave school. There's a weak one to stay."[71] Personal profiles of students who have quit school tell their own stories of boredom: "I just couldn't get any interest up for the classwork. It doesn't mean anything to me at all."[72]

The charge that students dislike or are bored with school is reflected in recommendations and programs that have attacked school curricula as irrelevant to the lives of potential dropouts. Particularly during the 1950s and early 1960s, academic subjects and college preparatory curricula were presented as the root of many students' boredom with school. "Courses," a 1952 article reports, "are out of step with the times. . . . [O]ur schools aren't preparing teen-agers with the everyday general education needed for their 'blue collar' life."[73] Students who were "below average," as well as those destined for working class lives, were deemed in need of special curricula, so that school could be made "interesting and meaningful for all students, not just those going on to college."[74]

The appropriate-curriculum argument, however, was rarely substantiated by direct evidence from dropouts' reports of their experiences in schools. Instead, it appears to have been a presumption on the part of authors and/or "experts" whom they consulted or quoted. In short, dropouts' reports of their boredom and dissatisfaction with schools were seldom more deeply explored. However, the idea that school structures and practices harm students, which has more recently been appearing in the popular press, is by no means an entirely new theme with regard to students' relationships with schools. A 1949 article, for example, mentions multiple transfers and grade retention as contributing to the problem,[75] and a 1966 piece describes the emotional scars left on young girls as a result of rejection by teachers.[76]

In addition, at least as early as 1965, the idea that school processes were serving not only to allow but, in some cases, to encourage students to drop out of high school began to be discussed. The dean of a Job Training Center is quoted in a 1965 article as saying that there are students for whom the "current educational system" holds "no place. . . . They're not really dropouts; they've been pushed out."[77] Noting the difficulties authorities have had in counting students who are not in school and getting them back in, a 1976 article noted that "many are not really dropouts but pushouts" whose expulsion or suspension led them to drop out or whose truancy was not pursued.[78] While the notion of the school "pushout" seems to have taken root in the academic literature, it remains a marginal theme in popular articles.

In general, the effects of school processes on students' decisions to quit school receive little attention. For example, the notion that schools may be largely to blame for students' dislike or boredom is rarely considered. In only one article did we find the suggestion that schools should be more interesting and enjoyable. When the responsibility of the school is acknowledged, it is usually treated as secondary to that of the students. A 1976 article, for example, observed that "school systems across the country are re-evaluating their programs," but later admitted that "for the most part, the effort to keep youngsters in school focuses on the children themselves."[79]

A somewhat increasing focus on school processes during the latter half of the 1980s may be inferred, however, from descriptions of some recent program efforts. A common theme in these recent articles is that schools are attempting to modify their organizational arrangements in order to cater to the needs of potential dropouts. Provision of flexible scheduling to allow students to work, smaller classes for more individual attention, and provision of prenatal and child care for pregnant girls and students with young children are some of the examples of the development of alternative structures within schools.

CONCLUSIONS AND IMPLICATIONS

Our analysis revealed that, although the popular print media has presented some mixed messages about dropping out and dropouts, the vast majority of articles (especially those in large-circulation magazines with broad readership) have reflected two consistent and common themes. These two related themes have important implications for the development of policies and programs aimed at addressing the problem and for our society's perception and treatment of dropouts.

First, in its presentation of the consequences and causes of, as well as the solutions to, the problem, the popular press has generally framed the issue of dropping out in terms of individual deficiencies rather than structural features of society or institutional shortcomings of schools. While the significance of dropping out is often explained in relation to economic and social consequences for the larger society, the underlying nature of the problem is almost exclusively portrayed as located in the individual's loss of employability, which is attributed to a lack of vocational or interpersonal skills or to negative personal attitudes. This deficiency image of the dropout is consistent with the press's representation of the causes of the problem—namely, individual personalities, temperaments, and abilities that interfere with the efforts of the school to educate at-risk students and the willingness of industry to employ them. These personal characteristics are often sympathetically portrayed, but by couching sympathy in terms of individuals who are victims of their own and their families' inabilities to deal with schooling and to be economically productive members of society, schools and other social institutions are largely exonerated of the responsibility for developing appropriate responses to the needs of such individuals. As a result, institutional features of schools and structural features of our economic system are rarely examined as part of the underlying causes of the problem.

This definition of the problem is reflected in the kinds of programs for dropouts which the periodical press has publicized, namely, those emphasizing the provision of job training and employment counseling. The predominance of articles that stress counseling and support in offering advice to parents on how to help their children stay in school and those that publicize "carrot-and-stick" approaches to retaining at-risk students similarly locate the problem within individuals. These approaches to the problem assume that school structures are basically sound and that students simply need to be motivated or helped to cope with school irrespective of the quality of educational services they receive.

On the other hand, the role of school processes in "pushing" students out of school has been implicitly acknowledged in some recent articles that described efforts by schools to create alternative organizational and/or instructional arrangements for at-risk students. Yet, even in these few articles, the contribution of school policies and practices to dropouts' decisions to leave is not made clear. Consequently, the presentation of alternative programs to prevent dropping out has not changed the predominant image of individual deficiencies as the primary cause of the problem.

In addition to ignoring school processes, the individual-deficit image of dropouts has left unexamined the possibility that broader societal problems contribute to dropping out. Increasingly, young people (along with people in all age groups) find themselves un- or underemployed, regardless of whether or not they have a high school diploma. That is, the assertion that completion of high school is a significant determinant of employability is becoming more and more untenable, especially in the cases of women and minorities. Framing issues of youth unemployment in terms of young peoples' family backgrounds, lack of education and/or skills, inadequate motivation, and so forth, without addressing the impact of economic conditions, serves to deny or marginalize such problems as social and economic inequalities in the larger society.

The implications of the image of dropouts as deficient individuals are profound. Popular images of educational problems and of the individuals who are part of such problems can be a pervasive influence on the decisions made by legislators, school board members, and other policymakers. When the image obscures or simplifies crucial elements of the problem, such as the contribution of school responses to the needs of at-risk students or the real prospects of youth employment, distorted or limited conceptualizations of the problem are likely to arise. Reform efforts based on such conceptualizations can hardly be expected to be broadly or consistently constructive.

The second concern that arises from our analysis is related to the deleterious image of dropouts as deficient individuals and the implications of this image for how our society views and feels about those citizens who do not hold a high school diploma. Overwhelmingly a negative or deviant image of the high school dropout has been presented by the press, especially since the dropout moved from being part of a statistical majority to being in the minority among young people. As economically and socially self-destructive, as threats to national economics and social stability, and as poorly motivated young people from dysfunctional and/or deviant backgrounds, dropouts have been presented as people of low social worth, unproductive members of society, and losers.

This tendency in the popular press has been challenged, but only in rare instances and then often with qualifications. A 1964 *Reporter* article, for example, blames "our penchant for categorization and problem making" for creating the image and the reality of dropouts as "a separate clan of pariahs."[80] Society, Brandes argues, has created the image of the dropout less out of concern for their welfare than out of discomfort with their presence as "inconsistent with our view of a free society that provides opportunity for all."[81] In a 1980 article in *Psychology Today*, Bernard Lefkowitz challenges the image of economic suicide, emphasizing that of the dropouts he met in the course of a Ford Foundation study, the majority "had demonstrated that they could find and hold a job. . . . Their own hopes and ambitions far exceeded what was expected of them by social planners, teachers, and economists."[82] The only time most articles profiled dropouts experiencing any kind of personal success, however, was after programs of intervention had "fixed" their problems or deficiencies.

Some research on dropouts suggests that counterimages of dropping out and of dropouts themselves are likely to be prevalent among minority students. African-American students, Ogbu[83] argues, form oppositional cultures which are, to some degree, based in their rejection of notions of equal educational and occupational opportunity, notions that are crucial to maintenance of the image of the economic and social value of the high school diploma. Minority dropouts interviewed by Fine and Rosenberg,[84] seldom the helpless victims portrayed by the media, also shared views that were highly critical of schools and schooling. Within such oppositional cultures, it is likely that images of dropping out of high school exist which are not only different from, but constructed in opposition to, those of the popular media.

In failing to address these competing images, the popular media has, first, presented at best a partial (in both senses of the word) view of high school dropouts. But in addition, students outside of well-defined oppositional groups have access only or primarily to the dominant negative views of dropouts. In interviews we conducted with white working-class dropouts, for example, we heard consistent echoes of these images, images that produced conflict in the way these young men and women thought about themselves and their experiences in and out of school. This conflict was evident as the young people struggled with notions of themselves as misfits and failures while simultaneously acknowledging their personal worth and the part their school played in their decision to drop out.[85]

We suggest that in order to better understand how and why dropping out happens, we need to begin to consider that young people are making decisions, not in a social vacuum, but rather within sets of socially constructed images and meanings. These images and meanings may or may not match those with which society is most familiar, such as those presented in the popular media. Without knowledge of young people's own conceptions of dropping out, how can we expect to communicate effectively with those whom we seek to keep in high school? Is it possible that in continuing to proffer messages that are in disjuncture with the realities of young people's experiences, schools and school people undermine their own credibility and even encourage the formation of counterimages that may thwart even our most well-intentioned programs?

Furthermore, the most broadly promulgated images may influence how dropouts and potential dropouts perceive themselves and relate to schools. How, for instance, might the strong messages that characterize the dropout as victim, for example, impact on students engaged in struggles with classes, teachers, and school processes? In what ways might images of personal failure and deviance enter into dropouts' decisions about their lives after quitting school? Finally, and most broadly, what do the overwhelmingly negative images of one-quarter of our high school students say about our commitment to developing what we self-righteously call "our most precious resource"?

NOTES

1. "Song for Dropouts," *Time* (10 April 1964), 76.

2. Varying methods and definitions used in computing dropout rates have produced inconsistent figures on dropping out. Using a commonly accepted definition of dropouts as individuals who have not received, or are not currently studying for, a high school diploma, a national dropout rate of 25 percent is most often cited in the academic literature. See, for exmaple, G. Wehlage, R. Rutter, G. Smith, N. Lesko, and R. Fernandez, *Reducing the Risk: Schools as Communities of Support* (London: Falmer Press, 1989).

3. *Readers' Guide to Periodical Literature* (New York: H. W. Wilson, 1990). The most commonly held popular index for nonacademic libraries, *Readers' Guide* now indexes articles in more than 150 magazines. See P. Vesenyi, *An Introduction to Periodical Bibliographies* (Ann Arbor, MI: Peirian, 1974).

4. The following articles comprise the study sample: E. Brumbaugh, "Dangers of the High School Age," *Independent* (14 October 1909), 873–77; M. Sumner, "What the Government Found When It Began to Study Children," *Survey* (16 December 1911), 1375–77; "What Children Who Leave School Really Need," *Survey* (24 May 1913), 273–74; "Children Straying in and out of School," *Survey* (23 December 1916), 340; J. Gwinn, "Stay-in-school Campaign in New Orleans," *American City* (May 1915), 404; J. Malone, "When Boys Leave School," *Review of Reviews* (December 1919), 627–30; L. Schilchting, "Lariat for Opportunity," *Survey* (15 December 1923), 331–32; H. Ormsbee, "School and Job in Philadelphia," *Survey* (15 April 1928), 116–17; "Hundred Child Workers," *Survey* (15 June 1929), 363–64; E. Stern, "Our New Lost Generation," *Woman's Home Companion* (March 1946), 4+; G. Zimand, "Don't Let Them Quit School," *Parents Magazine* (August 1947), 14; E. Stern, "Why Teen-agers Quit School," *Woman's Home Companion* (October 1949), 34–35+; G. White, "When a Boy Quits School," *Ladies Home Journal* (January 1951), 48–51+; J. Pollack, "What Happens When Kids Quit School?" *Parents Magazine* (August 1952), 44–45+; J. Hecht, "Calamity of Our Million School Dropouts," *Parents Magazine* (September 1957), 39+; "Academic Fallout,"

Newsweek (30 November 1959), 98; "Dropout Tragedies," *Life* (2 May 1960), 106A–13; "Hopeful Second Chance," *Life* (9 May 1960), 102–9; "Tragedy of Dropouts," *Ebony* (September 1961), 48–49; "Discussion," *Ebony* (November 1961), 13–14; D. Giese, "I Was a High School Drop-out!" *Reader's Digest* (December 1961), 203–7; "School Drop-out," *Good Housekeeping* (March 1962), 143–45; C. Brossard, "Teen-ager without a Job," *Look* (27 February 1962), 31–33; P. Bullock and R. Singleton, "What to do with the Drop-out?" *New Republic* (20 October 1962), 17–18; "Break for the Dropouts," *Business Week* (13 October 1962), 110–12; "School Dropouts Called Great American Tragedy," *Science News Letter* (7 April 1962), 217; "Only High School Grads Need Apply," *Business Week* (11 August 1962), 50–52; M. Koehler and A. Fontaine, "We Waste a Million Kids a Year," [three articles] *Saturday Evening Post* (10 March 1962), 15–23, (17 March 1962), 50–54, (24 March 1962), 58–59+; "Chicago's Answer for Dropouts," *Ebony* (October 1963), 81–82; G. Leonard, "Are We Cheating Twenty Million Students?" *Look* (4 June 1963), 36–40+; "Facts about Dropouts," *U.S. News* (26 August 1963), 10; E. Friedenberg, "Ideology of School Withdrawal," *Commentary* (June 1963), 492–500; "Discussion," *Commentary* (October 1963), 270+; P. Woodring, "Dropouts," *Saturday Review* (16 February 1963), 59–60; A. Maisel, "They Help Boys Want to be Educated," *Reader's Digest* (December 1963), 100–4; "Dropouts and the Draft," *New Republic* (17 August 1963), 3–4; "Reply with Rejoinder," *New Republic* (21 September 1963), 36+; E. Brandes, "Manpower Planning and the New Pariahs," *Reporter* (26 March 1964), 17–19; E. Velie, "No Room at the Bottom," *Reader's Digest* (April 1964), 169–70+; "Song for Dropouts," *Time* (10 April 1964), 76; A. Fontaine, "Remarkable Story of the Dropouts and the College Students," *McCalls* (March 1964), 36+; "The Day Our Boy Quit School and How We Got Him Back In!" *Farm Journal* (May 1964), 33+; "Changing Liabilities to Assets," *Business Week* (20 March 1965), 156+; W. VanTil, "Five Bold Ways to Attack the Dropout Problem," *Parents Magazine* (March 1965), 58–59; "Dad's Letter to a Dropout," *Good Housekeeping* (June 1965), 77+; "Our Readers Write about Dropouts," *Good Housekeeping* (October 1965), 24+; J. Miller, "It's a Dead-end Road for the Dropout," *Reader's Digest* (May 1965), 125–30; R. Hassenger, "Dropout," *America* (September 1965), 342–43; "Why Drop-outs Drop Out," *Science Digest* (January 1965), 20; S. Horwitz, "Employment Lab for Teenagers in Trouble," *Parents Magazine* (December 1966), 64–67+; J. Pollack, "Astonishing Truth about Girl Dropouts," *Parents Magazine* (September 1966): 66–67+; "Conversations Parents Never Hear," *Look* (20 September 1966), 61; B. Bard, "Why Dropout Campaigns Fail," *Saturday Review* (17 September 1966), 78–79+; "Technological Society Can Use Dropouts," *Science News* (25 June 1966), 509; D. Weldon, "Dropouts Anonymous," *Reader's Digest* (August 1966), 17–18+; R. Heilbroner, "No Room at the Bottom," *Saturday Review* (19 February 1966), 29–32; "Teacher's Dedication to Those Whose Search Has Failed," *Life* (28 April 1967), 76–79; P. Pierce,

"Street Academies: New Way to Reach the Ghetto Dropout," *Ebony* (August 1967), 158–60+; J. Sideman, "Death of a Dropout," *New Republic* (3 June 1967), 11–14; "Academies for Dropouts," *Time* (2 August 1968), 50; A. Eliasberg, "How to Stop a Dropout," *New York Times Magazine* (10 November 1968), 109–10+; "Letter to the Castle: Why I Want to Go Back to School," *Nation* (20 May 1968), 665–68; J. Featherstone, "Storefront Schools in Harlem," *New Republic* (7 September 1968), 21–27; A. Fisher, "White Rights versus Indian Rights," *Trans-Action* (November 1969), 29–33; J. Black, "Street Academies: One Step off the Sidewalk," *Saturday Review* (15 November 1969), 88–89+; B. Robinson, "Return of the Dropouts," *Motor Boat and Sailing* (December 1970), 44–45; "Second-chance Academy," *Ebony* (January 1971), 39–42; "Dropping out of School: Problem or Symptom?" *Science News* (6 November 1971), 310; C. Easton, "A Time to Fail; A Time to Succeed," *Parents Magazine* (December 1971), 44–45+; "How to Handle Dropouts," *Time* (22 October 1973), 98; "The 2.4 Million Children Who Aren't in School," *U.S. News and World Report* (22 March 1976), 43–44; "What's Being Done about the Dropouts?" *U.S. News and World Report* (2 June 1980), 64; B. Lefkowitz, "Making It as a Dropout," *Psychology Today* (December 1980), 106+; "Emotionally Bruised into Dropping Out," *Psychology Today* (December 1980), 102; "School Dropouts Learn a Lesson," *U.S. News and World Report* (19 December 1983), 11; "School Dropouts—State By State," *U.S. News and World Report* (3 June 1985), 14; "Hawkins Notes Prevention, Recovery Programs Key to Solving Drop Out Problem," *Jet* (8 July 1985), 22; "Teachers' Union Launches School Dropout Program," *Jet* (22 July 1985), 24; "Congressman Hayes Pushes Bill to Combat Dropout Rate in U.S.," *Jet* (26 August 1985), 39; G. Tapply, "What to Do When Your Teen Wants to Quit School," *Better Homes and Gardens* (June 1985): 30+; "Ford Foundation to Fight Dropout Rate in 21 Cities," *Jet* (22 December 1986), 24; "A Drop in the Dropout Rate," *U.S. News and World Report* (2 June 1986), 9; "High Drop Out School Plan Stirs Students to Excel," *Jet* (7 July 1986), 23; "Lionel Richie Wows D.C. Junior High Students," *Jet* (1 December 1986), 61; B. Thompson, "Dropping Out: The Once and Future Crisis," *Christianity Today* (17 October 1986), 32–36; "Saving Lives," *America* (4–11 January 1986), 2; M. D'Urso, "The A-Team," *Health* (July 1986): 18; "Bringing in the Dropouts: Symphonic Music Helps," *High Fidelity* (October 1986): MA8–MA11; L. Solorzano, "The Campaign to Lure Kids Back to Class," *U.S. News and World Report* (3 March 1986), 77–78; J. Baker, "Helping Dropouts Drop In," *Newsweek* (3 August 1987), 63; M. Oshin, "Top-grade Perks for Teens," *Essence* (June 1987), 38; "A Drop in Dropouts," *U.S. News and World Report* (23 May 1988), 13; D. Elkind, "Dropping out of School," *Parents Magazine* (December 1988), 221; B. Remmes, "Why Kids Drop Out," *Newsweek* (6 March 1989), 10–11; J. Rachlin and J. Shapiro, "No Pass, No Drive," *U.S. News and World Report* (5 June 1989), 49–51; G. Becker, "Tuning in to the Needs of High School Dropouts," *Business Week* (3 July 1989), 18; T.

Mason, "Can Business Throw a Net under Hispanic Dropouts?" *Business Week* (20 February 1989), 151+; P. Skalka, "No One's a Born Loser!" *Reader's Digest* (February 1989): 21–22+; L. Ransom, "Can the School Drop-out Problem be Solved?" *Jet* (9 October 1989), 12–13.

5. D. McQuail, "Processes of Media Effects," in *Media, Knowledge, and Power*, ed. O. Boyd-Barrett and P. Braham (London: Croom-Helm, 1987), 93.

6. E. Krug, *The Shaping of the American High School: 1920–1942*. (Madison: University of Wisconsin Press, 1972).

7. W. French, *American Secondary Education* (New York: Odyssey, 1967).

8. I. Kandell, *The Impact of the War on American Education* (Charlotte: University of North Carolina Press, 1949).

9. French, *American Secondary Education.*

10. M. LeCompte, "The Cultural Context of Dropping Out: Why Remedial Programs Fail to Solve the Problem," *Education and Urban Society* 19 (1987), 237.

11. G. Wehlage et al., *Reducing the Risk: Schools as Communities of Support* (London: Falmer, 1989).

12. A. Pearl, "Employment Dilemmas of Youth," in *The Value of Youth*, ed. A. Pearl, D. Grant, and E. Wenk (Davis, CA: International Dialogue, 1978).

13. J. Rachlin and J. Shapiro, "No Pass, No Drive," *U.S. News and World Report* (5 June 1989), 49.

14. "School Drop-out," *Good Housekeeping* (March 1962), 144.

15. "Only High School Grads Need Apply," *Business Week* (11 August 1962), 51.

16. LeCompte, "The Cultural Context of Dropping Out," 232.

17. C. Brossard, "Teenager without a Job," *Look* (27 February 1962), 32.

18. "Chicago's Answer for Dropouts," *Ebony* (October 1963), 81.

19. G. Hecht, "Calamity of Our Million School Dropouts," *Parents Magazine* (September 1957), 100.

20. Rachlin and Shapiro, "No Pass, No Drive," 49.

21. L. Ransom, "Can the School Drop-out Problem Be Solved?" *Jet* (9 October 1989), 13.

22. "Changing Liabilities to Assets," *Business Week* (20 March 1965), 162.

23. See, for example, J. Miller, "It's a Dead-end Road for the Dropout," *Reader's Digest* (May 1965); T. Mason, "Can Business Throw a Net under Hispanic Dropouts?" *Business Week* (20 February 1989).

24. Miller, "It's a Dead-end Road," 126–27.

25. W. VanTil, "Five Bold Ways to Attack the Dropout Problem," *Parents Magazine* (March 1965), 59.

26. Hecht, "Calamity," 39.

27. "Tragedy of Dropouts." *Ebony* (September 1961) 48–49.

28. A. Fisher, "White Rights vs. Indian Rights," *Trans-Action* (November 1969), 29–33.

29. G. White, "The Dropouts," *Ladies Home Journal* (January 1951), 51.

30. E. Stern, "Our New Lost Generation," *Woman's Home Companion* (March 1946), 4.

31. Ibid.

32. "Saving Lives," *America* (4–11 January 1986), 2.

33. E. Stern, "Why Teen-agers Quit School," *Woman's Home Companion* (October 1949), 94.

34. Brossard, "Teenager without a Job," 32.

35. G. Leonard, "Are We Cheating Twenty Million Students?" *Look* (4 June 1963), 36–40.

36. "Second-chance Academy," *Ebony* (January 1971), 40.

37. See, for example, P. Bullock and R. Singleton, "What to Do with the Dropout?" *New Republic* (20 October 1962); "Tragedy of Dropouts."

38. "High Drop Out School Plan Stirs Students to Excel," *Jet* (7 July 1986), 32.

39. "Hopeful Second Change," *Life* (9 May 1960).

40. "Chicago's Answer," 81.

41. "The 2.4 Million Children Who Aren't in School," *U.S. News and World Report* (22 March 1976), 43.

42. J. Pollack, "What Happens When Kids Quit School?" *Parents Magazine* (August 1952), 27.

43. VanTil, "Five Bold Ways," 59.

44. "Dropout Tragedies," *Life* (2 May 1960), 48.

45. Hecht, "Calamity," 100.

46. Leonard, "Are We Cheating," 38.

47. "Changing Liabilities to Assets," 158.

48. Pollack, "What Happens," 72.

49. Ibid., 45.

50. VanTil, "Five Bold Ways," 132.

51. The attention to dropouts' personal problems has only marginaly included pregnancy. In the articles under consideration, just six mention pregnancy, only in connection with girls, and all but one of the articles contains only a passing reference, such as "many girls drop out because of pregnancy."

52. Rachlin and Shapiro, "No Pass, No Drive," 49.

53. Bullock, "What to Do," 17.

54. Brossard, "Teenager without a Job," 33.

55. "What's Being Done about the Dropouts?" *U.S. News and World Report* (2 June 1980), 64.

56. Miller, "It's a Dead-end Road," 126.

57. "Dropout Tragedies," 106B.

58. J. Baker, "Helping Dropouts Drop In," *Newsweek* (3 August 1987), 63.

59. W. Tapply, "What to Do When Your Teen Wants to Quit School," *Better Homes and Gardens* (June 1985), 30.

60. B. Remmes, "Why Kids Drop Out," *Newsweek* (6 March 1989), 10.

61. Pollack, "What Happens," 27.

62. VanTil, "Five Bold Ways," 59.

63. See, for example, Mason, "Can Business Throw a Net"; "The Day Our Boy Quit School and How We Got Him Back In!" *Farm Journal* (May 1964).

64. See, for example, "Dropout Tragedies"; "What's Being Done."

65. "Discussion," *Ebony* (November 1961).

66. See, for example, Pollack, "What Happens"; P. Skalka, "No One's a Born Loser," *Reader's Digest* (February 1989); B. Thompson, "Dropping Out: The Once and Future Crisis," *Christianity Today* (17 October 1986); "Changing Liabilities."

67. A. Eliasberg, "How to Stop a Dropout," *New York Times Magazine* (10 November 1968), 112.

68. Thompson, "Dropping Out," 34.

69. See, for example, "High Drop Out School Plan"; M. Oshin, "Top-grade Perks for Teens." *Essence* (June 1987); Rachlin and Shapiro, "No Pass, No Drive."

70. Rachlin and Shapiro, "No Pass, No Drive."

71. Stern, "Why Teen-agers Quit School," 90.

72. Brossard, "Teenager without a Job," 32.

73. Pollack, "What Happens," 28.

74. "School Drop-out," *Good Housekeeping,* 145.

75. Stern, "Why Teenagers Quit School."

76. Pollack, "What Happens."

77. "Changing Liabilites to Assets," 162.

78. "The 2.4 Million Children," 43.

79. "The 2.4 Million Children," 44.

80. E. Brandes, "Manpower Planning and the New Pariahs," *Reporter* (26 March 1964), 17.

81. Ibid., 19.

82. B. Lefkowitz, "Making It as a Dropout," *Psychology Today* (December 1980), 106.

83. J. Ogbu, "Class Stratification, Racial Stratification, and Schooling." In *Class, Race and Gender In American Education*, ed. L. Weis (Albany: SUNY Press, 1988).

84. M. Fine and P. Rosenberg, "Dropping out of High School: The Ideology of School and Work," *Journal of Education* (1983), 257–72.

85. R. Stevenson and J. Ellsworth, "Dropping out in a Working Class High School: Adolescent Voices on the Decision to Leave," *British Journal of Sociology of Education* (1991), 277–91.

6 *New York Times*'s Coverage of Educational Reform: The 1950s and 1980s Compared

Okhee Lee and Michael Salwen

Educational reform has been a continuing national concern since the turn of the century. Debates about educational reform, especially during periods of perceived crisis, take place in social and political milieus that generate sustained public attention. This points to the need to understand how educational reform is reported in popular news media. This study compared the portrayal of educational reform in the *New York Times* during two periods of educational "crisis" in America—in the aftermath of the Soviet launch of *Sputnik I* on 4 October 1957 and following the release of the *Nation at Risk* report on 27 April 1983.

NEWS COVERAGE OF EDUCATION

Previous research of news media coverage about education indicates that, during most periods, the media devote little coverage to education.[1] In one of the most exhaustive studies, Gerbner analyzed national newspaper coverage of education from 1910 to 1960 and reported that, on average, about 4 percent of the "newshole" annually was devoted to educational issues.[2] Even this small percentage reported by Gerbner and replicated by others probably exaggerated the news media's attention to academic aspects of education, because much of the news coverage about education was devoted to athletics.[3]

When the state of American education becomes a "crisis," however, the media devote more attention to education than usual. The launches of Soviet *Sputnik* satellites in 1957 provide a striking example of how an event only peripherally related to education raised public consciousness of the deficiency of the nation's educational system.[4] Well before the *Sputnik* launches, there were debates inside educational circles about progressive education programs such as the Life Adjustment Movement.[5] The *Sputnik* launches, however, transformed what was an essentially closed, esoteric argument among scholars and educators into a public controversy.

During the 1980s, the fear that Japan and European nations posed a threat to America's economic prowess once again aroused national fears that American education was not adequately preparing its children for the future. A report issued by the National Commission on Excellence in Education, under the leadership of T.E. Bell, the Secretary of Education, was ominously titled, *A Nation at Risk: The Imperative for Educational Reform.*[6] The report stated the problem of American education in chilling terms sure to catch the attention of the news media and the public: "If an unfriendly foreign power had attempted to impose on America the mediocre educational performance that exists today, we might well have viewed it as an act of war. . . . We have, in effect, been committing an act of unthinking, unilateral educational disarmament." The report was followed by a plethora of national studies and reports that indicated that academic achievement among U.S. students had steadily declined since the mid-1960s and that U.S. students were performing at levels worse than their counterparts in other developed nations.

This study investigated how a respected popular news medium, the *New York Times*, portrayed education reform during the 1950s and 1980s. The study also investigated the newspaper's rhetoric during the two periods. Many journalism scholars have noted that the journalistic method is largely ahistorical, treating all news events as novel and without precedents.[7] Ironically, while journalists value novelty for its newsworthiness, novelty creates tension within news organizations, because the news media are unable to cope with novelty on a daily basis. Meeting the demands of newness on a daily basis precludes this as a realistic possibility. As a result, news coverage has become routinized so that similar events are reported the same way. This routinization of the news may consist of both standardized presentations and rhetorical devices.[8]

PROCEDURES

To investigate the *Times*'s coverage and rhetoric of educational crises during the 1950s and 1980s, the study analyzed (1) observable characteristics of the coverage and (2) rhetorical aspects of the coverage that could not be easily quantified but were needed in order to understand underlying aspects of the coverage.

The *New York Times*'s coverage of educational reform was examined for a six-month period, starting 4 October 1957, the day the Soviets launched the first *Sputnik*, to 4 April 1958. This coverage was compared with a second period consisting of six months of the *Times*'s coverage from 27 April 1983, when the *Nation at Risk* report was made public, to 27 October 1983. Stories were selected from *The New York Times Index* heading of "Education" that appeared under the subheadings of "Students," "Teachers," and "Schools." All stories—including newspaper stories, columns, editorials, and letters to the editor—were examined. A total of 280 news stories about educational reform were reported in the *New York Times* during both periods: 133 during the 1950s and 147 during the 1980s.

Each story was coded for (1) the problems facing American education, (2) their causes, and (3) possible solutions. These categories implied that the stories would be negative. Since it is possible that the *Times* might report positive stories about American education, a fourth category, praise, was also coded. After carefully reading the news stories, eleven categories were created to classify the stories in each of four domains of problems, causes, solutions, and praise. Multiple coding was permitted, so stories could be coded as having any of several problems, causes, solutions, or praise.[9]

FINDINGS

The five most frequently reported problems, causes, solutions and praise that appeared in the pages of the *Times* during the 1950s and 1980s are presented in table 6.1. As can be seen, the *Times* offered a large number of problem definitions and solutions during both periods. Only a small number of causes were reported. the *Times* and the sources cited in the *Times* were stingy in doling out praise.

Regarding problem definitions, the same five problems headed the list during the 1950s and the 1980s. The rankings of the five problems, however, are largely reversed. During the 1950s, the insufficiency of education in relation to international affairs was regarded as the most serious problem. It was followed by problems concerning the goals and pedagogy of American education as well as school curriculum. During the 1950s, the modification of goals and pedagogy was most commonly reported as the solution to the education crisis. In contrast, during the 1980s, problems concerning teachers (and teaching) and students (and

Table 6.1
Five Most Frequent Categories of Problems, Causes, Solutions, and Praise

		1950s	N		1980s	N
Problems	1.	International Affairs	37	1.	Teachers and Teaching	42
	2.	Goals and Pedagogy	23	2.	Students and Learning	39
	3.	Curriculum	20	3.	Goals and Pedagogy	16
	4.	Students and Learning	18	4.5	Curriculum	9
	5.	Teachers and Teaching	12	4.5	International Affairs	9
Causes	1.	Parental Support	11	1.	Teachers and Teaching	22
	2.	Leadership	9	2.	External Influences	19
	3.5	Goals and Pedagogy	7	3.	Leadership	8
	3.5	Schooling	7	4.5	Curriculum	7
	5.	External Influences	6	4.5	Schooling	7
Solutions	1.	Goals and Pedagogy	46	1.	Teachers and Teaching	69
	2.	Curriculum	33	2.5	Financial Support	37
	3.5	Students and Learning	29	2.5	Schooling	37
	3.5	Teachers and Teaching	29	4.	Curriculum	32
	5.	Financial Support	26	5.	Students and Learning	29
Praise	1.	Goals and Pedagogy	18	1.	Schooling	14
	2.	Schooling	6	2.	Teachers and Teaching	12
	3.	Teachers and Teaching	3	3.	Research and Academics	8
	4.	*	—	4.	Goals and Pedagogy	7
	5.	*	—	5.	Students and Learning	6

* = Four categories tied with N = 2.1

learning) were the two most often reported serious problems. Accordingly, solutions dealing with teachers and teaching were most often portrayed as necessary responses to the educational crisis.

As far as causes of the education crisis were concerned, the *Times* offered few explanations during either period. During the 1950s, no single cause received much attention. During the 1980s, causes focusing on teachers and teaching, and on external influences, received some attention. The small number of attributed causes of the education crisis in the pages of the *Times* during both periods is noteworthy, compared to the number of problems and solutions reported in its coverage. One would think that it is difficult to discuss problems of American education and offer solutions without examining the causes of the crisis in question.

During the 1950s, the *Times* dispensed little praise for American education. Only one category, goals and pedagogy, received some praise. The amount of praise increased somewhat during the 1980s. Matters dealing with schooling and teachers and teaching, respectively, received the most praise. These numbers are testimony to the supporters of American education who came forward to defend the embattled educational system during a time of harsh criticism.

Overall, the prominence of the various problems, causes, solutions, and praise regarding the education crisis in the pages of the *Times* were substantially different between the two periods. While the same concerns appeared during both periods, the emphasis clearly differed. During the 1950s, the education crisis centered on international concerns having more to do with goals and pedagogy, as well as with curriculum, than with teachers and students. During the 1980s, however, the crisis was viewed more as a domestic problem, and both its nature and solution tended to focus attention on teachers and teaching.

These quantitative findings are very broad, however, and suggest the value of exploring the coverage in greater depth. The major findings from descriptive analyses of the rhetoric of the news content during the 1950s and 1980s will be presented in the following sections.

DESCRIPTIVE ANALYSIS, 1950s

The 4 October 1957 launch of *Sputnik* dominated headlines for weeks and months after the event. A week after the first launch, the *Times* carried a story linking the *Sputnik* launch with matters of educational concern under the headline: "Satellite Called Spur to Education: Soviet Success Shows Need for a Major U.S. Effort" (12 October 1957, p. 3). By mid-November, it appeared as if all public leaders and public organizations felt obliged to respond to the crisis in American education. Even leaders and organizations not ordinarily associated with educational issues, such as military leaders, the mayor of New York City, former President Harry Truman, Vice-President Richard Nixon, novelist William Faulkner, the B'nai B'rith organization, the Foreign Legion, and union leaders were cited as education "experts" in the *Times*. Given the cold war between the Soviet Union and the United States, many of the prominent sources quoted in the pages of the *Times* drew heavily on the rhetoric of war.

The Critics

Critics of American education were to be found in all sectors of society, but they predominated in the military and the sciences. The critics viewed the educational crisis in international terms, as part of the cold war with the Soviets. They also saw the underlying philosophy of American education (i.e., goals and pedagogy) and school curricula as being at the heart of questions about the crisis, its problems, causes, and solutions. The debate concerned issues of (1) excellence versus equality as the goal of American education, (2) progressive education versus traditional drill and memorization of "basics" as pedagogical guides, and (3) sciences versus humanities in the school curriculum. The critics advocated excellence, basic skills, and sciences.

The critics of American education praised the "egghead," demanding more and better academic opportunities for capable and gifted students who would become future leaders, often at the expense of directing national energies toward low-achieving and even average students. For example, Dr. John F. Gunmere, chairman of the Secondary Education Board, said, "Schools should be permitted to concentrate scarce teaching resources on promising pupils. . . . Compulsory education should be modified so youngsters are not forced into school when they are incapable of receiving further education" (9 March 1958, p. 64). As another example, Dr. John P. Hagen, director of the U.S. *Vanguard* satellite program, gave a speech calling on the United States to establish an "intellectual elite" to lead the United States into the space age. Dr. Hagen, who called for stiffer high school science and mathematics courses and elimination of "frills" courses, said that "this nation needs to look to the egghead who will determine our progress in this new world" (1 February 1958, p. 7).

Some critics directly attacked the principles of progressive education. Ohio Senator John W. Bricker, speaking at a college convocation in Wilberforce, Ohio, lashed out against "professional pedagogues," adding that he objected to "teachers who were so fond of the label 'progressive' education that they considered as unimportant such subjects as mathematics and spelling" (14 November 1957, p. 27).

The *Times*'s coverage of educational reform during the 1950s was heavily tinged by the rhetoric of war and the danger of Soviet communism. Many critics viewed the *Sputnik* launches as "warnings" of the dire state of American education. The *Times* described how various interest groups and individuals described the *Sputnik* launches as "a shocker like Pearl Harbor, waking America up and making it buckle down" (17 November 1957, p. 8).

Perhaps most interesting is the set of persons quoted for their expertise on the state of American education. The experts were by no means uniformly from the ranks of education. For example, Rear Admiral H.G. Rickover, described in the *Times* as a "nuclear expert," became one of the nation's many self-proclaimed "education experts." Rickover traveled throughout the country and gave numerous speeches on American education. Typical of Rickover's speeches: "The launching of the *Sputniks* was a providential warning; we will disregard this warning at our peril" (23 November 1957, p. 8). Elsewhere in the same speech, Rickover blamed school curricula for America's unpreparedness in the space race: "If local schools continue to teach such pleasant subjects as 'life adjustment' . . . instead of trigonometry, French and physics, its diploma for all the world to see would be inferior" (23 November 1957, p. 8).

In a speech addressed to an audience of school administrators, Lawrence G. Derthick, United States Commissioner of Education, said "education had become 'the master weapon' in the 'cold war' and the United States must mobilize its educational facilities to combat the Soviet Union" (30 March 1958, p. 50).

Vice-President Richard Nixon threw himself into the debate over educational reform. Nixon aligned himself with the conservative critics and adopted their war rhetoric. Nixon called for more rigorous science and mathematics in the school curriculum, stressing that "Education constituted our most fundamental challenge as a result of Soviet scientific advances and that American military and economic strength could be no greater than our educational system" (16 December 1957, p. 1).

Besieged Defenders

Given our fear of the Soviets and the powerful war rhetoric coming from critics of American education, supporters were clearly at a disadvantage. How could they overcome the chilling rhetoric of their critics? For the most part, they did so gingerly, giving perfunctory approval to the value of science and mathematics as part of the educational curriculum. At the same time, they carefully pointed to the value of arts and the humanities in the curriculum. Some were also advocates for equal opportunity and progressive education. Interestingly, however, even the defenders drew on the rhetoric of war.

Like the critics, the defenders also saw a "warning" in the *Sputnik* launches. The warning, as the defenders interpreted it, was to give more attention to mathematics and science while also maintaining broad-based liberal education and humanities as the base of the curriculum. For example, Devereux C. Josephs, the head of the President's Committee for Higher Education and Beyond the High School, declared in a speech in New York that this nation's goal "does not end with survival, but with the justification of survival." Josephs added that if the United States seeks to achieve technical and educational superiority by using the same means as the Soviets, "we will shortly become indistinguishable from them" (14 February 1958, p. 26).

Some defenders called for equality of education in a democratic society. While admitting the importance of science and mathematics, as well as accelerated study for talented students, the State Board of Regents in New York still had this to say:

> The American system with its democratic goals of equality and of educational opportunity, freedom of choice for all youths based on our heritage of moral and spiritual values, constitutes democracy's most effective weapon for combating the military threat posed by the scientific and ideological challenges of the Soviet Union and its satellite nations. (22 November 1957, p. 17)

On the whole, most defenders did not directly attack their critics. In fact, they conceded the validity of many of their opponents' charges, but warned against taking their arguments too far. Occasional lone voices, such as Dr. Anne Hoppock, of the New Jersey State Board of Education, directly attacked the motives of the critics as "careless, misinformed or deliberately destructive critics who say our schools have failed. Crash programs may be appropriate for missile production, but not for teaching children" (27 March 1958, p. 35).

If the nation was looking for leadership on the national debate over educational reform during the 1950s, it did not find it in the Oval Office. President Dwight D. Eisenhower did not take a firm stand one way or the other on the educational crisis. Eisenhower's rhetoric at times sounded like that of the defenders of American education; but his defense was so restrained and ambiguous that he could have been interpreted either as a cautious defender or a mild critic. In line with conservative critics, Eisenhower agreed that American schools needed to place greater stress on science and mathematics. Eisenhower, however, also warned against emulating Soviet education, claiming that Soviet educational philosophy "postpones again and again the promise to each man that he will be allowed to be himself, and to enjoy according to his own desires the fruit of his own labor" (14 November 1957, p. 14).

Marion B. Folsom, Eisenhower's Secretary of Health, Education and Welfare, became one of the strongest and earliest defenders of American education. Speaking at a conference in Chicago, Folsom argued that despite "the dramatic advances of Soviet technological education," American education must continue to develop "broadly educated men in the humanities" (3 November 1957, p. 20). He warned Americans not to imitate Soviet education, which he said would be "tragic for mankind."

Typical of the rhetoric of the defenders of American education, Folsom felt obliged to counter the critics' harsh war rhetoric. The remarks of Folsom and other defenders either implied or directly stated that Soviet education focused narrowly on the sciences. The supporters of liberal education and humanities claimed that Soviet students were being trained to become uncritical servants of the state by means of a regimented, robotic educational system.

Both the defenders and critics seemed to accept the conclusion that Soviet education gave little or no attention to the arts and humanities. There were some efforts to correct this misperception, but, given the extraordinary war rhetoric during the 1950s, these efforts received little attention. For example, a letter to the editor of the *Times* from an associate professor of Slavic languages at Columbia University attempted to correct this misperception: "With all the sensational news about the thoroughness of scientific training in Soviet schools, I have seen very little discussion of the attention that Soviet educators give to the humanities. . . . Every ten-year-school graduate wishing to enter a Soviet university can expect to be examined, among other things, on Shakespeare's 'Hamlet' and part one of Goethe's 'Faust'" (23 November 1957, p. 18).

The Times *Takes a Stand*

The *Times* took a clear stand in the emerging debate regarding the value of the sciences versus the humanities in the educational reform debate. It ran an editorial entitled "The Educated Man" that was the subject of a number of subsequent letters to the editor (12 November 1957, p. 36). The thrust of the editorial was that science and mathematics, while valuable, should only be parts of a broad-based education:

> Scientists and technicians, yes, and the more the better. But the essential base, before becoming scientist or technician or anything else, is to obtain a glimpse of the broader horizons of life, the literature, the arts. . . . This is what we need, what we have always needed, and what we should make sure does not get lost in the sudden rally to the standard of science.

This editorial received a good deal of attention, based on the number of responses to the editorial that appeared in subsequent issues of the Letters to the Editor section. Most of the responses agreed with the *Times*'s view. Hyman Bookbinder, legislative representative from the AFL-CIO, applauded the editorial (18 November 1957, p. 30). Bookbinder added that extremists' calls for "crash courses" in the sciences at the expense of the humanities were part of a growing anti-intellectual climate: "The *Sputniks* have documented our specific lag in missile development. . . . But our lag runs right across the whole scientific and intellectual spectrum. If we had more Russian-speaking scientists and diplomats, for example, we might have known from public sources what our intellectual apparatus was not apparently able to tell us."

DESCRIPTIVE ANALYSIS: 1980s

During the 1950s, the Soviet threat loomed large in public discussions and press coverage about educational reform. An identifiable enemy made for clear and simple interpretations of the problems in, causes of, and solutions to the education crisis. During the 1980s, the foreign threat, when it was addressed, was more ambiguous than three decades earlier. While the economic threat from Japan and European countries surfaced in the press coverage, the threat was not concrete and certainly did not pose an immediate identifiable danger. Without a backdrop of a clearly defined foreign enemy against which to view America's education troubles, the problem of educational reform was exposed in terms of many more complexities. There appeared to be no "quick-fix" solution.

Even without a Soviet threat, war rhetoric found its way into the *Times*'s coverage during the 1980s. The tone of the debate over the education crisis and the war rhetoric had their roots in the government-sponsored report, *A Nation at Risk,* which used provocative and quotable expressions about American education, such as "a rising tide of mediocrity that threatens our very future as a nation and a people" and "unthinking, unilateral educational disarmament." These statements were quoted again and again in education stories that appeared in the *Times*. Although war metaphors served as a backdrop for education debates during the 1980s, the substantive issues that were debated were rather distinct from such rhetoric. After describing substantive issues in the *Times*'s coverage of education debate, the role of rhetoric will be described.

A Concern with Teachers

The most striking difference between the *Times*'s coverage of the education crisis during the 1950s and during the 1980s was the attention given to teachers and teaching during the 1980s. With the crisis and alarm that America's educational system lagged behind European nations and Japan, threatening "the military, economic, and social well-being of the country" (5 May 1983, p. 1), teachers and teaching were portrayed as being at the heart of the matter, both an important cause and a possible solution to the education crisis. Both critics and defenders of American education, when making comparisons to education systems in Japan and European countries, focused on this issue. Accordingly, most of the war metaphors concerned teachers and teaching in the classroom and school.

One issue involved the failure to recruit and retain qualified teachers. For instance, one story noted that among the students attending the 13 colleges on the University of Tennessee's main campus at Knoxville, those entering the School of Education ranked twelfth in test scores (14 June 1983, p. 16). In another story, a principal in a Hebrew School in Orlando, Florida, was convinced that the state-mandated teacher competency test was too easy. He gave what he said was a representative sample of the test items to his sixth grade students and found that they all passed the test (7 June 1983, p. 17).

Teacher training and certification requirements were identified as another major issue. Mary H. Futrell, president of National Education Association (NEA), said in an interview: "No one denies that there are teachers who aren't qualified to teach. . . . But the teachers' colleges that produced those people and the state education departments that certified them are responsible for putting them in the classroom, not us" (3 July 1983, p. 14). In a column, Charles Peters and Phil Keisling blamed teacher education programs for the poor quality of teachers: "Today one cannot teach in an American public school without a degree in education. Yet education courses are the academic equivalent of junk food—heavy on methodology and so devoid of substantive content that the best students avoid them" (13 July 1983, p. 21).

The problems with the quality of teachers and teacher training were frequently portrayed in war metaphors. Fred M. Hechinger, one of the *Times* education editors, stated: "There is no lack of generals who are calling for a campaign to improve the public schools. But what is lacking is an army of teachers trained to fight the battle for reforms. The nation's major universities, by largely abandoning teacher training, have done little to provide those important troops" (25 October 1983, section 3, p. 5). Hechinger's solution extended the war metaphor: "The generals would have to spend more time with their troops."

Since teachers were presented as central, contributing factors in the education crisis, the solution was often portrayed as having to do with teachers, especially their salaries and status. A teacher succinctly stated: "Teachers are poorly paid, do not advance, and are not given status. . . . In obscurity, one labors for a pittance" (1 May 1983, section 22, p. 26). This view was reflected in an editorial: "Much of the blame is placed on the teachers, and they are 'punished' for this by low salaries" (19 June 1983, section 11, p. 22). In one feature story, the *Times* reported that many teachers had to hold second jobs in order to survive. The story quoted an elementary school teacher who worked evenings as a cashier in an airport gift shop: "If I work until 1 o'clock in the morning and then get to school early, I certainly can't function at my optimum level" (4 June 1983, p. 7).

While no one disputed that teachers were underpaid and deserving of higher salaries and status, much of the debate centered on the controversial issue of "merit pay." This issue raised the question of whether all teachers should get across-the-board salary increases or only those teachers identified as qualified or even exemplary should get rewarded with merit pay increases.

The nation's teachers were split on the issue of merit pay. Although they conceded that rewarding good teaching was commendable, they were concerned about the difficulty involved in defining and evaluating good teaching. They feared that a merit-pay system would be used for political purposes. The nation's largest organization of teachers, the National Education Association (NEA), was squarely against merit pay. The American Federation of Teachers (AFT), a rival organization, was wary of merit pay, although it was not completely against the concept.

President Reagan took clear stands on education issues. While stressing excellence in American education, Reagan sought to arouse the attention of the public: "America is finally waking up to a threat to this nation caused by neglect of the most important function of our schools—teaching the skills that people need to succeed in life" (30 June 1983, p. 14). President Reagan proposed two major solutions to the education crisis: merit pay and a substantially reduced role of the federal government in American education.

President Reagan thrust himself into the merit-pay debate and called for the implementation of a merit-pay system. Reagan had criticized the NEA, after associating it with the Democratic party and liberal causes, for "clinging to" such standards as seniority and using "the number of college credits" in postgraduate studies to determine teacher salaries (16 June 1983, p. 24). When the *Times* covered the NEA's annual meeting in Philadelphia, the lead paragraph referred to Reagan's "presence" at the meeting: "The ghost of Ronald Reagan seemed to fill the vast Civic Center here for the five days of the National Education Association's convention" (7 July 1983, p. 13). The very day that the NEA concluded its meeting, Reagan gave a speech in California before the American Federation of Teachers, an organization generally more favorable to Reagan's polices, in which Reagan indirectly accused the NEA of "'brainwashing American children' by supporting courses on racism and nuclear disarmament in American schools" (7 July 1983, section 2, p. 1).

President Reagan also thrust himself into the debate on the role of the federal government in education. In line with his overall political philosophy, he repeatedly called for the federal government to play a smaller role in education and for local and state governments to assume the responsibility. Reagan's leadership—or lack of it—on educational matters was the subject of several commentaries. *Times* writer Flora Lewis claimed that it was ironic that the president could call the *Nation at Risk* report "masterful" (20 May 1983, p. 31). Lewis claimed that Reagan "missed the point" of the report, which asserted that the federal government has the primary responsibility for educating the nation's children. Lewis wrote: "He [Reagan] seemed to have read it selectively." Education editor Edward B. Fiske also reported that the administration, though praising those portions of the report with which it agreed, was in a "somewhat uneasy position: It is being asked to provide leadership in a field that it has declared is not really a concern of the federal government" (28 April 1983, section 2, p. 15).

The Rhetoric of War Revisited

The public debate on the education crisis during the 1980s started with the release of the *Nation at Risk* report. Many of the stories in the *Times* quoted the alarming rhetoric found in this report, which seemed to set the national agenda for the debate. *Times* writer Phil Gailey wrote: "It was that commission, created by the President, that brought the issue to the forefront of the political debate with an urgency not felt since the first Soviet space satellite shook American confidence in its public schools in 1957" (9 June 1983, p. 1). *Times* education editor Edward B. Fiske also noted, "The language [in the report] was frankly intended to make the improvement of education into a political issue at all levels" (28 April 1983, section 2, p. 15).

Unlike the 1950s, the "enemy" was unclear during the 1980s. Japan, other Asian nations, and European nations did not represent a direct military threat. As a result, war rhetoric during the 1980s was more clearly metaphorical, while actual war was portrayed as a real possibility during the 1950s. There was a clear understanding in the pages of the *Times* that the warlike rhetoric in the *Nation at Risk* report was neither spontaneous nor the result of genuine fear. There was a suspicion that various parties intentionally exploited war rhetoric in order to draw attention to America's education problems. The *Times* even carried several stories about how various parties, critics and defenders of American education, used powerful language to arouse public interest in the education debate. For example, Harold Howe II, a former United States Commissioner of Education, squarely attacked the rhetoric of *A Nation at Risk,* calling it "sensational," and suggested that "the high pitch of the rhetoric [was] designed for publicity" (28 April 1983, section 2, p. 15).

Overall, the tendency to use war metaphors in national reports on the education crisis was greeted with some skepticism. At a meeting, presidents of several prestigious universities referred to the harsh rhetoric as a "tactic of dramatizing in order to arouse public concern." Donald Kennedy, the president of Stanford University, said of the war-like rhetoric: "To use a Vietnam analogy, some seem to feel that we have to bomb the village in order to save it" (13 August 1983, section 3, p. 8).

To their credit, several editors of the *Times* during the 1980s were quick to point out the rhetorical differences in the education debate during the 1950s and 1980s (8 May 1983, section 4, p. 18; 10 May 1983, section 3, p. 4). Perhaps the *Times* education editor Fred M. Hechinger, noting the slew of dire reports about American education during the 1980s, best summarized how war rhetoric was being used to arouse public attention to educational reform:

> Only national emergencies seem to elicit major federal financing for education. The example of the *Sputnik* in orbit in 1957 has prompted Dr. Boyer to quip that a similar response was likely only if the Japanese put a Toyota into orbit. In a way, that is what happened, at least symbolically. Fear of Japanese competition may be translated into some federal dollars, but probably only for science, mathematics and technology. (4 October 1983, section 3, p. 8)

DISCUSSION AND CONCLUSIONS

This study compared the *New York Times*'s coverage of educational reform after the launch of *Sputnik* satellites in 1957 with the coverage after the release of the *Nation at Risk* report in 1983. War rhetoric set the tone of the debates during the 1950s and the 1980s. However, the educational debates existed within larger contexts that were incomparable during the two periods. During the 1950s, the military threat by the Soviet Union was immediate and, from the perspective of many members of the public, very real. As a result, the education crisis was portrayed as an international crisis marked by the urgent rhetoric of potential war. With the absence of a clear enemy during the 1980s, the education crisis was portrayed as a domestic problem. The metaphorical war rhetoric often appeared in the *Times*, but so, too, did criticism of such rhetoric as an attention-getting device.

What Was New and What Was Not

The *Times* must be credited with being aware of the historical context of public debates on education crises. Many stories during the

1980s referred to previous education-reform movements, especially those following the post-*Sputnik* movement during the 1950s. In one of his many insightful articles, *Times* education editor Edward B. Fiske compared the education crisis of the 1980s with that of the 1950s:

> The parallels between the current concern over educational excellence in this country and what happened after the Soviet Union launched *Sputnik* into orbit in 1957 are noteworthy. In both cases concern was generated by a perceived threat—military and economic—and in both cases much of the attention centered on math and science. (8 May 1983, section 4, p. 18)

Indeed, there were clear similarities in specific proposals for education reform presented in the *Times* during both periods—for instance, pursuit of both excellence and equality, more rigorous curriculum, higher standards for high school graduation and college admission, emphasis on science and mathematics, increases in teacher salaries, better discipline and motivation of students, better conditions for teaching and teachers, extended school years or days, and leadership and financial support for education.

However, systematic examination of content coverage in the *Times* indicates, as we have shown, that differences did exist in how the two crises were defined and addressed. During the 1950s, the goals and pedagogy of American education, along with school curriculum, were under attack. Solutions were to be found in curriculum changes and redefinitions of goals and pedagogy. During the 1980s, the coverage shifted to focus more on concrete and immediate concerns regarding teachers and teaching. In fact, the editors of the *Times* were aware of major differences between the two educational crisis debates. They repeatedly commented on these differences in terms of the altered international, political, and social context of education during the two time periods.

First, the overriding presence of the cold war accounted for the focus on international affairs of education during the 1950s. Cold war rhetoric helped define problems in education, and shaped discussion of the need to redefine the goals and pedagogy of American education, restructure school curriculum, and increase the financial support from and involvement of the federal government in education. Teachers and students were dwarfed by cold war rhetoric, and were largely left out of the debate in the *Times*. During the 1980s, in contrast, the cold war was in decline. No specific, single foreign threat could account for the education crisis. As a result, the education crisis was viewed as a largely domestic problem. Matters dealing with teachers and teaching dominated the *Times*'s coverage. For better or worse, teachers were seen "to make a difference."

Second, the *Times*'s coverage of educational reform also reflected the respective political contexts of the two time periods. During the 1950s, the federal government, under President Eisenhower, responded to the national calls for education reform by expanding its involvement in education and providing financial support, especially in the areas of science and mathematics. Among liberals and conservatives there was agreement that the federal government had to take the initiative in solving the crisis. During the 1980s, the conservative administration of President Reagan took a forceful role in thrusting its views about education into the national debate. Reagan argued against the federal government's involvement in education, and called for local school districts to take responsibility. Reagan also advocated a merit-pay system to encourage and reward good teaching.

The coverage during the 1980s also differed from the 1950s in terms of the social context of educational concern. In both cases, reform rhetoric centered on excellence emerged as a reaction to the social climate of each time period. As *Times* education editor Fred M. Hechinger noted, there was a significant difference in the concept of "excellence" between the 1950s and 1980s, although it was a 'favorite buzzword' during both periods (19 July 1983, section 3, p. 8). During the 1950s, excellence was pitted against those aspects of progressive education that had taken root in the education community. During the 1980s, pronouncements of concern for excellence contrasted with the struggle for social justice that dominated American society since the mid-1960s.

The *Times* occasionally shifted from its role as recorder and conduit of the views of the nation's elite and thrust itself into the debates. In its editorial pages and the columns of its own writers, the *Times* leaned toward favoring what would be described as the "establishment liberal" view during both periods. During the 1950s, it warned against the trend of incorporating science and mathematics into the curriculum at the expense of the humanities. During the 1980s, it decried the decentralization of federal government responsibility advocated by President Reagan. The *Times* called on the federal government to take an active role in solving the nation's educational problems.

In conclusion, this study has surveyed the *Times*'s coverage of education in periods of perceived crisis, and suggests the role played by the news concerning the perception of crisis itself. In this case, the perception of crisis was amplified by the use of war rhetoric to capture and focus the attention of the public on education debates during both the 1950s and the 1980s. Although the employment of war rhetoric was similar, the content of education stories in the *Times* was substantially different between the two periods. This suggests that newspapers such as the *Times* play a role in giving shape to the debates that take on a distinct character and focus at different time periods. While the *Times* may be commended for presenting a fairly broad spectrum of views representing the national debates on education during both periods, there clearly is a set of dominant issues and concerns that emerge during periods of perceived crisis. This study suggests that this dominant focus reflects aspects of the wider political and social context shaping what is considered newsworthy—a topic that warrants a much fuller analysis.

NOTES

1. T.L. Johnson, "The Portrayal of Education in *The New York Times Index*, 1970 to 1987, and in Prime Time Television Scripts, 1976 to 1986" (M.A. thesis, University of Pennsylvania, 1989); Michael Ryan and Dorothea Owen, "A Content Analysis of Metropolitan Newspaper Coverage of Social Issues," *Journalism Quarterly* 53; Guido H. Stempel III, "Content Patterns of Small and Metropolitan Newspapers," *Journalism Quarterly* 39.

2. George Gerbner, "Education about Education by the Mass Media," *The Educational Forum* 31.

3. Kaylene S. Baker, "A Content Analysis of the Educational News Stories Published in the 1976 *Des Moines Register*" (M.A. thesis, Iowa State University, 1988); George D. Cannon, "A Categorical Analysis of Educational Content Disseminated through Selected Mississippi Newspapers During 1970" (Ph.D. diss., University of Southern Mississippi, 1971); Luther W. Sanders, "A Content Analysis of Newspaper Coverage of Education News" (M.A. thesis, University of Tennessee, 1969); Stuart W. Showalter, "A Content Analysis of Three Dailies' Coverage of Higher Education Institutions within a Selected Metropolitan Area" (M.A. thesis, Ohio University, 1969).

4. Cheryl L. Marlin, "Space Race Propaganda: U.S. Coverage of the *Sputniks* in 1957," *Journalism Quarterly* 64.

5. Diane Ravitch, *The Troubled Crusade: American Education, 1945–1980* (New York: Basic Books, 1983); Willis Rudy, *Schools in the Age of Mass Culture* (Englewood Cliffs, NJ: Prentice-Hall, 1965).

6. National Commission on Excellence in Education, *A Nation at Risk: The Imperative of Educational Reform* (Washington, DC: Government Printing Office, 1983), p. 1.

7. Herbert J. Gans, *Deciding What's News: A Study of "CBS Evening News," "NBC Nightly News," "Newsweek" and "Time" (New York: Vintage Books, 1979).*

8. *Steven H. Chaffee, "The Diffusion of Political Information," in* Political

III PLOTTING LIVES

Narrative Accounts of School Experience

Stories sometimes take root in the imagination, hinting at horizons of possibility that might not otherwise have been conceived. In some cases, stories that portray school experience of exceptionally vivid kinds suggest horizons that are distinctly tied to what education can mean and can be. This section turns attention to the meaning and significance of narrative accounts of lives and events in school settings. In particular, these studies examine cinematic narratives of different kinds and consider their possible significance for the rather broad audience that engages them. Unlike the adolescent entertainments examined in Part I, school-based narratives tend to construct detailed, often optimistic, portrayals of what schooling can mean, while not purporting to inform their audience as the kind of sources examined in Part II do. As a result, narratives provide images—sometimes powerful ones—of what schooling might be, at least somewhere and for some people. The relationship of such stories to everyday experience provokes a set of questions, both about the kinds of stories that seem worth telling and how understandings derived from narratives interact with other aspects of lived experience.

Chapter 7, "A Brotherhood of Heroes: The Charismatic Educator in Recent American Movies," by Paul Farber and Gunilla Holm, examines the representation of the educator-hero in contemporary American films. This study demonstrates a common structural device at work in seemingly diverse films, and discusses how this device works to satisfy certain desires while marginalizing large numbers of educators and their concerns and accomplishments. In chapter 8, "Conformity,

Conflict, and Curriculum: Film Images of Boys' Preparatory Schools," Gary N. McCloskey describes important examples of movies portraying boys' preparatory schools. These films are discussed in relation to the way they frame issues of conformity and change pertaining to students being prepared to assume roles of power and authority in society. Chapter 9, "Miracle Working: Film and the Image of the Exceptional Student," by Arlene S. Sacks and Gary N. McCloskey, describes prominent themes and characteristics of movies that center on the education of exceptional students. These films are then analyzed in relation to larger issues regarding the actual problems and difficulties faced by students with special needs.

These studies raise into view stories that resonate in the public consciousness, raising questions about how such stories challenge or reinforce the way people tend to make sense of schooling. For practitioners, these works suggest the importance of reflecting on what popular narratives indicate about collective longings and fears regarding education. Vivid narratives speak to what is possible, giving form to vague hopes about what school experience might be like or how it might be transformed. Stories convey attitudes and expectations about schooling, while suggesting—whether darkly or hopefully—where things are heading or what individuals might achieve. Within the patterns and interactions of actual practice, such attitudes and expectations are an uncertain element. Stories provide images that can inspire individuals to transcend the limits of routine experience, strive to emulate the heroes whose tales are told.

But everyday experience may also be perceived as more bitter when set in contrast to dramatic stories in which familiar school settings are transformed, energized, or at least made a little more interesting. Gripping stories can, in short, encourage renewed faith and idealism or harden attitudes of apathy and resignation—or, indeed, do both. And it is this very ambiguity that intrigues us most, for it opens pedagogical possibilities of an extraordinary kind. From a pedagogical perspective, inquiry focused on the construction of stories set in schools has great potential for thinking about the meaning education typically has for those involved and the kinds of transformed possibilities we tend to respond to in works that capture the collective imagination. Through critical discussion of school-based stories, what can those involved in education learn about themselves, each other, and the institutions that bring them together? There is great potential here for reflective inquiry into the taken-for-granted world of schooling.

It is also the case that wider circles of discussion and insight are affected by the kinds of narratives explored in this section. Our collective heroes and villains set the parameters for debate, and these parameters, in turn, are conceptualized in terms of particular narrative accounts of what is taking place in schools. Consider, for example, the way many recent discussions of urban education became framed in relation to stories about fuch figures as Jaime Escalante and Joe Clark, stories disseminated through the popular media, including the films *Stand and Deliver* and *Lean on Me,* respectively. Such stories can be instrumental in the way perspectives crystallize and issues are articulated. The stories that are widely told matter, and so, too, does it matter how, at the level of public discussion, we think through the stories we tell, and what these in turn tell about us, our longings, and our fears.

This is a wide field for inquiry. The studies presented here explore themes and issues pertaining to a fairly broad scope of cinematic narratives. As in previous sections, this provides the basis for exploring a range of related topics. Inquiry into other films is clearly possible, as is examination of noncinematic narratives, such as novels and short stories that vividly portray the lives of teachers or school experience. Importantly, within the context provided here, there are numerous examples of particular works that could be plumbed in closer detail, especially with regard to their pedagogical significance. Both in schools and as a concerned public, close critical study of popular stories about school experience can play a role in our becoming more aware of how we make sense of schooling. The studies in this section seek to frame some of the possibilities for thinking about how stories serve to etch in our shared horizons—at once enabling and limiting ways of thinking about—what schooling is and can be.

other adults) who happen to be portrayed. These movies barely engage the teachers and principals that they typically reject or ignore; teachers and learning alike are simply never a subject worth talking about, except, perhaps, as an object of what Marc Crispin Miller has called the "promiscuous ridicule" of many recent Hollywood movies.[3] As a result, while they are implicitly critical of education and those involved in it, they are not so much subversive as simply dismissive. So far as schooling is concerned, they seem, if anything at all, to warn against taking it too seriously, commending instead a casual disinterest and disengagement.

A small number of movies, however, invite consideration of the experience and perspective of one or more educators engaged in school-related activity. In his review of films centered on adolescents, Considine describes the emergence of depictions of a teacher-hero.[4] Recent American movies seem to have given a boost to this phenomenon and reached out to acknowledge the occasional principal as well; hence, we use the term "educator-hero."

What do educator-heroes do on screen these days? In two instances, the stories of living men are told: Jaime Escalante's work in teaching mathematics to inner-city Hispanic students—as documented by the successes of Garfield High students on the Advanced Placement calculus test over recent years—is the subject of *Stand and Deliver*.[5] The widely publicized struggles of Joe Clark to reform an urban high school (Eastside High, in Paterson, New Jersey), through force of personality and methods that polarized his community, are depicted in *Lean on Me*.[6] Clark's battles pale beside the entirely fictional account of Rick Lattimore (Jim Belushi) in *The Principal*,[7] an action movie about taking charge in Chicago's end-of-the-line high school for students kicked out of everywhere else. In *Teachers*,[8] the burnt out Alex Jurrel (Nick Nolte), once Teacher of the Year, makes a comeback and finds the courage to fight on in the interests of the kids, while Robin Williams's Mr. Keating in *Dead Poets Society*,[9] although banished in the end for urging his affluent students to resist the stifling conformity of their position and seek their own true voice, stays around long enough to see his best hopes affirmed despite the tragic suicide of one of his favorites. In a movie that is anything but tragic, Mr. Shoop (Mark Harmon) overcomes his own incompetence and lack of interest to discover with his students what education is really all about in *Summer School*.[10] Eddie Layden (Steve Landesberg) stumbles into the job of conducting a shoddy high school marching band and brings them to the heights of skill and camaraderie in *Leader of the Band*.[11] Two coaches—Norman (Gene Hackman) in *Hoosiers*[12] and Molly McGrath (Goldie Hawn), the only woman to appear as educator-hero in the movies we viewed, in *Wildcats*—overcome personal problems and lots of flack in taking ragtag teams to the top.[13] In one other notable case, William Hurt plays a teacher of the deaf in *Children of a Lesser God.*[14] As a teacher, he warrants a place on the list insofar as his work with students is concerned; he literally stands on his head to win over his class, and is the very essence of the charismatic and successful teacher. But since the picture presents him with only one true challenge—and she is not in his class—his work as a teacher is too much a matter of background for him to emerge a hero in the way that all of the others we have mentioned quite clearly do.

Many stirring and upbeat moments of care and success in educational settings emerge from these stories. In them, Hollywood can at least be said to balance somewhat the bleak or dismissive scenes of schools and teachers that predominate in other movies set in schools. But is this truly so? We need to look more closely at this set of educator-hero movies if we are to weigh their individual and collective merits with respect to the way education is understood and addressed in contemporary American society.

Our focus, then, is on what this set of stories about educator-heroes offers, with respect to public discourse about education. In this regard, we follow Wayne Booth's suggestion that a revival of ethical criticism is in order.[15] Booth promotes and models an approach to criticism that takes seriously the consequences of particular stories on those who read them. He encourages use of a language of friendship in speaking of stories. Adopting Booth's metaphor for thinking about stories, then, we ask with regard to the educator hero movies, What kind of friends are these?

EARNING MEMBERSHIP IN THE BROTHERHOOD OF EDUCATOR-HEROES

The above description of the surface features of the movies under consideration suggests considerable variation in plot and content. But this is misleading in certain important respects. There is also a strong commonality running through the movies in question, a commonality without exception in the set of movies centering on the work of educators. We contend that what these movies share in common warrants close attention as we consider their meaning and value with regard to educational interests. What is the core held in common?

Trials of a Hero

To locate the common core, we can begin with a movie that many would likely regard as an exemplary teacher's tale on film, *Stand*

and Deliver. It seems both to address hard problems facing teachers and to offer an edifying view of what good teaching can accomplish. To explore it further, let us begin with a pivotal moment not far from the end. The test results of Jaime Escalante's Advanced Placement calculus students have been called into question, all having succeeded but with a similar pattern of errors. Escalante suffers the spiteful reaction of the woman who is head of the math department. She bemoans "the mess this school is in," and has apparently placed a letter of resignation in Jaime's mailbox for him to sign. Even Escalante's car has disappeared from the school parking lot, apparently stolen.

Jaime Escalante trudges home, slumps down, and announces to his wife, "I may have made a mistake trying to teach them calculus. . . . They learned if you try real hard nothing really changes. . . . They lost confidence in the system they're finally qualified to be part of." He contemplates resignation: "I could make twice the money and have people treat me with respect." For all his earlier toils and joy, only dejection remains. We confront a burnt-out hero. What hope is it now reasonable to harbor?

Escalante's emotional resignation dissolves when some of his students show up with his refurbished car, a token of the love of which, only moments before, his wife had sought to remind him. The moment is pivotal in that it provides the vital link between Escalante's vigorous efforts and their culmination in a union achieved with his students, between his various trials as one who would make a real difference and his vindication as one who has done so. It is a moment that reverberates in film after film as students step forward to acknowledge, embrace, and restore the spirits of the one person who has awakened them to the good they could achieve in their lives.

How does Jaime Escalante reach this point of satisfaction pivoting on despair? This story stands apart from the others we will consider in its presentation of a multifaceted challenge faced by its central figure. It is a chronicle of Escalante's battles on several fronts. Some of these are quite standard: His first class of students confronts him with an array of postures and attitudes ranging from the bored and the sarcastic to the intimidatingly sullen and aggressive, exemplified by Angel, a student whose conversion from hood to triumphant scholar provides a central story line. The students are antagonists at first, to be sure, and gaining their trust and respect is one challenge, but not the only one. On the first day Escalante encounters another. First, he finds on his arrival that, while he has signed on to teach computer classes, he has been reassigned to math, as the school has no computers. Then, barely having achieved with much effort a degree of order, the bell rings, prematurely as it turns out, and chaos quickly returns. The message is delivered clearly to him on his first day that the management of urban high schools—this one at least—is no friend to his best intentions as a teacher. Later we learn of a reassigned physical education teacher's struggles in teaching math, witness a substitute for Escalante (a music teacher by training) fail with his class, and shudder to hear the way the head of the math department speaks of the limited potential of the students at Garfield, saying at one point, "You can't teach logarithms to illiterates." This fabric of problems at the level of the school's organization is compounded by a run-down and crime-ridden school environment, a lack of support in the community from parents whose own lives are sympathetically portrayed as bent on the struggle to survive in a harsh working-class environment, and the cool efficiency of a corporate testing empire that raises doubts about the accomplishments of Escalante's students once they do succeed and, by doing so, reveals the hierarchy of achievement and social status that schools normally legitimize and reproduce. As Escalante exclaims in repudiation of the ETS officials, "These scores wouldn't have been questioned if my kids didn't have Spanish surnames and attended barrio schools."

Escalanate thus faces challenges, and the movie poses problems, at every level in schooling: interpersonal and classroom, school environment, community, and in the institutional hierarchy of corporate America that ranks the output of schools and anticipates the reproduction of standard patterns of inequality. Escalante's situation invites questions about student failure and disaffection, but places these in relation to problems of social class and ethnicity and the way schools perpetuate inequality in ways that would likely overwhelm even the best efforts of most well-intentioned teachers.

With such challenges, we come to appreciate Escalante's character. He rises to the challenge, establishing himself with his students early on. The second time we see him, the chaos of day one is gone. Dressed in an apron, he chops through an apple with a large kitchen knife, seizing the attention of most of his students; they, and the more resistant Angel, who succumbs later, will be under Escalante's spell through the rest of the film. He whispers softly to a quiet young woman, establishing a vital link with her, and takes on the tough guys who contest his turf with wit and steely nerves. "This is my domain," he says, and no one can really doubt it. He's tough, but he is not only tough, as he goes on to say, "This is basic math, but basic math is too easy for you. I'm going to teach you algebra because I'm the champ." He cares, and points out that algebra is worth something to them, since if all they could do was add and subtract, they would wind up frying chicken for a living. Angel reluctantly (but correctly) answers an initial question posed by Escalante; once hooked, neither he nor the other students ever again doubt that their teacher knows what it is in their best interests to do (however difficult it is to stay with him). Nicknames begin to proliferate, and a warm sense of membership in the community of Escalante's class emerges. His domain is secured. Later we will see Angel plead to remain part of it after a minor infraction puts him out—the world Escalante creates in this classroom becomes for the students portrayed in the film the center of their lives.

But the classroom is seemingly the easier part for Escalante. We witness him bravely confronting parents about their views on education for their children, and he speaks with dignity—if not always with happy effect—with other teachers and the testing authorities, always an advocate of the students and a voice on behalf of just and genuine change. Finally, the character and courage of this teacher are revealed as he fights back—against his doctor's orders, soon after a heart attack—to lead his students in final preparation for the AP calculus test, the test that marks the last hurdle before their undisputed entry into the world beyond the barrio.

This brings us to the pivotal moment described above. As his students' scores are contested, his vision darkened, Escalante thinks about getting out. Such despair is quickly dispelled. His wife answers his comment about a lack of respect with the observation that his students not only respect him—but also love him. And when Angel and a few others arrive honking the horn of Escalante's now spiffed-up car, he realizes that the machinations of the larger society, however cruel, cannot touch the wellsprings of his life as a teacher, the love of his students. A flurry of preparations follows as his students ready themselves to retake the AP exam with only one day's notice. They cram and sweat together (it's summertime) and Escalante cooks a meal for some of them at his home. Together they can overcome the wrongs that have been done to people of their kind and proudly knock down the doors of exclusion and prejudice. The students retake the test, and there is no surprise. When the results come in, all have once again passed. As Escalante stands by, his principal (quietly supportive throughout—a rather exceptional celluloid principal) records the results coming over the phone, and Escalante's face expresses a deep satisfaction. It is a strength of this movie that we see neither gloating nor a sentimental bath of hugs and hollers. Instead, the self-effacing teacher, his work done for this year and for these students, walks away alone down the long empty hallway toward the light outside, the only sign of his pleasure a sudden arm thrust of private celebration. We read, as he departs, of his successes to come, the increasing numbers of students Garfield High has brought through the AP calculus exam. The small, lone figure leaves a changed world behind as he exits.

Echoes of Escalante

Stand and Deliver addresses a range of matters of real concern to those working to enact some progressive vision in public education. Escalante's trials, if not his triumph, are borne by many who do what they can to bring about healthy change. But it would be premature to leave the analysis at this point, for *Stand and Deliver* is but one of a number of movies heralding the return of the educator-hero. As a film, it contains a structural similarity to the others that suggests that its more challenging message may be overshadowed by what the common formula of this diverse set of movies in fact delivers.

The formula set forth in *Stand and Deliver* and other films like it may be interpreted as follows. One man engages the attention of an assortment of students somehow foreign to him, odd and challenging. The man has a vision of what the young need (although they do not know they need it), and he struggles with obstacles that make it difficult to convey what it is—obstacles, moreover, that bring him to the verge of quitting. The students awake to what is happening, and express the love and respect they have come to feel for the man in time to dispel despair and remove all thoughts of resignation. Once realized, the love—and the talents it unleashes—transcends the problems encountered, and the man's hope and vision are vindicated. True educators will strive on, while transformed students will fulfill their hero's dreams (without losing whatever unique charm and individuality they had in the first place). The promise of joy and success into the future lingers at the close.

Consider *Summer School*, a movie that follows the pattern as surely as *Stand and Deliver* does, while presenting us with a teacher-hero seemingly opposite to Jaime Escalante. The Mark Harmon character, Freddie Shoop, when we first see him, is a gym teacher counting down the last few moments of a school year with a crowd of students equally eager to depart. Under some compulsion, he reluctantly agrees to solve an administrator's problem by teaching a summer-school remedial English course for assorted losers, airheads, and burnouts who have failed a minimum-competency test. Utterly uninterested in being there, Shoop's challenge, at first, is to make the best of a bad situation for all concerned. There is no test of character in this; he shows up in shorts and shades, gets into a swearing contest with his students, and gropes about for things to do, eventually taking off on field trips to a farm, a go-cart track, and an amusement park. The challenge changes, however, as he begins to care for the kids. At first he is ironic; trying to impress a committed teacher, Robin, into accepting a date with him, he says, "Inside each bad kid is a good kid. You just have to reach down through the sleaze and slime. We're unsung heroes." Shoop begins to truly believe this line only after he's threatened with the loss of his job for all the goofing off. In order to keep his job, he must get them to pass the test. His supervisor notes, "It's called teaching." When next we see him, Shoop's suit sends the message to the students that he is serious now. He wants them to study. They respond with a deal. They will do some minimal work and he will do something for each in return: driving lessons for one, Lamaze class for another—he even allows one young spaced-out surfer girl to move in with him.

As this scenario unfolds, he becomes a friend; genuine affection builds, and the students are learning (a little at least). It is a very different domain from Jaime's, but, in both cases, a special fabric of relationships develops between teacher and students. The character of Shoop's concern is exemplified by his willingness to take the blame for two of the students when they are about to be arrested for drinking on the beach, as he offers himself for arrest in their place. The students help him before the judge, but, back in class, time is running out before the test. His job is still on the line.

It is at this point that the scope of Shoop's trials dramatically escalates and his character as a committed teacher fully emerges. His appeal to the students to work harder is met by their desire to extract more goods from him in return. The pivotal moment arrives. "I can't believe this greed," he says, adding, "All I'm asking for is a little extra effort; the problem is you're so happy being failures." Seeing the scope of the challenge that he now truly wishes to confront, Shoop storms out, quitting in anger and frustration.

Seeing Robin on his way out, Shoop then echoes Escalante, saying, "I never got through to anybody." Shoop is finished. But the students cannot let that happen. They cleverly conspire to rid themselves of the substitute teacher by recreating *The Texas Chainsaw Massacre* for their substitute; then, in full, bloody makeup, they seek out Shoop on the beach. One pleads, "We can't pass that test without you. We'll study in school, after school, whatever it takes . . . but we need a teacher." And Shoop has proven himself to be their man.

Faith restored, we see the students studying in all kinds of ways and places. They give it their best. When the test results come in, they are not so great—these kids are losers after all, at least academically. But as Shoop points out in the culminating scene, where he is called before the principal to account for all that has occurred, including the fact that the average grade was below passing, "There's more going on here than test scores and grades." All had improved markedly, and parents testified to such engagement in learning as they had not seen before. These kids have never found school satisfying before. They haven't lost any of their wacky charm, but they are ready to start learning and make something of themselves. Like Escalante's more academic crew, these kids are okay, and they are on their way to being successful. The reluctant, unprofessional, but truly caring teacher made the difference. Shoop is granted tenure, the music swells, and the joyous celebration commences.

The surface details shift again in the Joe Clark story, *Lean on Me*, though the triumph feels the same in the end. *Lean on Me* shifts the scene to an urban-jungle high school. It is noted at the outset that "the battle of one man, Joe Clark, is the subject of our story." The challenge is quickly made clear. With the opening credits, we see a young Joe Clark at Eastside High in 1967, working smoothly with a group of eager students in a social studies class. Following a disreputable union deal "selling out" and transferring Joe from Eastside High in exchange for minor pay increments, the school is portrayed as it "was" twenty years later. To the accompaniment of Guns 'N' Roses's "Welcome to the Jungle," the camera explores a hellish place. In three minutes' time, the camera pans over the following: a fistfight in the hallway; filthy, graffiti-covered corridors; a window smashed out in a lavatory; a teacher frisked; drug use in another lavatory; one girl attacked by several others, who strip her to the waist and send her screaming into the crowded hallway; a female teacher accosted by a thug; a large drug and cash transaction taking place in a doorway; drugs being sold in the cafeteria; guns present there, along with a fight; a male teacher, attempting to break up the fight, being brutally beaten and carted away in an ambulance; and, finally, at day's end, with the corridors emptied, a young man is stuffed in a locker and left wailing for help in the now empty building. The three minutes demonstrate how the school has become hell in twenty years.

The boy in the locker is a symbol. He is Sams, an example of just the kind of person Joe Clark saves from incarceration in the confines of a failed school and, later, imprisonment in the larger world. Clark, an outsider respected for his tough willfulness, is recruited to come back as principal. Clark's well-publicized battles to take command in the school, beginning with the permanent expulsion of hundreds of students he considered incorrigible, are dramatized. The depiction does not stray too far from the public image of Clark gained through various news magazines: an extremist in the cause of order and renewed school discipline, vilified by some, admired by others.

But while this movie touches on the range of Clark's activity, including scenes of Clark lording it over humiliated teachers and students, the challenges facing him are portrayed only in the most shallow ways. Once the law-less students are expelled, for example, the school is scrubbed in other ways as well and the setting seems more like a country club than a high school: lots of warm woodwork and green plants around the place, while the remaining students are bright, cheerful, and good-hearted—as exemplified by Sams, whom Clark was able to reach only after marching him up to the roof and terrorizing him with the vision of falling away to the street. The students are not the problem (once you cast out the bad apples); they readily accept Clark's appeal to be part of a resurrection and overcome the predictions that they are doomed to fail. His major challenge is the intransigent political order; certain teachers who resist Clark's commands but eventually either shape up, grateful for the change, or disappear; and those trouble-making parents and citizens who resent Clark's methods (although we learn almost nothing in the movie as to their concerns, we mostly see the scowling face of their leader, Mrs. Barrett, a woman who gets on the school board and plots Clark's downfall).

The major effort facing Clark is to demonstrate that the school has been turned around by way of success on the state minimum-skills test. Everyone is concerned and excited about reaching the cut-off score of 75 percent passing the test and demonstrating minimum academic skills. Clark sends them into the test with a prideful pep talk: They can show the world what they're made of. But, before the results come in, he is arrested for refusing to remove the chains from the school's emergency exits—his determination to keep the drug dealers out is used against him by those who want him removed.

The pivotal moment finds Clark in jail mulling over his fate. He has fought the good fight, but the resistance to reform was too great. A lone man, for the first time stilled, sits in a cell. He hears his friend, the superintendent who hired him, say, "You accomplished a miracle; those kids have a light in their eyes that was never there." But the words do not break the sense of sadness and defeat. Unlike *Stand and Deliver* and several other educator-hero movies, the despair at this pivotal moment is not so much in Clark—he is too proud for that—but in us, the viewers, who are given to see the tragedy of his unjust treatment and the great loss his silencing represents. We do not wait long for our delivery, and Clark's. A torch-light parade of students, by the hundreds, approach the courthouse chanting "Free Mr. Clark." They rally outside the building, disrupting the Board of Education meeting that debates Clark's future as principal, and drawing out Mrs. Barrett, the conniving school board member, to try and disperse them. She tells the students they'll soon have a good principal, to which Sams replies, "We don't want a good principal. We want Mr. Clark." Another says, "Mr. Clark has been like a father to us." The Mayor worriedly urges Clark to leave his cell and send them off, and Clark steps forward to do so, for their safety. Humbly, Clark urges respect for the law, but the students will not disperse. Then the news comes: Eastside High has reached its goal of 75 percent passing the minimum-skills test. Clark glories in dismissing the mayor with the remark that he should tell the state authorities now to go to hell. Barrett and the mayor leave, bickering. Sams rushes up the steps into Clark's arms, the school song swells grandly, and Clark wades, free, into the mass of joyous students (though one might wonder why he is now released, since he wasn't charged with failing to produce adequate test scores on a minimum-skills test). Love and pride are evident everywhere. The final freeze frame of the film captures Clark's smile of triumphant satisfaction, embracing the students he has saved and who, in turn, have saved him. In this scenario, we see again the charismatic outsider create a bond of love and trust with students, overcome adversaries, and, saved from defeat and despair by the awakened and adoring students, join with them as the problems they face dissolve.

In *Teachers,* Nick Nolte's burned-out Alex Jurrell, once an inspiring teacher, we have learned, faces trials of a more personal kind. He is a teacher for whom the school has become a burden; his idealism has vanished. He stands alongside a motley assortment of colleagues, ranging from the high-strung neurotic incompetent to the master of drill and routine, nicknamed Ditto (who actually dies in class without his well-programmed students even noticing) to the temporary, inspired service of an escapee from a mental ward who, among other things, "becomes" George Washington and Abe Lincoln in the course of his much-appreciated lessons. Jurrell groans through his days in a school that doesn't seem to include enough people who really care, and struggles to keep his own sense of concern alive. Facing a hearing on the school's record of just passing some illiterate students along, Jurrell must decide whether he will blow the whistle and strive again to generate real reform; he rediscovers in the process, what it would take for his work to once again have meaning. As with Shoop, we are not sure whether Jurrell has the character to overcome the challenge he faces. School officials and peers—among them his former pal, Roger, now a bureaucratic functionary in the school—lean on him to resign. He is presumably a threat to the established, corrupt order.

Jurrell's moment of truth arrives as he surveys the faces of corruption. He cannot take it anymore and decides to quit: "Nobody cares. I'm out, I'm through fighting. I can't make a difference." As he packs up to leave, all of his students show up and take their seats in the classroom. Eddie, the tough kid only Jurrell could reach, asks if he's going to stay. Jurrell, tears in his eyes, starts walking, stopped only by the former student who has come back as a lawyer to try the case of the school's failure. She strips off her clothes to stop him, challenging him also to do the crazy thing and continue as a teacher. Alex relents, curses his adversaries, and rejoins the loving throng of students who now bask in his presence. The final freeze frame captures Jurrell and Eddie in happy embrace, two feisty, independent souls who will now work together to resist what is wrong with the school.

We see again the despair and defeat of an outsider—in this case, an outsider by virtue of his unique qualities as a caring person and inspired teacher—dispelled by communion with students, the special wellspring of genuine relationships in school settings. What their triumph will lead to is unimportant. What matters is the feeling of solidarity they achieve.

The Principal is less reassuring in this regard. Nevertheless, as the outsider brought in as principal to reclaim an urban-jungle high school from the thugs and drug dealers—in this case, a hard-drinking teacher who is transferred from his position and targeted for the impossible job after smashing up a sports car with a baseball bat—Lattimore (Jim Belushi) does win the battle in the end to oust the worst brutes from the building. But it does not come without a cost. The challenge, as with *Lean on Me*, is obvious. Lattimore clearly does not lack courage. He gathers all together in an assembly and vows, "No more," then confronts the vicious gang leader, Victor Duncan, to reinforce the message. Each considers Brandell High his own turf.

The crisis of faith and despair arrives when Lattimore breaks through to Neil, a kid who has done jobs for Duncan. Neil also says, in effect, "No more" to Duncan, and is nearly beaten to death for having done so. At Neil's hospital bedside, Lattimore intones the now familiar lament. He expresses his sorrow, saying, "I thought I was doing something good. I don't know why I thought I could change things there—I can't, I just can't, man." Neil proceeds to invoke, with a mild rebuke echoing Lattimore's own earlier challenge to him, the community of fellow battlers in the good fight. Lattimore, awakened to his duty, returns to the school, issues the fateful challenge to Duncan and his gang, and proceeds to the action. He survives the brutal attack of Duncan's gang, tossing Duncan out the door unceremoniously, saying "No more" as he does so, and sees him taken away by the cops. It may not be the last battle, but, amidst the rubble, there is some solace in the spirit of true and caring relationships on the right side in the struggle. Lattimore has stood tall, fulfilling the trust Neil placed in him. With his friend, Jake, the security guard, Lattimore contemplates the next round. They'll be back the next day, the good fight defining the meaning in their lives.

In *Dead Poets Society,* we find ourselves at the other end of the social spectrum, in an exclusive prep school. The new English teacher, John Keating, played by Robin Williams, enters and challenges the taken-for-granted sense of what the school is all about. Like Jurrell in *Teachers*, he raises questions of meaning, though he does so in a way that is more intellectual in its focus (as befitting the setting). His challenge is complacency and the students' lack of awareness about the most vital questions in life. He strives from the first day to awaken in them a love of learning and life: Tearing pages of academic rot from their standard texts, he challenges them to seize the day (*carpe diem*). Successes follow as Keating arranges a variety of occasions for questioning the paths of conformity. "This is a battle, a war, and the casualties could be your hearts and souls." Keating urges his students constantly to look at things in a different way: "When we read, don't just consider what the author thinks; consider what you think." He offers therapy for the spiritual oppression of the privileged: "Strive to find your own voice." This is never clearer than in a rousing scene in which Keating helps release shy Todd from his inhibitions by inducing a "barbaric yawp," then sits back with others in surprised delight as Todd delivers a fit of inspired, spontaneous verse. Later, Todd's voice will do for Keating what Sams's hug did for Joe Clark, marking the moment of final satisfaction for the hero who set the student free.

Keating's trial as a hero is not in working with students; they are in the palm of his hand. The headmaster is another story. At one point, Keating says to him, "I always thought the idea of education was to learn to think for yourself," and is rebuked with the comment that he should rather provide tradition and discipline: "Prepare them for college and the rest will take care of itself."

This, of course, Keating cannot accept. And after the tragic death of one of his students—Neil, who commits suicide in response to the psychological violence of a repressive father unable to accept the free spirit in a son who has found joy and freedom as an actor on the stage—the headmaster makes Keating a scapegoat and ousts him.

The spiritual crisis arrives for Keating, not in his removal, but in quiet reflection at Neil's desk. He grieves the loss, and agonizes with the knowledge that Neil's awakening, and thus his demise, was in part his own doing. As in *The Principal*, the educator's despair follows not failure but success. Each of the two characters named Neil—one nearly murdered, the other a suicide—was set on a path of destruction through the power of an educator calling him to a vision of some higher ground.

For Keating, the delivery from despair comes as he prepares to leave while his students suffer the once-discarded rot from the poetry text under the stern command of the headmaster who has taken Keating's place. Todd, in a show of support for Keating, abruptly stands on his desk to say farewell to his "Captain." Others follow the lead as the headmaster scrambles to stop them and bring order to the classroom. As the music swells, we see from Keating's perspective the boys who have joined the community of free men that Keating represents, towering above him on their desks with newly awakened dignity, while those who lack the courage cower meekly, heads down, under the headmaster's authority. Keating is shown from the boys' perspective, small and frail in the doorway, but justly proud. He is the teacher who has made them grow so large and free. He now can leave, knowing that his teaching has transformed them, at least some of them, forever. He and the film's audience know the truth: that, in rare cases, teachers build relationships that transform those who partake in them, even if the rest of the world and its ways remain bleak and unchanged.

Finally, the three movies about extracurricular teacher-heroes warrant mention for the ways in which they participate in the theme of personal struggle and triumphant delivery for a teacher who creates transformative bonds with a set of once aimless or misguided students. In *Leader of the Band,* Steve Landesberg plays a down-on-his-luck musician, Eddie Layden, who manages to stumble into a teaching post working with a hopelessly awful high school marching band. Confronting their lack of skill and interest, he might just bide his time and collect his salary, but he cannot. Rather, he takes his students to task and awakens in his players a genuine interest in music. As he begins to get through to them, the band improves, although not fast enough. After being outshone by a better-funded and classier band, Eddie loses his job. The pivotal moment finds him in a sleazy hotel in town. Suddenly the band arrives, in full gear, and plays up a storm outside his hotel window. It comes as no surprise that Eddie rejoins his students and leads them to triumph in a major contest, having now become the best band in the region.

The two movies centering on coaches diverge only slightly from the pattern. In *Hoosiers*, Gene Hackman plays Norman, a basketball coach long exiled from the game, who gets one last chance to coach again, in a small Indiana town. His strict methods and determination to have the game played right alienate his players and irritate the townsmen who scrutinize the team. Norman expresses his resolve, saying, "There's a lot of talent, raw and undisciplined; I'm going to break them down, then build them back up." His chance to do so is threatened, however, because his methods initially alienate players and observers alike. While Norman suffers the shortsightedness of the townspeople as they meet to fire him from the job, a local star player suddenly announces his resolve to rejoin the team only if Norman stays. The star recognizes Norman's vision and saves him in time for it to be enacted. The team begins to win, going all the way through the Indiana championships to win the title, an accomplishment of mythic proportions. As in the portrayal of Joe Clark, there is little doubt or despair in Norman, even when he sees his hopes about to be dashed, but the viewer feels sorrow in watching a good man brought down. Once restored, Norman is steadfast, and, as his team advances, each triumph they achieve is his as well, a tribute to his firm authority, discipline, and ability to promote a feeling of camaraderie they presumably had never experienced before. Once the basis was established—in a kind of disciplined community of effort and respect—there was no stopping them.

Finally we come to *Wildcats*, in which Molly McGrath (Goldie Hawn) finds herself thrown into a situation in which her detractors expect her to fail as football coach of a large, unruly, urban high school. She relishes the chance to coach, to use her knowledge and love of the game, and weathers the abuse which is rained on her by the vulgar crew she is given to coach, finally gaining their respect through sheer determination. She refuses to retreat from their insults. Like Norman, Molly is able to bring back a star player and lead the team to a string of victories. This is enough, until her ex-husband tries to remove her daughters from her care, owing to the kinds of people she is now associating with. Molly despairs of leaving the school and her team, but decides she must. The decision is a personal defeat for her and has the effect of deflating her team during the city championship game. At halftime, the team challenges her to fight on, and, recognizing the higher purpose of keeping faith with her students, she accepts, standing up to her ex-husband and sparking the team's resurgence with her spunk. The ex-husband backs down, the team wins, and all enjoy the moment as the losing coach—the very creep who set her up to fail (so he thought) in the first place—is deposited in the mud by one of Molly's players. The final freeze frame shows her on the shoulders of her triumphant team.

Molly represents one notable change from all of the others: The hero is a woman. But the change is not as stark as it might seem. In Molly's story, the challenge confronts her precisely on the point of her difference from the other heroes, as an apparently fragile woman cast into a rough and threatening male (also poor and largely black) world. Molly nearly resigns following the first crude confrontations, but manages to gain the respect of her team. Interestingly, she does so through a show of physical strength, by challenging them to outlast her in running around the track. Whipping the lot of them, Molly suddenly seems tough enough, and further demonstrates her toughness in subsequent rigorous practice sessions. Molly emerges as the exceptional woman educator-hero by being tougher than the boys and men she encounters. She earns her place in the "brotherhood" of educator-heroes.

LEARNING FROM THE EDUCATOR-HERO

What can we make of these movies that work to raise our spirits about good people achieving fine things in schools? In virtually every case, we see a man, some sort of renegade or outsider, enter hostile territory, find a way to earn the trust and respect of students, and build bonds with them which make some tangible victory possible. Meddlesome antagonists are clearly identified in the process and rebuffed in the end, though, in most cases, not before they manage to bring the hero to despair over ever making a difference or finishing the job he (or she) has set out to do. We watch assured, however, that the hero has built bonds of love with students sufficient to rescue him from doubt and deliver all to triumph together in the end. When all is said and done, we walk away with the sense of finished business: The game has been won, the school has been saved, the test has been passed, the villains once encountered are history, sometimes slinking off in ignominy, as in *Lean on Me,* or left on scene looking ridiculous and small as in *Dead Poets Society.* Problems overcome in triumph dissolve before our eyes.

What is missing here? For one thing, as Todd Gitlin has recently remarked, "Hollywood movies have largely been blind to the working of institutions. Where they excel is with villains."[16] These pictures leave everything outside the frame of the relationships we exult in virtually untouched, including the larger institutional realities that provide the backdrop for what we see. Hence, while most of Clark's kids do pass a minimum competency test, we are given no inducement to think of the institutional reality that still faces them as students, living in poverty, functioning at the lowest levels of the social hierarchy that looms over them. Their limited chances in the world outside Eastside High is a cloud we never sense in the picture. Even in the case of Escalante, whose achievements are certainly laudatory, one might wonder about the other students in Garfield, taking courses from teachers out of their field, held to lowered expectations of less heroic figures, not taking the advanced classes. His satisfaction is deserved, but it is no excuse for anyone else to be satisfied with the larger picture of unchanged inequality and hopeless failure just outside the frame in this work. As Gitlin suggests, these more troubling institutional realities are squeezed out of the frame by the sharp focus on those villains who play the foil to our heroes.

A second observation stems from Wayne Booth's efforts to advance an ethics of fiction.[17] Booth suggests several criteria for use in thinking about the ethical consequences of narratives. He frames each criterion in terms of a continuum of possibilities of particular kinds. One continuum that is especially relevant in the case of the fictions we are discussing is the continuum between what Booth calls "familiarity and otherness." Stories can sometimes deepen or transform our sense of that which we might otherwise take for granted as part of the familiar, or challenge us to come to grips with domains and perspectives that are foreign to us. But stories can also fail to do either of these things and instead reinforce one's existing vision of the familiar and the foreign. All of the movies we are considering focus on educators who are, in some sense, outsiders encountering an array of students initially at odds with them and in a setting where other adult figures offer conflicting views of what is taking place. The scenario is very rich in possibilities for the consideration of "otherness," multiple, even conflicting, perspectives, values, and understandings. Instead, we encounter characters who quickly fall into either the camp of the near and good or that of the enemy (or irrelevant). The outsider figure of the educator-hero often seems peculiar, but only in ways that prove him (or her) to be worthy of the students' respect, and students who do not enter into the union created are seen to prefer (and thus deserve) some realm of crime or empty drudgery. The spotlight falls on characters who know where they stand in relation to the polarities of good and evil established by the presence of the hero. One is rarely forced to think about the reasons why anyone does what she or he does or what their different understandings might consist of. Hence, we deal almost exclusively with characters who seem very familiar, and whose potential otherness—the possibility of genuinely conflicting views among reasonable and sympathetically presented characters—we never experience in these tales.

A second criterion that Booth proposes for evaluating the impact of stories is pertinent here as well. It is defined in terms of a continuum between hierarchy and reciprocity. This criterion concerns the extent to which the reader is invited to reciprocate in creating the meaning of events and actions in the story, as opposed to having them handed down, hierarchically, from the knowing author. In the case of these stories, it is very clear that the viewer is given everything he or she is supposed to think or feel. All the tools of the film maker are used so as to minimize any doubts about whom we love and hate, what we want to happen, when we are to feel glad or angry, and so on. There is an absence of ambiguity and complexity, anything to work out a view on, mull over, or argue about. The framing of the story, the use of music, the presentation of characters—all are consistently designed to produce a specific response in us as viewers. Was Clark right to boot those students out? In the universe of *Lean on Me*, there is hardly a moment to question it. Should we tear the pages out of the poetry text? The presumption favors the charismatic star. There's never any doubt about what we should feel, whom we care about or reject, and what we resent. Nor is the viewer left with something to mull over for another day, reinterpret, or inspect. Judgments are quick, automatic, and overwhelmingly clear. In terms of reciprocity, all the viewer is left to do is smile in the end.

Finally, it is worth our while to consider the role of wish fulfillment in these movies. Marc Crispin Miller has surveyed recent American movies and observed that they center on the satisfaction of simple wishes around which the stories are contrived.[18] Because of market considerations including the increasing use of movies to carry the product names of advertisers (who often advance payment for the message while the picture is in production), movies are increasingly driven to gratify viewer wishes and dissolve into pleasant, simplistic endings. What kind of wishes are fulfilled in this set of movies? Above all, it seems to be a wish for meaningful personal interaction in a setting more often experienced as unfulfilling or empty. Time after time, we witness the saving grace of genuine love and care between students and teacher or principal, the transcendent moment when all—central characters and audience alike—share in the satisfaction of something true and lasting having happened. It is something that the surrounding fools or villains cannot take away or diminish in the slightest way; whatever else the school might be (typically not much), at least it allows this. And we walk away wishing it could happen everywhere while knowing it never could. In several cases, this wish is paired with a wish for achievement: the reassuring sense that a troubled group of students, whether bright but nonachieving Hispanic kids, inner-city blacks, or white suburban burnouts might finally get on track for a future, thanks to the work of the one teacher who really cares. Even in the apparent exception of *Dead Poets Society*, where the students already are high achievers on the track of success, we witness them as they gain a new definition of success at the top of the social-class hierarchy, one that frees them to really live and achieve full standing as human beings; they overcome a form of poverty, we are persuaded, as surely as Jaime Escalante's students will do, or Joe Clark's. In the end, it is a wish for transformation: If only we could find or create that kind of relationship that transforms unhappy or unsuccessful students into winners, and caring educators into charismatic leaders, full of love, pride, and triumphant satisfaction for the good they bring about. Education can be saved, it seems, if enough caring and charismatic men turn their attention to the task.

What shall we conclude, then, with regard to the question raised at the outset as to whether education finds a friend in these films? The first thing to note is that whatever else might be needed, efforts to improve schooling are a matter of subtle and discerning deliberation about the aims and purposes of educational practice. There is not much to mull over in these stories on that front. The richly textured, complex, ambiguous fabric of thought about education is scarcely hinted at in these films. We do not walk away from these movies with much need to think or sort out our feelings. We know where we stand.

Beyond that, while it can be said that these movies about educator-heroes do uplift the spirits, their value in this regard is dubious. For while the message is conveyed that transformative action is possible, that action seems always to be a product of special heroes, working alone—often even entering from outside and never fitting in. Transformation is always a product of masculine charisma and unique interpersonal relationships. And the nature of the transformation, oddly enough, is typically limited to success in the system or just in feeling good about things with people you like. Both the source of transformation and its end are thus cut off from conceptions of any wider sphere of interests or power, no hint of change in the system itself or even of a need to think about it. Nor is there any suggestion of shared work among adults of good will to achieve any transformative ends together. Escalante walks off alone into the sunset. Other good teachers might emulate his efforts and transform the prospects of some other group of deserving kids, but the focus and method of change is always personal, the private dealings of a bunch of good people who find themselves happily together, cut off from and superior to a world whose workings they must largely accept. The great majority of more ordinary relationships—both problematic and decent—between students and teachers in schools, and especially the work of women in education, are simply not worth noticing. The ordinary is irrelevant in schooling. And women either act as obstacles to the work of charismatic men (as in the examples of the head of the math department whom Jaime Escalante must overcome and the villain trying to derail Joe Clark) or find their place offering comfort and support to the heroes at moments of weakness and need (as does Escalante's wife and Clark's assistant principal).

In the end, these stories portray the institutional order as empty but unavoidable, requiring the infusion of some special set of interpersonal interests and intrigues to help the time pass and awaken our senses. The educator as hero reminds us that sometimes adults can be a part of relationships that have meaning for students in school, and even that some learning might result from that relationship. But apart from those special gatherings of spirit and care, the rare drama enacted when a man of vision builds bonds of love and trust with students, there is not much to think about; the rest of what goes on in school just leaves us cold.

NOTES

1. See, e.g., S. Cavell, *Pursuits of Happiness* (Cambridge, MA.: Harvard University Press, 1981) p. 1.

2. See our "Adolescent Freedom and the Cinematic High School," in this volume.

8 Conformity, Conflict, and Curriculum: Film Images of Boys' Preparatory Schools

Gary N. Mc Closkey, O.S.A.

In describing the variation among schools in different sectors of society, Samuel Bowles and Herbert Gintis posit a "correspondence" between economic and educational systems.[1] Herbert Gintis, summarizing this correspondence principle, states:

> There tends to be a correspondence between the educational system and the economic system. People who go to ghetto schools in the inner city experience the same types of education, the same types of personal relations, and the same attacks on their personal dignity as such individuals experience on the lower end of the economic spectrum when they actually go out to get jobs. Middle-class children, on the other hand, go to middle-class schools, where they are treated in a manner very similar to the types of positions they will have in society as active participants in the economy. Upper-class students, to continue the analogy, experience the types of freedom and develop the forms of personal dignity and effectiveness to control their lives that they will later use when they are controlling the lives of others in the world of business.[2]

Joseph Murphy, in reflections on differences in higher education, sees lower- and middle-class higher-education institutions as places where "something watered down is being offered, that the cut-rate product is as fresh and unappetizing as the offerings of a poor inner-city market."[3] On the other hand, elite higher-education institutions are places where one "has a right, even an obligation, reinforced and rewarded in the classroom, to have an authoritative opinion and to express it. Thus, the children of the wealthy are taught to be competent wielders of the power that they are being trained to inherit."[4] According to Elizabeth Vallance, even though this circumstance is evident to the theorists, it is "unacknowledged"[5] and thus a hidden curriculum in the schools themselves.

While the popular film image of life and education in elite boys' preparatory schools reinforces an impression that entrance into these schools is related to entrance into the halls of societal power, these same films also convey the image of an institution hostile to individual freedom and personal dignity. These films show people punished, or at least muted, when they exercise the freedom and voice the theorists presume the people in such schools have. Elliott Eisner terms those items that "schools do *not teach*" or do not allow to take place in schools the "null curriculum."[6] This essay will look at how films about boys' preparatory schools portray a popular understanding of a null curriculum, one centered on the lack of freedom to initiate change and exercise voice with respect to change. Further, this essay will analyze problems that result from the null curriculum of these schools as it is portrayed, as well as implications that popular film images may have for understanding boys' preparatory schools.

The films that were analyzed for this study were *Goodbye Mr. Chips, Zero for Conduct, Tom Brown's Schooldays, if . . . , A Separate Peace, Another Country, Making the Grade,* and *Dead Poets' Society.*[7] These movies were chosen through a review of the descriptions of more than 18,500 movies presented in Leonard Maltin's *TV Movies and Video Guide.*[8] In order to focus the analysis, there was a decision to limit the study to exclude religiously affiliated and military preparatory schools because of possible complications of additional subcultural motifs connected to these schools. Focusing on nonsectarian and nonmilitary preparatory schools left the eight movies under study as the population of films in this genre.

PRESSURES TO CONFORM

Dead Poets Society begins with a ritual in which the values of "Tradition, Honor, Discipline, and Excellence"—the essential values of Welton Academy, the prep school portrayed in the film—are displayed as paramount concerns. In a sense, these are the values that work against change in all of the films reviewed in this essay. The presentations that follow are not complete synopses of the movies but rather highlights of the films which relate to the theme of change. The films are reviewed in chronological order.

Goodbye, Mr. Chips *(1939)*

Goodbye, Mr. Chips presents the life of the venerable Mr. Chipping of Brookfield School, providing glimpses of his lengthy teaching career. This film shows how his original desire to change from teacher to master is undermined early in his career. The "powers that be" view him as a classroom teacher not as one of the masters. He has difficulty giving up his ambition and accepting the position assigned to him, until his wife helps him to see teaching as an exciting and even heroic profession. She specifically enables him to forge a vision of his life and work which will eventually support him through the grief of her death and help him build a stronger sense of purpose in his work at Brookfield. Finally, after a long career, he is asked to assume the role of headmaster during the dark days of World War I, and brings to this administrative role the sense of stability and acceptance of tradition that he has found in teaching. One is left at the end of the film with the impression that his children, "thousands of them and all boys," have benefited enormously from his having been stymied when he had first wanted to advance to the position of master. His students are seen as learning better lessons from his patient acceptance than they would have learned had he achieved his ambition early in his career. Brookfield's curriculum of tradition has been preserved and the undesirability of hasty change underscored.

Zero for Conduct *(1947)*

Unlike the Brookfield School, which is presented as a very humane setting, the French boarding school presented in *Zero for Conduct* is a horrific place. Discipline and punishment are the hallmarks of this school. The initially docile students increasingly desire a change in the circumstances in which they find themselves. This finally culminates in the students' unapologetic disruption of their science class. In contrast to the students who shared polite teas with Mr. Chips, these students demand change, in one scene crying out, "Down with the School! Down with teachers! Hurrah for Revolt! Liberty or Death!" The final act shows students rising up to bombard Alumni Day visitors with old books, tin cans, and shoes. In this case, the desire for change has brought about anarchy. The system is left in shambles when freedom and change creep in.

Tom Brown's Schooldays *(1951)*

In a sense, the Rugby School presented here is a middle ground between Mr. Chips's Brookfield and the French boarding school of *Zero for Conduct*. Dr. Arnold, the headmaster, recognizes the negative world of discipline and punishment in his school and sees it as his job to bring about a change in the school's curriculum in order to create a more humane setting of the sort found in Mr. Chips's Brookfield School. It is not an easy task. As he comments, "Changing things is a so often discouraging business." In Arnold's pursuit of new institutional goals, Tom Brown, a young student, becomes a central figure because of his innate gentle humanity. He becomes, for Dr. Arnold, an icon of the Rugby School's achievement of new institutional goals.

An interesting part of this dynamic is that the changing of institutional goals envisioned by Arnold is to be achieved, for the most part, by the students themselves. There are few times when the masters have a role in bringing about this change. Mostly they are portrayed as opposing Arnold and his efforts. Dr. Arnold is depicted as being fearful of openly discussing change. As a result, students are on their own against the reigning bullies. They must make the difference in order to survive. In fact, Tom Brown does more than survive. When a younger student whom Tom is supposed to protect is endangered, his prayers aid in saving the younger student's life. As Dr. Arnold hoped, Tom grows to become a force in the reforms that shape the school into the new Rugby.

if . . . *(1968)*

In *if* . . . , we find the scenario of *Zero for Conduct* transplanted into a more contemporary English school. However, this updated setting is more violent and nihilistic. Conversation among students gives rise to statements such as, "When do we live?" and "Violence and revolution are the only pure acts" and "War is the last possible creative act." Even adolescent introduction to sexuality is presented in violent animalistic terms. Students try edging toward suicide by seeing how long they can last with a plastic bag over the head. Each action is seen as an attempt for freedom and choice in a rigid system that allows no leeway.

Unlike *Zero for Conduct*, this movie portrays the struggle as occurring primarily among the students. Some students, with the support of the school staff, are the perpetrators of discipline and violence. Others find themselves, in the terms of the movie, first in "resistance" and then as "crusaders" "going forth to war." The group that becomes crusaders starts out as merely unhappy and devoid of any real desire for change or freedom from the roles they are expected to assume. Treatment at school, which they perceive as demeaning, moves them toward revolution. This struggle can be seen as coming to a head in their participation in the quasi-military exercises that are part of the school's tradition and values. During the five hundredth anniversary celebration for the school, when statements of official speakers—such as "There is nothing the matter with privilege"—describe the dominant values taught by the school, the rebellious segment of students start a fire in the celebration assembly. When the participants in the celebration run from the smoke and fire, they are met by machine-gun fire from the rebellious students, who have discovered in the school a cache of arms left over from the war. The rebellious students exercise freedom and opt for change. The result of such overt action is the destruction of the school itself.

A Separate Peace *(1972)*

The films described thus far have related to difficulties centered on the tension in elite schools between their traditional order and values, on the one hand, and desires for freedom and change on the other. *A Separate Peace* relates a story about struggle and change that is more personal in nature. The setting is the Devon School prior to World War II. The story centers on Gene's recollection of his days at the school and his relationship with his friend Finney. He recalls how fear, anger, and senseless rivalry led him to the impulsive act of shaking a high tree limb on which he and Finney are standing in preparation for a dive into water below. Gene's impulse causes Finney to fall and break his leg.

Gene struggles with why he has given in to his impulse and how to tell Finney of his action. In the midst of this struggle, war is declared. As high school students, Gene and his comrades prepare for the duty of enlistment. Finney feigns disinterest, but later confesses his depression at being unable to serve due to the severity of the break in his leg. Other members of their group begin to suspect Gene's part in Finney's accident, and hold a mock trial. Leper, a former student who is now A.W.O.L. from the service, remembers at the trial that Gene jumped twice, the first jump causing Finney to lose his balance. Finney is shocked by the revelation and leaves the trial very upset. On the way back to his room, he loses his balance and falls down a staircase, breaking his leg again.

Gene struggles, finally, to tell Finney of the impulsive action he has not been able to talk about previously. Even though Finney says he understands, Gene never recovers his own equilibrium. Finney dies unexpectedly in the operation to set his leg. The doctor sees the death as part of the larger social picture, bridging the separation between Finney's operating room and the war. Gene, however, understands it only personally and recalls his not crying at Finney's funeral because, to some extent, Finney's death was his own. With one impulsive jump, choosing to act outside of the stable norms of his school, his life is changed in ways that cannot be reversed. The schooling that would have provided fully for his future, had he remained within the normal bounds of conduct, becomes instead the backdrop to an independent action that shapes his destiny to an even greater extent than the war that raged in the distance and shaped the history of the time.

Another Country *(1984)*

In an approach similar to *A Separate Peace*, although less purely personal, *Another Country* is presented as a flashback to schooldays. It involves, in part, a presentation of struggles between capitalism and communism from the 1930s to the 1970s. Guy Bennett, an Englishman who functioned as a spy for the Soviet Union, reflects on his preparatory-school life. Guy, through his emerging homosexuality, along with his friend Judd, who is enamored of Marxist philosophy, struggle as outsiders in their preparatory school. Their choice to act freely rather than in approved ways relegates them to marginal status and causes them to wonder about the kind of loyalty fostered in school. Since loyalty is accorded only to those who conform to certain norms and roles, questions arise in their minds. If there is loyalty, to whom is it given and how is it obtained? If there is treason, who, or what, loses in the treasonous act?

In their reflections, Guy and Judd wonder about their role in being educated to keep "the whole thing going." Despite their role as outsiders acting freely and promoting change from the values the school teaches them, they find parts of prep-school life very attractive—in particular, cricket. This leaves them with what they term "Judd's Paradox." Judd especially likes the game, but, in some ways, sees it as a "fundamental part of the capitalist conspiracy" into which school life is inducting them. Although direct connections are not made to spying for the Soviet Union, they undergo a change at preparatory school that is implied to be a significant part of later political choices to spy. The refusal to conform to the role that is taught in school continues in life. Bennett, because of his overt homosexuality and the reaction of his peers to his demeanor, discovers that no matter what else he does, from the perspective of his schoolmates he has chosen goals that make him "not quite one of us." He sees the school's role as one of determining who is in and who is out. Further, despite his efforts, any connection with him is purely an alliance of convenience on the part of his peers. Such an alliance disappears when there is no longer a need for him, in relation to the group's goals of continuing the status quo. In later life, Guy observes that all he really misses in Russia is the cricket.

Making the Grade *(1984)*

In *Making the Grade*, the only comedy in this group of films, Eddie Keaton seeks to escape the clutches of his loan shark. He runs into

Palmer Woodrow, who is looking for someone to take his place at school. Having flunked out of other schools, Palmer does not wish to attend a school of last resort. Eddie hits on the idea of taking Palmer's place in order to hide out.

With the help of Palmer's friend, Randall Weatherby, Eddie changes in response to his role in school life to such an extent that he is able to say to Palmer, "I'm better at this than you are." Eddie's change is so effective that, at graduation, he is awarded the Hoover Memorial Award for his work under the name of Palmer Woodrow. Even though Eddie feels it necessary to own up to the fraud, he now sees himself as more capable than his elite peers to lead and prosper in the ways fostered by "their" school. The character who starts out thinking he will change the school is changed by it.

Dead Poets Society *(1989)*

The most recent of the films, *Dead Poets Society*, takes place at the mythical Welton Academy in the late 1950s. John Keating arrives as the new English teacher, bringing with him new ideas. He strives to enable his students to have, express and act on their own opinions. Through the works of free thinking heroes such as Whitman and Thoreau, Keating strives to enliven his students to cultivate their own ambitions so that, like Thoreau, they will come "to live deliberately" and "to suck the marrow out of life." With activities such as having students view the world from atop his desk, Keating attempts to offer them the experience of a curriculum at variance from the prescribed one by looking "at things in a different way."

When his students discover and express curiosity about his experience of being a member of the Dead Poets Society while a student at Welton, Keating senses some success in his quest to open their minds in ways not fostered by the prescribed curriculum. However, with that success, Keating has opened Pandora's Box. Each of the members of the re-formed Dead Poets Society begins to explore his own free choices, some more deeply than others. The feelings engendered by the society lead some of the students to take unapproved risks. Knox seeks the affection of a young woman who is already the girlfriend of the local high school quarterback; Todd begins to feel free to express his deepest feelings; Charley challenges the administration; and Neil acts in a Shakespearean play against his father's express wishes. This particular act of freedom and independence leads Neil's father to withdraw him from the school, in turn bringing Neil to commit suicide as the role and education his father imposes on him become too much to bear. The suicide leads to an investigation and Keating's dismissal for failure to follow the norms of the school. Reflecting institutional pressure to conformity, the Dead Poets Society is censured and blamed for the tragedy. As Cameron observes, "Schools go down over things like this." Scapegoats and victims are identified.

At the end, the four pillars of the curriculum of Welton Academy have seemed to turn from tradition, honor, discipline, and excellence to what the students have sarcastically identified at the beginning of the film as travesty, horror, decadence, and excrement. Upon Keating's departure from the school, a number of his students continue to confront the institution by standing up on their desks and saluting Keating, citing Whitman's line, "Oh Captain, My Captain" in a fashion reminiscent of the earlier, happier days of the year and in defiance of the headmaster. The students' action riles and threatens to overwhelm the headmaster, who has replaced Keating in order to reestablish a curriculum of conformity among the students.

PROBLEMS AND THE NULL CURRICULUM

There is reason to believe that elite prep schools function to promote capacities for freedom and choice for those who attend them. Still, in the context of prep-school movies, such capacities are often treated as anathema in these schools. Despite the presence of change as integral to the narratives, little room for individual freedom and choice is allowed in the dynamics of life in preparatory schools as portrayed in these movies. The culture of these schools is consistently presented as resistant or hostile to individual initiative. These films thus construct an image of a null curriculum in elite prep schools. Despite a null curriculum related to change, choice, and freedom, in each of the movies, difficulties with these pervasive realities demonstrate that there are more factors operative in these school settings than the approved programs make readily apparent. Each of the schools has an order and structure. The outdoor vistas are pastoral settings with broad, open spaces. Yet into these peaceful and bucolic settings arrives the unexpected, the unexplained, and, in some cases, the tragic and unwanted. Each of these settings contains within itself contradictions of its image and institutional goals.

Such contradictions in school settings are unique neither to these stories nor to boys' preparatory schools. As Catherine Cornbleth observes:

> Contradiction and normative variation are inherent in schooling as in other social institutions in heterogeneous or changing societies. Schools proffer contradictory messages and possibilities for interpretation and

> action. Among the contradictions of contemporary schooling are discrepancies within and between curriculum documents and curriculum practice, discontinuities among the messages of schooling and other social institutions, and the paradox of the schools' role in affording both liberating opportunities and constraints on personal autonomy.[9]

From this perspective, contradiction and normative variation can be found in all schooling. What is interesting in these movies is that these schools are portrayed as places in which there is no allowance for paradox. Constraints on personal autonomy exist while, through the null curriculum, there is a lack of liberating opportunities. Here there is a contradiction between the access to power in the larger world that these schools provide and the lack of freedom they allow within them.

Perhaps the null curriculum constructed in these narratives stems from the limited range of students found in this type of school. Sara Lawrence Lightfoot, commenting on actual private schools that can be termed "good" high schools, notes that

> in most private schools, diversity is limited to token groups of working-class and minority students, but the proportions remain small enough so that the homogeneous culture is largely unchallenged. It is expected that the unusual students, not the curriculum or pedagogy, will have to be transformed.[10]

In such a limited atmosphere, there is a focus on certain ways of doing or not doing things. This narrow focus minimizes, according to Lightfoot, the types of playful interchanges we find between student and teacher in such movies as *Goodbye, Mr. Chips* and in Keating's classroom in *Dead Poets Society*. She describes intellectual play in private schools:

> Certainly, such intellectual play is both rare and fleeting in any environment. It requires a creative and challenging teacher, a trusting and relaxed relationship among students, and a direct engagement with the material. Play is unlikely to occur in a highly competitive or combative environment because it requires the collaboration and elaboration of ideas, one building on the other. Play is unlikely to occur in a classroom where teachers are dominant and powerful and students passive and accommodating. And play is unlikely to be found in schools where students are worried about their own survival. It requires abundance, certainty, and the assurance of a future.[11]

The fragile nature of playful interaction in real school situations demonstrates a nonfictional substance to the contradictory pressure for conformity evident in films such as *Zero for Conduct*, *if . . .* , and *Another Country*, as well as the development of the action in *Dead Poets Society* after the suicide.

The cinematic portrayal of a null curriculum in prep schools is one putatively designed to prepare students for social standing and power in the larger society. However, the imposed limits of tradition do not seem, in these films, to have the power to insulate students from the influence of factors the schools do not allow to be part of their educational agendas. The null curriculum would deny powerful aspects of life in order to cultivate student characteristics associated with a clear sense of elite understandings and roles. Maxine Greene has suggested, with regard to similar types of neglect, that they result from an emphasis on the "givenness" of most school programs:

> The schools with their traditional presumption of a "normal" world and an official meaning-structure, have not only emphasized the givenness of what is taught, they have customarily neglected the distinctiveness of viewpoint, unless it seemed desirable to tap into individual interests, the better to connect individuals with what was thought of as heritage, funded experience, or the accumulated experience of the race. . . . Participation was not as important as accommodation, even in cases of explicit individualization.[12]

In the prep schools portrayed in movies, accommodation is more important than participation. The neglect of personal viewpoints, resulting from the pressure to accommodate, may be why Neil, in *Dead Poets Society*, comes to see life as futile in contradiction to his father's "given" project for a full and happy life for him. The revolutionaries in *Zero for Conduct* and *if . . .* see violence as the only creative answer. Guy Bennett finds spying to be a proper role for the outsider in *Another Country*. Because individuals are called upon to conform to institutional roles and goals, maybe Mr. Chips, Tom Brown, Gene in *A Separate Peace*, and Palmer and Eddie in *Making the Grade* all see their experiences of change and choice as personal crises rather than part of education. Schooling is not seen as preparing, explaining, or assisting them in their personal changes. Protagonists risk contradicting their true selves by changing goals and conforming to the structures of the schooling they participate in.

This emphasis on the "givenness" of these celluloid educational programs not only conveys the sense of a null curriculum but also presents such schools as devaluing the individual. This presentation gives form to Maxine Greene's observation that

> preoccupied with priorities, purposes, programs of "intended learning" and intended (or unintended) manipulation, we pay too little attention to the individual in the quest for his own future.[13]

The lack of concern for the individual's viewpoint and the "givenness" of the educational program are presented in these film images as things that are in the very nature of the schools described. But it is the presence of conflicting viewpoints that makes the movies work. Since change, freedom, and choice always remain part of the lives of people with power (as those in prep schools are destined to be), these movies suggest the tension between the null curriculum that denies them and the explicit and hidden curricula of these schools. The result, in many cases, is that the "given" unravels and comes into question. In *Zero for Conduct* and *if . . .*, we find the gradual breakdown of the students' sense of purpose resulting finally in a disconnectedness that is resolved only through a revolutionary process of destruction. In *Tom Brown's Schooldays*, Dr. Arnold's purposes are constantly in danger of collapse. It is only the power of Tom's personality that sustains them. In *Another Country* and *Dead Poets Society*, there are portrayals of a struggle in which unaddressed questions and the unrecognized strength of the "givenness" of school tradition lead to destruction of individuals and the apparent triumph of the established order in its quest for conformity.

For Gene in *A Separate Peace* and Eddie and Palmer in *Making the Grade*, the personal issues in focus are separated from systemic concerns. The project of schooling is only a backdrop for them. In these cases, the experience of the schooling portrayed does not affect the direction of their lives. Their personal choices are what shape—negatively for Gene and, in the end, positively for Eddie and Palmer—the experiences they draw from their schooling. In the end, we simply do not know where they are situated with respect to questions of power and conformity in the schools they attend.

The "givenness" of the agenda in these schools defines what is and what is not appropriate within their explicit curricula. What is not appropriate becomes the null curriculum and is thus repressed. Students are able to learn how to solve and understand certain problems of life and to make choices pertaining to the given problems. However, the changes these protagonists experience concern matters not always defined as acceptable. By focusing on unaddressed concerns, the protagonists provide vivid examples of what Donald Schon calls 'problem setting." For him, this is the

> process by which we define the decision to be made, the ends to be achieved, the means which may be chosen . . . a process in which,

> interactively, we *name* the things to which we will attend and *frame* the context in which we will attend to them.[14]

Often, the characters stand unprepared to deal with problem setting because of their lack of experience. While trying to prepare students for status and power by way of their explicit and hidden curricula, the null curriculum evident in these stories discourages students from having the power to name the important experiences in their lives and to frame the ways they would seek to address the conflicts they confront. The givenness of tradition, which these schools provide, does not foster capacities for naming and framing matters of authentic concern. As a result, these prep schools present the ironic contradiction of trying to keep their elite students unprepared for life.

IRONY AND UNRESOLVED CONTRADICTIONS

While irony is clearly part of films, theater, literature, and art, it is rarely if ever part of the discussion of organizations such as schools. The relationship between preparatory schools and unprepared people is indicative of the use of irony in the films in this study. The film makers involved with these movies visualize the relationships involved in ways that draw on two ironies connected to the development of western education. The first of the ironies is that structures designed to aid in the development of human efficacy become traps. The second irony concerns the avoidance and denial of conflict in a process that is unavoidably conflictual. To understand how structures meant to assist become traps, an observation by David Hogan concerning working class education may be helpful. He says that there is an

> enormous irony, however poignant and tragic, in the fact that it was the way of life centered on the union, the voluntary association, the school, the church, the saloon, the neighborhood, the machine and the party that the working class developed in the course of its struggle to survive and control the conditions of its own existence that in the long run locked it into the dominant structures, institutions and mentalities of bourgeois society.[15]

For the elite who utilize the preparatory school as an entree to power, there is a limit to the questions they can ask and the control they can exercise. According to Terrence Deal, private schools are cohesive cultures; such cohesion "can become a constricting vise."[16] The prep school of these movies, like the public school in some ways, ends up trapping those the school is designed to empower. In the terms used here, the null curriculum, with its denial of authentic individual choice and corollary pressures to conform, threatens a kind of powerlessness.

For Mr. Chipping, the ironic resolution comes in accepting his role as teacher, which is a contradiction of his desire. However, in accepting this trap, he is rewarded with love, children, and the headmastership. These goals are implied to be out of his reach without this twist of fate. Acquiescence, rather than freedom, helps him achieve his true goal eventually.

More painful traps can be found in *Another Country* and *Dead Poets Society*. In *Another Country*, according to the character Guy Bennett, "empire builders" are constrained by a system that wants them to be nothing more than impotent "empire rulers." The inability to bridge the gap between desire and conformity leads to marginalization. This marginal experience seems to be the seed for Guy's later involvement with a spy network. The gap leads to attempts to overthrow the powers that be in the whole society and an eventual self-imposed exile from it. In his spying, Guy, the scion of the aristocracy, becomes the agent allied against it. Guy, the devotee of cricket (a fundamental part of the capitalist conspiracy), in the end breaks from the trap by becoming a fundamental part of the communist conspiracy. In *Dead Poets Society*, John Keating seeks to inspire students to be like Thoreau and live life so as not to find at death that they had not lived. His support of nonconformity leaves him facing a student's suicide. The suicide stems from the student's despair over being apparently trapped by the power of others over him. Keating, who sees his students "seize the day" by standing on their desks in defiance of the headmaster's order, is faced with the realization that they are being returned to the trap of conformity to societal meanings. The exercise of the freedom to which he introduced them likely will be overturned by a return to an even greater pressure for conformity and dominance and the elimination of those too unruly to be controlled. In both *Another Country* and *Dead Poets Society,* freedom is portrayed as ironically carrying a higher price than submission to control.

The second irony builds on the first. An area of limitation in the education of the students in these movies is the denial by the schools of the reality of conflict. In particular, conflict flowing from the trap of conformity is suppressed. Limitations in addressing conflicts, according to Michael Apple, are inherent in all of western education, not just prep schools. In schools,

> a basic assumption seems to be that conflict among groups of people is *inherently* and fundamentally bad and we should strive to eliminate it *within* the established framework of institutions, rather than seeing conflict and contradiction as the basic "driving forces" in society.

> While some of the better schools and classrooms are alive with issues and controversies, the controversies usually exhibited in schools concern choices *within* the parameters of implicitly held rules of activity.[17]

The lack of recognition of conflict, as part of the null curriculum, may then flow from a general avoidance of any type of conflict. While lip service may be paid to the idea of conflict, these films suggest how the reality of conflict is denied as part of the null curriculum of prep schools.

Conflict is most clearly a part of the lives of the students of *Zero for Conduct* and *if. . . .* Supposedly being schooled to lead, they experience instead discipline and punishment, imposed so as to eliminate conflicts concerning how and why they might lead. Learning from the violence of their experience, the students in these movies use violence to take hold, as people of their class are expected to do, of their destiny. Ironically, discipline and punishment increase the conflict, thus destroying the school and creating for these students a likely criminal destiny unbecoming of people of their social station.

Tom Brown epitomizes the irony to be found in *Tom Brown's Schooldays*. The weakest of the lot, Tom eventually becomes the strongest and imparts his strength to others. As a student, he is expected to conform to the expectations of the institution, while at the same time he experiences the conflict engendered by his role as a change agent in relation to those expectations. Although Dr. Arnold does not like the old ways, he desires to avoid and eliminate conflict. He therefore enlists Tom to do what must be done, shifting the locus of conflict onto Tom in the process.

Gene in *A Separate Peace* and Eddie and Palmer in *Making the Grade* also expose the irony of schools that deny conflict even as they purport to foster growth. Their stories reveal the school's failure to help them deal with the important circumstances in their lives. For Gene, there is no real future after prep school. Finney's death, the moral equivalent of his own, renders life after prep school devoid of meaning. Eddie, on the other hand, must struggle to play the game that those born to it take for granted. His achievement ironically demonstrates that subversion of the system can be more productive in attaining its ends than conformity to it can be.

In the end, the ironies in these movies related to the trap of control and the avoidance of conflict come to light through the portrayal of these schools as places bent on control and full of conflict. The null curriculum promising a path of status and power by way of conformity and the denial of conflict is exposed as a sham, withholding from students real control over their lives. Ironically, they seem to be places intent on achieving ends very different from those Gintis describes in speaking about schools for the elite, where students "experience the types of freedom and develop the forms of personal dignity and effectiveness to control their lives that they will later use when they are controlling the lives of others in the world of business."[18]

CONCLUSION

The popular-culture medium of films should never be mistaken for reality. Often enough, films portray stereotypes that, as Gunderson and Haas caution, serve, "not so much as an indicator of reality, but as an indicator of 'reality' as seen by the public."[19] Given the irony at the center of these films, the "reality" that is seen by the public differs sharply from Gintis's description of upper-class schooling. Certainly the ambience and aura of these schools are much more attractive than those of ghetto schools. What is the lived reality? How much freedom, how much dignity, and how much control is afforded to those living and working in these schools? While these are the quintessential schools of choice of the marketplace,[20] the images of these films raise questions about the limits of choice.

While the hidden curriculum of socialization into social class is acknowledged by the schools in these film images, these films suggest a null curriculum at work in schools of this kind. This null curriculum does not acknowledge the price that those participating have to pay in this socialization and the types of experiences they are unprepared to face by virtue of the world they are being socialized for. Signithia Fordham, in an analysis of data on African-American students in private schools, identifies at least one area in which real schools have a null curriculum like that of the film schools. She observes that in private schools,

> for African-American adolescents, learning to cope with the "burden of 'acting white'" is (or becomes) an academic imperative, an undeniable breach of the Self. Ironically, this academic imperative is also the quintessential element in African-Americans' post–civil rights era identity implosion.[21]

In her research, there is evidence of a pressure to become "raceless" resulting from an avoidance of (null curriculum about) real differences in the experiences of blacks and whites in our society. The pressure to conform in the face of individual difference is seen by the subjects of Fordham's study as a "burden." Such a desire seems analogous to the conflict identified in this study as resulting from the absence of real parts of students' lives from the curriculum. The mythical price of the null curriculum in the films studied here thus appears to have a corollary in real counterparts among the subjects of Fordham's study. As they experience the hidden curriculum of entree to power in their schooling, they also experience the burden of the null curriculum of "acting white," that is, denying that race relates to power in our society.

When connected to studies such as Fordham's, the film images are not so easily dismissed as mere media stereotypes. Whether public image or lived reality, further study as to the accuracy of the popular image seems to be needed in order to understand whether there is a null curriculum in real prep schools. Movies such as those discussed here may provide indicators of the prep-school experience with respect to such a phenomenon. As the film portrayal of boys' prep schools shows, a null curriculum shaped from realities that are not taught and that are often denied can exert a formative impact on the experience of education. Sometimes that impact is powerful in maintaining the system. At other times, the impact is experienced as painful for those involved. What is clear is that inquiry centered on the null curriculum is vital if we are to understand the meaning of education that denies the realities of change, conformity, and conflict. The cinematic treatment of life in prep schools provides an avenue for inquiry of this kind.

NOTES

1. Samuel Bowles and Herbert Gintis, *Schooling in Capitalist America* (New York: Basic Books, 1976).

2. Herbert Gintis, "Education, Personal Development, and Human Dignity," in *Education and the American Dream: Conservatives, Liberals & Radicals Debate the Future of Education*, ed. Harry Holtz, Irwin Marcus, Jim Dougherty, Judy Michaels, and Rick Peduzzi (Granby, MA: Bergin & Garvey, 1989), p. 56.

3. Joseph S. Murphy, "Some Thoughts about Class, Caste, and the Canon," *Teachers College Record* 93 (2): p. 272.

4. Ibid.

5. Elizabeth Vallance, "Hiding the Hidden Curriculum: An Interpretation of the Language of Justification in Nineteenth Century Educational Reform," in *The Hidden Curriculum and Moral Education*, ed. Henry Giroux and David Purpel (Berkeley: McCutchan, 1983), p. 10.

6. Elliott E. Eisner, *The Educational Imagination*, 2d ed. (New York: Macmillan, 1985), p. 97.

7. Sam Wood (director), *Goodbye, Mr. Chips,* 1939; Jean Vigo (director), *Zero for Conduct,* 1947; Gordon Parry (director), *Tom Brown's Schooldays,*

1951; Lindsay Anderson (director), *if . . .*, 1968; Larry Peerce (director), *A Separate Peace,* 1972; Marek Kanievska (director), *Another Country,* 1984; Dorian Walker (director), *Making the Grade,* 1984; Peter Weir (director), *Dead Poets Society*, 1989.

8. Leonard Maltin, ed., *TV Movies and Video Guide* (New York: New American Library, 1989).

9. Catherine Cornbleth, *Curriculum in Context* (London: Falmer Press, 1990), p. 49.

10. Sara Lawrence Lightfoot, *The Good High School* (New York: Basic Books, 1983), p. 360.

11. Ibid., p. 361.

12. Maxine Greene, *Landscapes of Learning* (New York: Teachers College Press, 1978), p. 70.

13. Maxine Greene, "Curriculum and Consciousness." in *The Hidden Curriculum and Moral Education*, ed. Henry Giroux and David Purpel (Berkeley: McCutchan, 1983), p. 168.

14. Donald Schon, *The Reflective Practitioner* (New York: Basic Books, 1983), p. 40.

15. David Hogan, "Education and Class Formation: The Peculiarities of the Americans," in *Cultural and Economic Reproduction in Education: Essays on Class, Ideology and the State*, ed. Michael W. Apple (London: Routledge, 1982), p. 45.

16. Terrence E. Deal, "Private Schools: Bridging Mr. Chips and My Captain," *Teachers College Record* 92 (3): 423.

17. Michael W. Apple, *Ideology and Curriculum* (London: Routledge, 1979), p. 87.

18. Gintis, "Human Dignity," p. 56.

19. D. F. Gunderson and N. S. Haas, "Media Stereotypes in Teacher Role Definition," *Action in Teacher Education* 9 (2): 28.

20. John E. Chubb and Terry M. Moe, *Politics, Markets, and American Schools* (Washington DC: Brookings Institution, 1990).

21. Signithia Fordham, "Racelessness in Private Schools: Should We Deconstruct the Racial and Cultural Identity of African-American Adolescents?" *Teachers College Record* 92 (3): 471.

9 Miracle Working and the Image of the Exceptional Student

Arlene S. Sacks and Gary N. Mc Closkey, O.S.A.

In a review of the film *Awakenings*, David Sterritt reflected on the power of the tapestry of case stories in the book on which the movie was based, and wondered:

> How could this be made into a Hollywood movie? Simple: Narrow the focus to a wistful "human interest" story concentrating on one colorful hero, hire two of the world's most charismatic stars to play him and his doctor, and condense the other awakenings into a batch of colorful cameo performances. Call it over-simplified, call it manipulative, but it's bound to sell tickets, and that's what counts in Hollywood.[1]

In a similar way, the themes of films have also been "oversimplified" or "manipulated" with respect to our conceptions of the education of the exceptional student. Movies dealing with exceptional-student education, developmental disorders, and disabilities and impairments also do such condensation in a way that sometimes provides a positive learning experience and develops a bond between the "handicapped" character and the larger public. If this is a positive bond, such films can nurture public awareness, concern, and support. Yet, in such cinematic oversimplification and manipulation, some potential aspects of the relationship are cut out. In describing relations in which reality is oversimplified and manipulated, Anne Wilson Schaef, an analyst of dependency relations in societal structures, identifies a process of invalidation that occurs. In her experience, there is a "process of invalidating that which the system does not know, understand, cannot measure, and thereby cannot control."[2] In this process of invalidation, "large areas of perception and knowledge are lost."[3] Also in this process, participants "give the system the power to make the known unknown."[4]

Certainly, very familiar films such as *Mask, Rain Man, Children of a Lesser God, The Miracle Worker,* and *David and Lisa*—as well as less familiar films such as *Gaby: A True Story, A Test of Love, A Time to Live, Choices,* and *Amy*—have attempted to connect themselves to public concern for individuals who are now identified as exceptional students.[5] If Schaef is right, what has been lost in the oversimplification and manipulation? What "knowns" have been made unknown? The popularity of these films attests to the widespread reception and, one may assume, acceptance of the manipulated images presented. Films about exceptional-student experiences, like other media of popular culture, often represent particular interests or viewpoints. Yet, as Maxine Greene observes about the treatment of schooling more generally, "Messages of this sort (often embedded, of course, in the 'positive images' so insistently purveyed by the media) are not being articulated, confronted, or subjected to critique."[6] This essay will explore the relationships highlighted by, and aspects of the relationships that have become hidden due to, the simplifications and condensations of the films. Finally, some conclusions will be drawn about the difficulties in current exceptional-student education which these films exacerbate by helping to hide aspects of the reality of educating exceptional students.

MAJOR FILMS

Since the 1960s, there has been an increasing awareness about, and development of programs for, disabled students. During this same time, such exceptional students have also been the subject of films about their struggles. Testifying to the height of public awareness is the fact that four of the ten films we have identified have received Academy Awards (*Mask*, *Rain Man*, *Children of a Lesser God*, and *The Miracle Worker*). A fifth (*David and Lisa*) is a cult classic among latter-day black-and-white films. The popularity of these films suggests a wide acceptance of their message and portrayals. We now look at these five films before we move to the minor films we see as extending and reinforcing the messages and portrayals of the five major films.

Mask

In the film *Mask*, Rocky Dennis is afflicted with a disorder called "craniodiaphysealdysplasia." This disorder is best explained by viewing it through its three roots—cranio, diaphyseal, and dysplasia: *Cranio* pertains to the cranial or head area; *diaphyseal* pertains to the shaft of a long bone; and *dysplasia* pertains to incomplete or aberrant development of a part, system, or region of a body—in this case, the head, face, and clavicle.[7] The film explains that Rocky was diagnosed with the disorder at age four, when too much calcium was depositing around his skull. This occurs in approximately 1 in 22,000 births, and is commonly called "lionitis."

The film presents Rocky as a high-functioning adolescent. A great deal of his strong self-esteem is attributed to his advocate mother and supportive friends, who, as members of a motorcycle gang, are social outcasts. It is the depth of the love of the significant adult, the mother, that draws the viewer to support her advocacy for her son. The strength of her determination becomes clear when she confronts the principal of the local school to which Rocky has just been assigned. The principal wants to place Rocky in a separate, special school for handicapped students, simply because of the way he looks. Rocky's mother insists that he stay, and proceeds to explain Rocky's rights and to display appropriate documentation, including his last report card, demonstrating that he has been in the top fifth of his class. This experience shows the mother's ongoing struggle over school placements for Rocky. The principal demonstrates the desire of the school to hide, rather than mainstream, the exceptional student.

Another such situation occurs when a new doctor wants to tell the mother, once again, that, because of his lionitis and its pressure on the brain, Rocky should be limited in intelligence, life expectancy, and abilities. Her response is to shock him into understanding that she has been told this since Rocky was diagnosed and that he should be at least retarded or dead by now. The mother, as the significant adult, serves two functions: (1) She is the advocate of her handicapped child, and (2) she is a critic of the schooling situation who rallies support among the viewers while demonstrating not only the rights of the handicapped but also the responsibility of society. The main character, Rocky, has been created by the writer and director to: (1) Demand dignity while evoking sympathy and (2) serve as an example of how much potential there is in persons with handicapping conditions. Toward these ends, the film maker risks having the main character viewed in a skewed fashion. For example, Rocky is not only an unexpected high achiever in spite of his lionitis, but he also wins the graduation awards in mathematics, history, and science, and he evokes speech from a friend who, up to that point, has appeared to be mute. In contrast with the school's initial desire to hide Rocky in another, special school, it now parades him as a model mainstreamed student. Rocky's accomplishments lie somewhere between total fantasy and the normal experience of people with his disorder.

Successful experiences for Rocky extend to a summer camp where, as a counselor, he teaches a blind girl to "see" through the use of her sense of touch. To sense colors, for example, she touches the blue of ice and a hot potato depicting red. Rocky uses cotton balls to convey the sense of billowy clouds. When the girl's parents come to pick her up, however, they meet Rocky and scoot her away as quickly as possible upon seeing him. They have judged him from the features of his lionitis, not from his accomplishments. As they pull away, Rocky's mother and friends pull right up to ensure that negatives are never unreconciled for very long.

This question arises: What knowns become unknown in the manipulations of this movie? Rocky's support system and achievements present a pleasant picture to the viewer. This surely masks, however, what we know about the difficulties faced by those with severely handicapping conditions. Outside of the movie framework, we certainly know that it is unrealistic to expect all such students to be success stories. Still, it is difficult for parents, family, and friends who cannot be super advocates, or for handicapped people who cannot be super achievers, to reconcile their efforts with those depicted in the movie. Thus, the problem for the significant adult becomes a questioning of why his/her child is not able to do these things. This is a strange question if we recognize the medical facts manipulated by this movie. Likewise, for the handicapped person, the problem becomes one of accepting a level of accomplishment less than that of the class valedictorian. In addition to those immediately involved in cases such as Rocky's, a question arises concerning other viewers enjoying the fairy tale. If movies such as *Mask* are to succeed in generating greater advocacy and support due to greater public awareness, how does that support and advocacy move beyond the fantasy and relate to the harsher and manipulated reality of severely handicapping conditions?

Rain Man

A situation similar to the one found in *Mask* can be seen in *Rain Man*. The main character is Raymond, a high-functioning autistic man who is a resident of Wallebrook Institution. Autism is

> a severe childhood disturbance characterized by bizarre behavior, developmental delays and extreme isolation. . . . The behavioral features are often appropriate for interventions employed with students who have emotional disturbances.[8]

At times, this film does a good job of portraying the characteristics of this autistic savant by presenting a variety of situations in which his extraordinary abilities and severe disabilities are displayed. The problem with sensory input and how it is processed is exemplified many times. Raymond's need for absolute routine and the absolute terror at a break in his routine are presented throughout the film.

Wallebrook Institution, where Raymond lives, offers him a place where his daily routine is never changed. Raymond's caretaker is a young man who helps him through his day and accompanies him wherever he goes. The institution is protective of him and sympathetic to his needs. Removal of the autistic Raymond from Wallebrook Institution is accomplished because of his unquestioning, childlike trust for his younger brother, Charles, who, for his own reasons, questions the appropriateness of the institution in meeting the emotional needs of Raymond. Although his chronological age is that of an adult, Raymond's childlike dependency easily puts the younger brother in the role of the significant adult and, ultimately, the advocate. The movie's depiction of Raymond screaming at the interruption of repetitions, ranting at the thought of flying, due to his knowledge of the statistics of accidents, and his mortal fear of highways all demonstrate his need for supervision and a caretaker or significant adult advocate.

As in *Mask*, the film uses a family member, Raymond's brother Charles, as a significant adult who successfully serves as an advocate on the exceptional person's behalf. Charles's actions also imply a criticism of the particular institution while demonstrating the need not only for respecting the rights of the handicapped person but also for expanding the responsibility of society. Again, as with Rocky in *Mask*, Raymond as a character is created so as to (1) be able to demand dignity while evoking sympathy and (2) serve as an example of the kinds of talents and strengths handicapped persons such as Raymond have. However, the shaping of the character makes viewers suspend disbelief, making what is known unknown in order to enter the world of the film. One must set aside what is known about autism to enjoy seeing Raymond help Charles beat the house at the casinos in Las Vegas, for example. The level of communication for someone who is by definition living in "extreme isolation" is at odds with the experience of high-stimulus, nonroutinized gambling tables. Similarly, the dance scene between the two brothers and the kiss between Charles's girlfriend and Raymond involve an unrealistic amount of touching and socialization for someone who we know should be evidencing "bizarre behavior" and "developmental delays." Even though Charles tries to care for his brother's needs to the best of his abilities, he finds that the emotional stress is more than he can handle, and he returns Raymond to the institution. Is this return symbolic of a reality that the known, even when made unknown, will reappear in some form to make us face reality?

The impact of a model of such a high level of social and physical communication and success outside of a stable institutional setting can be devastating for parents, family, and friends of autistic persons. If there is to be success, the full picture of reality must be taken into account. If not, the fantasy, and whatever positive effects it may have in generating heightened awareness and support for the autistic, must be weighed against the impact of any misconceptions and disappointments that result from the film's tendency to simplify and distort what is known.

Children of a Lesser God

In *Children of a Lesser God*, Sarah, the main character, is deaf.[9] In contrast to most of the other films discussed in this study, the actress playing the handicapped person is, like the character, deaf. At the school for the deaf where most of the action takes place, Sarah has achieved a level of independence through work as a custodian after graduation from the school. High levels of success are portrayed for other students in the film. The educational programs for the deaf and hearing impaired are cast in a consistently positive light. The significant adult is not a family member but John, a teacher who, while becoming Sarah's lover, is portrayed as desiring to be an advocate for all the handicapped persons he encounters. He takes his students and Sarah to new levels of experience, particularly in teaching his students to dance to rock music by feeling the impulses through large speakers. His teaching the students to sing in a rock performance—as opposed to just signing the words—is an important success for the supportive parents who have all come to watch their children. Although he claims to use the total communication approach, which involves the training of all possible communication forms (speech, signing, finger spelling), as opposed to just signing, the teacher in *Children of a Lesser God* displays a definite preference for the oral approach. The fact that this remains a highly controversial issue among the hearing impaired is never really addressed in the movie.

An instance of misdiagnosis, itself a common occurrence, is part of the film's plot. Sarah's skepticism about her improving her ability to communicate relates in part to being originally diagnosed as mentally retarded[10] based on the lack of "normal functioning" resulting from deafness. Unfortunately, the deaf have often been misdiagnosed in the past by ignorant practitioners as being mentally retarded due to their inability to speak coherently at expected developmental levels. Overcoming her skepticism, Sarah allows John, the teacher, to intervene as a significant adult, enabling her to reach new levels of progress.

What is the known that is made unknown in this movie? Perhaps the most serious unaddressed issue in the movie is the price handicapped persons pay in order to be accepted. For Sarah, the price of John's advocacy, criticism, and acceptance is the need to appear "normal." In an effort to please and to appear "normal" in her functioning, Sarah teaches herself to play poker rather successfully, for example, and otherwise do things necessary to please a hearing world. She is portrayed as most successful (most normal) when demonstrating her ability to leave the relationship with John and live independently, thereby making possible the reestablishment of a life with John based on full equality. Sarah and John must find a place, outside of the school, where he will not push her to speak in order to communicate, since she has determined the normality of oral communication to be inappropriate for her, as an individual. This determination is presented as stemming from reactions to her speech beginning in childhood. Could she have appeared to be normal if she had had another childhood?

The narrative ends, of course, with them together as equal adults. However, there is no real discussion of the problem of "normal appearance." It is no longer a relationship based on a pairing of handicapped and advocate/critic. Sarah has become her own advocate and critic of the schooling process by leaving the limiting atmosphere of the school. John is still supportive. Like *Mask* and *Rain Man, Children of a Lesser God* spins a tale that entrances the viewer to support the success while overlooking some unreality regarding levels of functioning and ability to cope with disability. We know the messages regarding the appearance of normality that the handicapped and nonhandicapped alike receive from society. Unreality results when we oversimplify the struggle for anyone to stand against the norm as their own advocate and critic of institutions.

The Miracle Worker

The Miracle Worker is another cinematic learning situation in which the main character, Helen Keller, blind[11] and deaf[12] due to a fever in infancy, is offered a chance in life due to the intervention of a teacher/advocate. Helen Keller is fortunate to have affluent parents who are caring and perhaps exasperated enough to give up some of their power to her teacher, Annie Sullivan. Sullivan, visually impaired herself,[13] was a student at the Perkins School, an institution for the handicapped.

This hiring of Sullivan is the last attempt on the part of the parents to help Helen before sending her to a school for the mentally defective, because of her bizarre behavior. Such a facility was not an unusual school placement for the period. Examples of her behavior include beating up other children as well as physically threatening her new baby brother. The scenes between Helen and Annie are truly "fantastic." It takes a knock-down, drag-out fight for Helen to sit at the table and to use a spoon. It takes two weeks of Annie and Helen living alone in a converted storage shed, without the interference of loving but permissive parents, and the withholding of food for Annie to get Helen to spell "cake." The famous water scene at the pump where learning finally occurs is done with music and fanfare. The audience is spelling and saying the word with Helen as her brain is putting out proof that the messages have gone in and that thought is taking place.

Once again, we see the significant adult as an advocate for successful learning for this multihandicapped student, and as a critic encouraging viewers to rally against institutionalizing the handicapped person. Viewers are again reminded that a true advocate's sense of responsibility endures regardless of how many discomforts or slaps in the face are required. The image of the main character, Helen, is again fashioned so as to mask the depth and hardship of the struggles that persons with such disorders must suffer before they are able to become a functional part of their families and the larger society.

As a multihandicapped person, Helen Keller's life is an extreme case when compared to the other films discussed. However, as in the case of the other films, the most extreme difficulties dissolve in order to clear the way for the movie to win the hearts of viewers with its story-book ending as Helen becomes a great communicator despite the lack of hearing and vision. This movie contributed to the process through which Helen Keller has become an icon of overcoming obstacles in life. The overcoming of obstacles in the movie seems to resolve all issues, yet one wonders what is lost among the hidden and now unknown aspects of this life. In giving Helen Keller her due, have we lost sight of the social and financial conditions that make such accomplishments possible?

David and Lisa

David and Lisa takes place in a residential-school setting. Using black-and-white film and focusing on bizarre images to depict the thoughts and perceptions of the emotionally disturbed adolescents who attend the school, the film makers emphasize the unusual nature of the story. This reinforces the reality that the emotionally disturbed exhibit "an inability to build or maintain satisfactory interpersonal relationships" and "inappropriate types of behaviors or feelings under normal circumstances."[14] The film derives its name from the two main characters and focuses on their relationship.

David, who is seventeen years old, dominates the relationship. Depicted as severely emotionally disturbed, he believes that touch can kill, and therefore gets hysterical when anyone touches him. In public he appears arrogant and difficult, a near-genius and an excellent student. Although David is antisocial in his behavior and thus unable to develop "satisfactory interpersonal relationships," he spends a great deal of time watching Lisa. She is fifteen years old, makes rhymes for communication, stomps up and down, has wide mood swings, and displays a personality disorder in which she acts as another persona, Muriel. David calls Lisa an adolescent schizophrenic. In between his observations of Lisa's drawing, playing, and rhyming, David pays visits to the significant adult in the film, the psychiatrist, with whom he chooses to demonstrate a somewhat equal relation by calling him by his first name, Alan. The low-key, almost monotone, psychiatrist appears dull. This portrayal, along with the use of black and white, is meant to suggest the type of impression the world makes on the mind of the emotionally disturbed. David focuses on a broken clock in the psychiatrist's office. He dreams about the clock, enlarging it to great proportions. The clock seems to symbolize David's feeling of being overpowered by the school as well as by the concept of death. He has dreams of rigging the clock so that it chops off the head of one of the staff who touches him by accident. David is preoccupied by time because it keeps going on and brings him closer to death. He believes that if no one touches him, they cannot hurt him, and thus he will not move closer to death. In this way, interpersonal relationships are seen as deadly. This is a symptom of David's emotional disturbance.

A dimension of reality is brought into the film when the class takes a trip into town to see Christmas decorations. While waiting for the train, the class encounters a man and his family. This encounter turns into an altercation, and the man shouts at them, "You're a bunch of screwballs spoiling the town." The students' reactions, particularly facial expressions, show pain, anger, and frustration. The viewer is drawn to advocacy by feeling the hurt inflicted by "normal" people.

Atypical for a relationship undertaken by an emotionally disturbed person, David breaks through Lisa's communication block by speaking to her in her own rhyming pattern; they rhyme back and forth. However, when he returns to his usual behavior and yells at her for unkind behavior exhibited to another boy, she runs away from the school. David is the only one who knows where to find her. Alan, the psychiatrist who has observed David's success with Lisa, encourages him to find her. When Lisa is found, she finally speaks to David without rhyming. He tells her she did not rhyme and she is not under the control of Muriel, the persona which pushed her to say strange things. She says, "I'm me. Lisa is Muriel." He says, "Lisa, take my hand." She does.

As in all of these films, conflict is resolved. Again, the known, involving deep struggles for wholeness, is made unknown. In a fairly simple way, David draws normal speech out of Lisa, while Lisa enables David to allow touching. The only reference to the depth of struggle each is engaged in is the celebration of the moment with music to identify the breaking of the barriers to interpersonal relationships for persons with an emotional disturbance. The viewer joins those believing that emotional disturbance can be overcome through advocacy and support, appropriate placement, and good psychiatric care. Thus, the built-in message of the film is the need for society to replicate David and Lisa's support for one another and thus enable the emotionally disturbed to function well in the greater society. However, one does not see, in this movie, those patients who do not make the breakthrough. What becomes masked in this situation is the reality that we often do not know what constitutes an appropriate placement, nor good psychiatric care, for many people who struggle with emotional disturbances.

THE MINOR FILMS

In addition to the five Academy Award/cult-classic movies, there are five movies in this genre which are of lesser notoriety: *Gaby: A True Story, A Test of Love, A Time to Live, Choices*, and *Amy*. However, with respect to the nature of this type of film, these five minor films continue and reinforce the pattern of portraying extraordinary examples of advocacy for, and breakthroughs by, handicapped persons.

Gaby: A True Story

In *Gaby: A True Story*, the title character has cerebral palsy. Cerebral palsy is defined as "an abnormal alteration of human movement or motor function arising from a defect, injury, or disease of the tissues of the central nervous system."[15] The problem in the central nervous system, which controls motor behavior, makes it impossible for the brain to send impulses with the correct messages. The movements exhibited are therefore jerky and uncontrolled. Speech is frequently affected, and the person with cerebral palsy cannot communicate normally. Often, the incorrect inference is made that the jerky, uncontrollable movement and or uncommunicative speech must mean that the person with cerebral palsy is retarded or incapable of learning.

In this film, Gaby's relatively affluent parents, who have fled from the Nazis in Europe, give birth in Mexico to this child with cerebral palsy. Florenza, one of the housemaids who works for them, becomes the significant adult in Gaby's life. After portraying initial obstacles from her family, the movie presents Gaby's support system within the home as increasingly positive. It is school that proves to be her biggest obstacle. Here the school assists society in hiding exceptional students by keeping them in a dead-end learning situation. Gaby's parents act as advocates for her by criticizing the school officials and supporting Gaby's demand for the right to take an equivalency examination for graduation, which she passes.

The film makers provide Gaby with an almost normal social development that seems unimpeded by her physical difficulties and the social stigma attached to cerebral palsy. She has two boyfriends: one with whom she has a sexual experience despite her physical limitations and another who helps her publish her writing despite the limitations of her communication. Ultimately her parents die. Gaby attends the university and publishes a book about her life (on which the film is based). She and Florenza adopt a baby girl. With the requisite inspirational music playing in the background, Florenza and Gaby are each shown taking part in encouraging the child's development, thereby becoming a family.

As in the previously analyzed films, the handicapped person shows great ability, and the viewer, in knowing this person in this way, comes to feel an admiration for the handicapped character. This may result in further advocacy and criticism of problematic schooling situations. But, again, such responses are based on the portrait of a handicapped person depicted in a skewed fashion. What is particularly skewed (made unknown) in this film is the likelihood of such success in overcoming the power of an entrenched system. Further, in this film, the issue that for some parents is their greatest concern—what happens to the handicapped child after the parents' death—is glossed over, and thereby minimized or denied, by the image of Florenza simply devoting her life to Gaby.

A Test of Love

As in *Gaby: A True Story, A Test of Love* provides another example in which the prevailing conditions for learning in an educational setting must be confronted and overcome. Brentwood Hospital, a residential institution for the mentally retarded, made dying the easy way out. Annie, the main character, is diagnosed as being mentally retarded[16] and having cerebral palsy.[17] She is given six months to live because she cannot be fed. Jessie, the significant adult who supervises student teachers at the hospital, views the program and schedule as having a negative effect. She gets some money and support for change from the institution. Most of the children have not been outside of the hospital since they were three years old. They are put to bed at 4:30 P.M. and are expected to lie there until the next morning.

Jessie begins her effort to transform the institution by singling out Annie. Watching the child's reactions and responding to those which are contrary to those responses expected from someone with such disorders, she begins her effort. Placing colorful posters above the children's cribs, she provides a more stimulating environment. Through efforts such as playing music in the wards, she tries to convince her skeptical boyfriend that Annie is not mentally retarded—the physical difficulties of cerebral palsy are what create the false impression. Jessie's crusade provides the catalyst for larger changes that occur. Eventually, Jessie fights a custody battle with the hospital for Annie. Even though the institution had made improvements over the years, the officials of the hospital were afraid that radical change might bring about its demise. In the end the hospital does close. In the battle, Annie's parents side with the institution.

Jessie is triumphant in court. In typical fantasy format she rushes off to sweep Annie into her arms. Jessie, her boyfriend, and Annie become a family. Annie overcomes the physical difficulties of cerebral palsy and proceeds to earn a B.A. from Deacon University. This demonstrates the actual mental ability of many persons with cerebral palsy. While advocacy and criticism are once again portrayed as successful, with the advocate and model handicapped person triumphing over an institution, no consideration is given to the possibility of failure and the parents' concern about the hurt their child might suffer. Such questions are undercut by portraying them in a negative light and simplifying the story to one of undeniable success.

A Time to Live

In *A Time to Live*, the main character is affected with muscular dystrophy, "an hereditary disorder that causes loss of vitality and progressive deterioration of the body as a result of atrophy, or the replacement of muscle tissue with fatty tissue."[18] From the beginning of the movie, the physician tells the parents of the main character, Petey, that he can live into the third decade but will ultimately die of pneumonia when the muscles in his lungs atrophy. The significant adult in the movie is his mother, although the father is also highly supportive. The mother is told that, although muscular dystrophy is a male disease, it is transmitted by the mother. The film makers create a plot in which the superadvocate parents go to great lengths in visiting specialists, even going to a faith healer. The mother devotes her entire life to taking care of Petey. Fortunately, the father is a well-paid attorney. The mother's schedule involves getting up at 6 A.M., and striving to overcome the effects of muscular dystrophy by exercising, dressing, washing, and feeding Petey to get him ready for school. In contrast to the family's devotion, the school is portrayed as a place of obstacles for Petey. For example, while in an unfamiliar wheelchair, Petey bumps into a boy who then applies the wheelchair brakes. Unable to move his hands because of muscle atrophy, Petey cannot release the brakes, and the school day continues without him.

The family's effort to keep Petey developing is superhuman. Unfortunately, as is the case for most children with this disease, despite advocacy and criticism of inappropriate treatment and education, the muscular dystrophy prevails, and he dies gallantly. As in each of the other films, the determination of Petey and his family provides a model situation. What becomes hidden here is any true sense of the cost of this family's struggle. We witness scenes demonstrating their extraordinary communication skills and total devotion, but learn little of the pain and sacrifice such families must endure.

Choices

In *Choices*, a film about a hearing-impaired high school football star, the school situation provides an atmosphere that can either encourage the boy or destroy him. John's hearing impairment,[19] which occurred at the age of eight due to a swimming accident, is almost total in one ear and 50 percent in the other ear.

The significant adult in this film is the boy's father, although his friends and coach are also extremely supportive. While he plays football, John appears successful as well in his academic work, socialization, musical ability on the violin, and self-concept. A new physician for the school district, backed by the school board, decides that the hearing impaired should not play football, and disqualifies him. The father has raised him to believe, and continues to reinforce, the concept that he is normal. Yet, because the institution has labeled and limited him, John begins to lose faith in himself. After problems with drinking, drugs, cutting school, family arguments, and a car theft, John comes to his senses. He even faces honestly the severity of his hearing loss.

As with other films of this genre, the ending seems to resolve all the issues. In the final football game, John is put in without the board's permission as the team is losing. He leads the team to victory. The film then flashes to John playing the violin in a musical performance, tuxedo and all. The movie notes that laws have been amended, since John's experience, to support the rights of individuals who are disabled. The viewer is encouraged to reflect on the importance of such rights by way of the focus on the importance of athletics in John's healthy development. This is the basis for criticism of the school's placing of obstacles in the path of the handicapped. Again, the hidden reality is that a hearing impaired, scholar-athlete-violinist who can beat the odds hardly is representative of the norm.

Amy

Amy is somewhat different from the other films in that the main character is not handicapped. The focus is on the difficulties of the advocate. In some ways, this is the flip side of *Children of a Lesser God.* The school situation dominates as the children and their education are analyzed throughout the film. The children are attending a residential school for handicapped children from poor mountain families. Without the school, we are given to understand, these children would be shut away, by themselves, in dark rooms.

The school is for the deaf and blind, and Amy is an oralist teacher for the deaf. As such, she believes the deaf children should speak, not just sign. She has conflicts with the teachers who are not oralists. Amy wants the oralist philosophy to prevail so the children will be able to communicate orally with those outside the deaf world. The other teachers want the children to sign, apparently to accept their lot and live among their own. As a result of Amy's work, there is a touching scene between a deaf boy who learns to say "mother" for the first time to his blind mother, who comes to the school. She has never seen her boy, but now she can hear him, and thus they can communicate despite their respective handicaps.

A physician who helps the school becomes Amy's support in advocacy. He helps her understand her life direction and assists her with the children. In the end, the film is a wonderful success story for the development of a woman's ego, the oralist philosophy of deaf education, and the goal of mainstreaming deaf children with normal children. But issues still remain unaddressed. Viewers are not aided to see the difficulty of gaining acceptance for new programs in schools, particularly after false starts. Another factor that becomes masked is the reality that advocates with little training rarely have such immediate success, or even any success at all, when faced with trained teachers following ingrained methods. Finally, while the oralist versus sign language controversy is solved here, it remains an issue that divides informed parties in our society.

CONCLUSION

Each of the ten films discussed raises unrealistic emotional expectations. These relate to expectations about the success of education in assisting handicapped persons as well as expectations about the success of advocacy. Thus, each movie extends the accusation Sterritt levels against *Awakenings*: "It makes you laugh, cry, and marvel. But it also simplifies and falsifies all kinds of issues."[20] The simplification and falsification in the movies about exceptional student education can be reduced to two elements. First, much of what is invalidated (known but left out of account) in these movies is medical fact. The medical facts tell us that these characters are not typical of the groups of exceptional students they supposedly represent. In these representations, the complexity of medical situations faced by these persons is falsified and thus invalidated. The second simplification is in the portrayal of the system being fought—in these films, an individual school or institution. This simplification falsifies the reality that these individual settings are and have been almost always part of a larger system that determines policy.

With respect to simplifying the medical reality, the unknowns can complicate the ability to deal with the current design of exceptional-student education programs. The reality that most handicapped children now face is a program of exceptional-student education in which public-school systems provide the institutional setting. Increasingly, during the thirty-year period when these films were made, public-school systems have, by law, become responsible for education of exceptional students. With the passage of P.L. 94–142, provision by the public school of the "most appropriate" education of exceptional students, in the "least restrictive environment," became compulsory. Also, with the passage of P.L. 99–457, that obligation was extended to include students below the normal school age. The way the most appropriate education and the least restrictive environment are determined is through the development of an Individualized Education Program (IEP) mandated by P.L. 94–142 or an Individualized Family Service Plan (IFSP) mandated by P.L. 99–457.

The contents of such plans are not designs for dealing with emotional relationships. Rather, they provide for structured educational settings based on the medical needs and conditions of students. In these plans, objectives are established by a professional, multidisciplinary team to ensure that the specific, primarily medically based, needs of the exceptional student are met. In the film presentations, such efforts are unrepresented, and schools are often portrayed as part of the problem. Invalidating the medical facts creates difficulties in answering a number of questions. Are the advances being made by schools to meet educational and medical needs sufficient? Have these films been effective in addressing real experiences and concerns, or have they raised emotional expectations unrealistically high with regard to what exceptional students and their closest advocates can achieve in the face of medical difficulties and limitations?

Beyond the expectations of advocates and exceptional students with regard to the assistance of programs in overcoming medical deficiencies, the roles of advocates and exceptional students in decision making seems oversimplified, again, with respect to recent developments in exceptional-student education. In both the IEP and the IFSP, the role of advocate can be frequently more difficult than the circumstances portrayed in the films. Even though the advocate can be a participant, the whole society, through law, places the responsibility on the professional, multidisciplinary team designated by the public-school system to state in the IEP and the IFSP the most appropriate education and least restrictive environment for the handicapped student. For the advocate, who may disagree with the educational and medical assessment of the professional team, it is not enough to object. The advocate, in a sense, must fight the legally supported system, rather than a single institution, and disprove the recommendations of the team by providing direction to a more appropriate educational plan. Some of the films suggest advancements in the education of exceptional students. However, in the reality that becomes hidden or unknown in these films, when an advocate believes there has been an error in assessment, that advocate is in the same position that Helen Keller's family was in almost a century ago, as portrayed in *The Miracle Worker*. The advocate will, in most cases, have to hire professionals as miracle workers to disprove the efficacy of the recommendations and aid in better education. Having the resources available to engage miracle workers to contest the recommendations of whole educational systems is not something that a poor or even middle-class family can easily afford. Many of these families may end up emotionally destroyed in the face of the reality of a system's power.

As a result of the changing educational climate of the last thirty years, including significant changes in the laws passed and the influence of popular support (generated, in part, by the success of these movies), an increasing number of exceptional-student education programs have provided greater access to programs for exceptional students. Despite this success, the common tendency of film makers to manipulate emotions in the movies examined here invalidates what many know, and leaves some realities hidden. Full success will never be possible without confronting and overcoming these realities. The simplifications of the circumstances of the handicapped and their families invalidate what is known about the medical complexities and the power of educational systems faced by most exceptional students.

As Sterritt observed about *Awakenings*, "Watching it diverts attention from the problems' complexities and creates an illusory sense of involvement and understanding. That's a dubious achievement."[21] Schaef would probably be stronger in evaluating these circumstances, because they fit not only her definition of the process of invalidation but also her definition of denial, that is, refusing "to see what we see and know what we know." Rather than contributing to the freeing of the exceptional student, by invalidating and denying elements of reality, these movies may be supporting the creation of another form of control over the abnormal and unwanted. In evaluating the hold on people exercised by problematic systems and societies, Schaef posits that "denial is the means by which that hold continues."[22] Thus, even though each of the movies analyzed here featured a successful resolution of its conflict, the conflicts presented in the films do not address the full scope of what we know about the experiences of exceptional students and those who are advocates for them. While the interests of control in society have been regularly served by messages in popular culture, the growing complexity of the processes of culture and popular media have made such interests and messages, according to Maxine Greene, "far more complex, far more mystifying, far more manipulative than the statements about social ills that motivated critical thinking in the past."[23] Hopefully, increased critique and analysis can make these engaging "human interest" stories more transparent. In this way, perhaps, persons struggling with disabilities might be less subject to the processes of invalidation and denial through which popular-culture images reduce their reality to something "that's bound to sell tickets"[24] while demanding a miracle worker more than ever.

NOTES

1. David Sterritt, "'Awakenings' Shortcuts Fact to Stir Emotion," *Christian Science Monitor* (7 February 1991), p. 13.
2. Anne Wilson Schaef, *When Society Becomes an Addict* (New York: Harper & Row, 1987), p. 108.
3. Ibid.
4. Ibid.
5. Peter Bogdanovich (director), *Mask*, 1986; Barry Levinson (director), *Rain Man*, 1988; Randa Haines (director), *Children of a Lesser God*, 1986; Paul Aaron (director) *The Miracle Worker*, 1962; Frank Perry (director), *David and Lisa*, 1962; Luis Mandoki (director), *Gaby: A True Story*, 1987; Gil Brealey (director), *A Test of Love*, 1984; Rick Wallace (director), *A Time to Live*, 1985; Silvio Narizzano (director), *Choices*, 1990; Vincent McEveety (director), *Amy*, 1980.

The movies analyzed here were chosen after a review of Leonard Maltin, ed., *TV Movies and Video Guide* (New York: New American Library, 1989).

From the 18,500 movies reviewed, those that focused on a situation concerning the education of an exceptional student were identified. In addition, only movies that had made it to the home-video market were investigated, in order to ensure that a wide audience might have been affected by the presentation. That dual analysis yielded the ten movies analyzed in this study.

6. Maxine Greene, *Landscapes of Learning* (New York: Teachers College Press, 1978), pp. 170–71.

7. S. I. Landow, *International Dictionary of Medicine and Biology*, Vol. I (New York: Wiley Medical Publications, 1986), pp. 663, 784, 882.

8. Edward L. Meyen, *Exceptional Children in Today's Schools* (Denver: Love Publishing, 1990), p. 514.

9. Deafness is a "condition in which the sense of hearing is so lacking or drastically reduced as to prohibit normal functioning; the auditory sense is not the primary means by which speech and language are learned" (Ibid., p. 515).

10. Mental retardation is "a condition in which significantly subaverage general intellectual functioning is manifested during the developmental period and exists concurrently with impairment in adaptive behavior" (Ibid., p. 519).

11. Blindness is defined as "having only light perception without projection or being totally without sense of vision. Educationally, the blind child learns through the tactile and auditory materials" (Ibid., p. 514).

12. Previously defined in relation to *Children of a Lesser God*. See n. 9.

13. Being visually impaired is "a measured loss of any of the visual functions such as acuity, visual fields, color vision or binocular vision" (Meyen, *Exceptional Children*, p. 524).

14. Ibid., p. 27.

15. Ibid., p. 514.

16. Previously defined in relation to *Children of a Lesser God*. See n. 9.

17. Previously defined in relation to *Gaby: A True Story*. See n. 15.

18. Meyen, *Exceptional Children*, p. 520.

19. A hearing impairment is defined as "a deficiency in the ability to hear. It may range from a mild loss to a total lack of hearing ability (deafness). At the level of severe loss, defined as 70–90 dB measured on an audiometer, hearing impaired individuals require extensive training in communication methods" (Ibid., p. 517).

20. Sterritt, "'Awakenings' Shortcuts Fact," p. 13.

21. Ibid.

22. Schaef, *Society*, p. 138.

23. Greene, *Landscapes of Learning*, p. 171.

24. Sterritt, "'Awakenings' Shortcuts Fact," p. 13.

IV FLARES AND SNAPSHOTS

Telling Images of School Experience

In the preceding sections of this volume, we have sought to show that there is not one relationship between schooling and popular culture but many. Sometimes tangential to popular images of youthful concerns, sometimes the focus of media coverage, and sometimes the context of popular tales, aspects of schooling are subject to diverse treatment in the forms of popular culture. In each category, fairly definite lines of analysis and inquiry suggest themselves. While such categories help to frame important kinds of questions, they leave out of account vital and diverse examples of texts that resist any such scheme. The reason for this concerns a widely remarked characteristic of contemporary, postmodern culture. A central feature of postmodern culture is the extent to which people increasingly attend to multiple, shifting, and fragmented domains of meaning. In this context, numerous sites exist for popular-culture texts to register with diverse audiences in more fleeting and less predictable ways. This section includes studies suggesting the variety of popular modes that feature direct but limited and highly focused attention to specific aspects of school experience. The works in question typically involve an interplay of entertainment value and pointed, telling images designed to spark some shared insight, convey a bit of truth, or make a point about school experience. The works in question are not constrained to simply dismiss, report on, or sustain a vision of school experience; rather, they function more playfully and anecdotally. Like flares, the works operate by highlighting particular, widely shared observations and insights in popular forms that make quick recognition and common assent possible.

The following studies suggest the terrain of possible inquiry. In chapter 10, "Carnival, Pop Culture, and the Comics: Radical Political Discourse," Olga Skorapa analyzes the treatment of educational themes in newspaper comics. Building on Bakhtin's theory of carnival, this analysis suggests the power of comics to open avenues of inquiry into schooling and their potential as sources of alternate visions of class, race, and gender in education. Chapter 11, "Educational Cartoons and *Phi Delta Kappan* Magazine, 1950 to 1990," by Eugene F. Provenzo, Jr., and Anthon Beonde, looks at the cartoons included in the educational magazine *Phi Delta Kappan.* While this is a periodical for professional educators, the popular form of the cartoon provides a clearly alternative route to the raising of specific views and issues concerning the teaching profession, bureaucracy, and higher education. Finally, in chapter 12, "Education 1st!: Using Television to Promote the Schools," Lynn Nations Johnson and Gunilla Holm examine a highly publicized effort to offer a proeducation-oriented week of television programming by the major networks and cable stations in the United States. This chapter analyzes the way programs formally designated as presenting proeducation themes and issues registered diverse connections to and points about schooling, often at odds with the publicized intent of the week-long event's sponsors.

From these studies questions arise about the array of such popular "flares" and how they function in the collective imagination about schools. Such flares as these can both highlight common stereotypes and spark arresting challenges to our thinking about schools. The chapters suggest the ubiquity of particular, telling characterizations of school experience and their potential significance in marking the terrain. How thoroughly do we learn what to expect, doubt, or laugh at in school settings, by way of the kinds of popular snapshots we are considering here? As Milan Kundera has suggested, there is often no better way to make a serious point than by the off-hand or humorous remark. Can particular flares be used pedagogically to open up discussion of common perceptions about schooling and its problems? The power of particular examples of popular texts to open space for fresh insights and critical dialogue about the shared world of school practice is a vital matter to explore in greater detail.

Inquiry in this category is pertinent as well insofar as the larger world of public understanding and discussion about schooling is concerned. What do, or what might, diverse popular images contribute to public attitudes, expectations, and deliberations? How can we learn better to explore the most telling images and characterizations of schooling, exposing both their stereotypes and penetrating insights? The studies in this section chart a small part of a wide domain. Studies of related works are warranted, as are more detailed analyses of particular ones. How do the variety of particular images, seemingly mere snapshots of school experience, affirm, challenge, or awaken us in our thinking about schools? This, in short, is the pedagogical path that opens here, learning to apprehend the meaning captured in even the most fleeting glimpses of school experience.

10 Carnival, Pop Culture and the Comics: Radical Political Discourse

Olga Skorapa

> Fear is the extreme expression of narrow-minded and stupid seriousness, which is defeated by laughter. . . . Complete liberty is possible only in a completely fearless world.
> —M. M. Bakhtin

In my efforts to help undergraduate students understand the concepts of ideology, hegemony, liberation, and oppression, I have been trying to contextualize these definitions in texts they understand, read on their own, and can teach from. Through our reading of popular texts, it becomes possible to tease out many of the ideologies/power/meanings woven together within the culture and to discover the complexity of interactions as individuals and groups compete for power/meaning. To this end, my students and I bring into the classroom many popular-culture texts to analyze and critique from magazines, newspapers, television shows, movies, and videos.

THEORETICAL JUSTIFICATION

Comics, in particular, work well for this kind of study: Simultaneously visual and written texts, they are widely available, often extremely funny, and blatant in their reification of the dominant ideology and their resistance to it. (In this way they "mediate" the dominant culture.) Comics' position in opposition to the newspaper, to "real" books, and to "real" art makes them particularly rich as sites of multilayered dialogic (within dialogues) interaction, oppression, resistance, and meaning(s).[1] In opposition to the high-culture texts they parody, comics exemplify the spirit of carnival as it has (de)volved through history in its popular forms.[2] In this chapter, I critique comics about education as popular-culture texts using their carnivalesque qualities as the basis for my critique. In doing so, I draw on the work of the Russian literary critic Mikhail Mikhailovich Bakhtin.

In his analysis of the narrative writing of Rabelais, Bakhtin outlines the theory of carnival: During the festivals of medieval Europe, hierarchy, order, and formal structures were overturned with energy and abandon by the common people. Writing in the midst of severest government repression under Stalin, Bakhtin lauded the beneficial aspects of laughter within the folk tradition, expressed through carnival in the work of Rabelais. Acts of rebellion and resistance against the church and the monarchy, these forms utilized scatology, parody, and farce in the forms of low comedy to counter the oppressive and corrupt practices that dominated these institutions. The obvious parallels between medieval Europe and Stalin's Russia gave Bakhtin's work special significance for its time.

Bakhtin deplored the fragmentation and dissolution of carnival in the development of early modern Europe, when its multiple forms devolved into single festivals, rituals, and fairs with few of the aspects of the original. Chivarie,[3] farce, improvisation, plays, puppetry, busking, and parodies of sacred or exalted writing in both Latin and the vernacular were epigonal reprises of the days and weeks spent in madcap feasting and merriment described in Rabelais's novels of medieval Europe. In addition to his analysis of Rabelais, Bakhtin illustrated his conclusions with examples from comedic writing from across time and the continent: Cervantes, Aristophanes, Balzac, Boccacio, Brecht, Goethe, Moliere, the *Comedia D'el Arte*, Shakespeare, Voltaire, and others who are less familiar to modern readers.

Bakhtin was writing when Soviet Russia was creating the single party line for literary endeavor—that of Socialist Realism—as defined exclusively in the work of Maxim Gorky.[4] In that genre, he found little to inspire him, for its narrow analyses failed to acknowledge the potential for growth, resistance, and renewal inherent in the tradition of carnival and absent from both the Renaissance and (by implication) Stalinist Russia. His position in opposition to the party line left Bakhtin constantly vulnerable to the repressive practices of the government, for, to the censors who controlled intellectual activity, it was apparent that his writing was not exclusively about Rabelais.

The premise of this paper is that carnival as defined by Bakhtin in *Rabelais and His World*, in the form of the carnivalesque (that which is similar to and originates in carnival), can be found in contemporary forms of popular culture. I consider comics to be carnivalesque, because they are imbued with the spirit of resistance and comedy that Bakhtin found in Rabelais's *Gargantua and Pantagruel* and throughout the genre of the novel. The novel, to Bakhtin, was comprised most importantly of the dialogues it contained. That was important because he found in dialogue the opposition to the authoritarian word "in the same way as carnival is opposed to the official culture."[5] Like novels, comics are also composed of dialogue, and they, too, are texts that mediate the dominant ideology and culture. Bakhtin's analysis of folk culture within the writing of Rabelais provides a useful tool for analyzing these texts: "Bakhtin's vision of the carnival has an importance greater that any of its particular applications . . . for [his] book is finally about freedom, the courage needed to establish it, the cunning required to maintain it, and—above all—the horrific ease with which it can be lost." According to Holquist, "Carnival laughter 'builds its own world in opposition to the official world, its own church in opposition to the official church, its own state in opposition to the official state.'"[6]

CRITIQUE OF THEORETICAL JUSTIFICATION

One of the major problems that I find with Bakhtin's work, however, is that he does not include an analysis of the experience of women or children in his literary critique, nor does he discuss their existence in the genre of comedy except as minor characters participating in the carnivals of Rabelais's writing and the bodily source of carnival's regenerative capacity.[7] This lacuna, the lack of consideration of women or children, renders Bakhtin's conclusions flawed, both when he was writing and when I apply them to the critique of contemporary texts and ideas (and it mirrors the failure of classical Marxism to unwrap layered oppressions of gender, race, class, production, reproduction, etc.)

In contemporary culture in which the "objectivity" of dominant men is recreated in opposition to the "subjectivity" of women and other disempowered groups, the carnivalesque *also* rests in subjectivity, the conflict between the dominant culture and its unofficial parody within popular culture.[8] Comics are seldom the object of either art or news, but represent some kind of shared culture outside the "official" world. The unofficial world of comics, however, also includes the domination of women by men, poor by rich, race by race, children by adults, and animals by humans and other animals. These patterns are illustrated in newspaper comics, with few exceptions—notably *Cathy* and *Brenda Starr* as texts that mediate gender, *Herb and Jamaal, Outland*, *Bloom County*'s supporting cast of Ronald-Anne and Oliver Wendell Jones and his family as African-American characters who mediate the meaning of race, and minor characters in *Doonesbury* and *Bloom County* who are poor or homeless. Children (who are almost always white male) in conflict over unequal distribution of power are often subjects within this medium. (Berke Breathed's treatment of Ronald-Anne, Milo, and Binky as "fully human" subjects with anxieties, political attitudes, and jobs is a notable exception in a medium that rarely allows children out of their narrow socially prescribed roles, the possibility for alternative realities inherent in the form notwithstanding.)

In comics, even more than novels, the written text occurs in the form of dialogues between characters or between character and reader, when the character is engaged in "thought" or soliloquy with the balloon of words over his head. In addition to their written texts, comics also provide pictorial representations that present another level of meaning, as texts in themselves. This layering of meanings between the written and the visual text gives the reader complex and conflicting signs to negotiate while reading. In addition to these complex negotiations, newspaper strip comics themselves as opposed to comix (the "underground" or subcultural rendering of the genre), single-frame representations, or comic books—are popular narrative media printed in newspapers, which are sources for "objective truth" in our culture. (Despite the problematic nature of considering the newspaper as "objective" or in any construction of the word "truth," its use as a referent by the courts, politicians, and some historians as documentary evidence for "real" events legitimates its function as the quasi-official voice of the dominant culture.)

Comics, then, in their position within the medium of the newspaper, can be understood to serve as a parody or subtext to the "truth" presented in the newspapers in which they are printed. Like the carnival, newspaper comics are, more or less consciously, in dialogic opposition to the authoritarian word of the newspaper. In recent years, *Doonesbury, Bloom County*, and, in the 1992 presidential election, *Cathy* have often provided very conscious critiques of the official media coverage of the Bush nee Reagan administration. They also comment more or less regularly on politics, fashion, celebrity, and many of our most important national symbols. Other strips—*Blondie, Beetle Bailey,* and *Garfield*, for example—rather than pointing up the inconsistencies between the official reading of the culture in the dominant voice and its reality, appear mostly to reify the dominant discourse. These strips cannot be read *solo voce*, however, for, within the genre of the comics, irony is consistently apparent even in the most banal texts, as in Miss Buxley's awareness of her objectification by General Halftrack and the other soldiers in *Beetle Bailey*.

A third level of critique in reading comics is the assumption that comics are texts directed at children, when, in fact, they are being read by most newspaper readers.[9] Because they are partially visual as well as written representations of the world, and because of our cultural assumptions about "literacy," children, in their supposed illiteracy, have been the assumed audience of comics. In their visual-narrative forms, comic strips coincide with our cultural designation of childhood as subjective and illiterate or partially constructed and quasi-literate. Simultaneously, they mediate the meaning of childhood through the visual and written texts and the actual reader (all those who read the paper) in opposition to the pretended reader (children). Within this construct of pretended audience, the activities in which children are assumed to participate are frequently the subject of these narratives.[10] Home, families, playgrounds, neighborhood streets, and schools are the scenes of these carnivalesque critiques of childhood and schooling presented in opposition to the adult worlds of work, military, and marriage also represented in the strips. Comics frequently serve to recreate rather than resist unequal relations of power between adults and children. For comics, notwithstanding their form and their contextual opposition to the official word of the newspaper, are still popular-cultural-commodity texts (PCCTs), and are created specifically to sell papers and their dominant ideology.[11] Comics are written/drawn by adults, and mediate the meaning of childhood in relation to adulthood in the dominant culture from the perspective of adult, predominantly male, artists. Humor is used as a vehicle within this genre and elsewhere to challenge and reproduce the existing power relations of a culture.

COMICS AND SCHOOLS

Often, the setting of comic strips about childhood, schooling, and the critique of schooling presented on the newspaper comics page runs the gamut from glorification of existing social and cultural structures in comics like Bil Keane's *Family Circus* to biting political critique. In the early 1970s, in Garry Trudeau's *Doonesbury*, Joanie Caucus brought feminism to the daycare center where she worked, spreading equality and rebellion among the four-year-olds until the little girls were calling their fathers MCPs (male chauvinist pigs).[12] In *Peanuts*, the cast has for years been bombarded with meaningless assignments, inane tests, and humiliating interrogations.[13] Television's Bart Simpson, created by Matt Groening, follows in their footsteps, though he takes the critique even further to include an outspoken insolence to the institution never uttered by his more daunted forebears.

Generally, these comic-strip stories of schooling are often subplots to the narratives concerned with a more complete ideology of childhood, or are told about children only in relation to adults. *Peanuts* and the other strips suggest critical interpretations of schooling. These strips demonstrate political critique from liberal (*Funky Winkerbean*, for example, drawn by Tom Batiuk), to anarchist (*Calvin and Hobbes*, drawn by Bill Watterson), to Nihilist (*Life in Hell* by Matt Groening, where Groening is even less constrained than in *The Simpsons*). Unlike the other two strips, which are daily features in mainstream newspapers,

Groening's *Life* appears in strip or single-frame form in entertainment or alternative newspapers. Both *Calvin and Hobbes* and *Life in Hell* are also published separately as books. These various comics present visions of children, childhood, and schooling with successively less nurturance and more oppression from the adult world, and are drawn successively more from the point of view of a particular child.

Batiuk's *Funky Winkerbean* is drawn in a realistic, noncombative style within the genre of comic art: simple line drawings with recognizable backgrounds typical of high school settings of ceiling tile in music rooms, chain link fences around the field, bleachers, rows of lockers, and desks. Set in "average white middle-class" high school, the characters participate in many of the rituals of schooling—sports, band, gym, hanging out in the hall or teachers' lounge, cheerleading.[14] The teachers and students are not usually depicted at odds with one another, and their difficulties are mainly in the context of unexamined acceptance of the dominant ideological constructs that exist in schools: the problems within the school are construed as social or psychological rather than political: how to get dates (boys), how to sell band candy, turkeys, and raffle tickets, how to motivate students (coach and band director), and the various interpersonal relationships which develop within these contexts.[15]

The main characters in this strip are the band director, who is always drawn wearing his band uniform; Funky himself, (seldom seen) average white male kid, straight hair and nondescript clothes; and the school nerd/geek/dweeb, Les, who wears glasses. Women are included as minor characters: ditzy blonde majorettes and cheerleaders, the wife of the principal (a teacher), incompetent musicians in the band. Adults and children do not differ substantially from one another in representation, displaying proportional size, with teachers generally bigger than students and women smaller than men. Teachers and students are mostly white; the principal is an older white man who wears glasses and a suit; the superintendent, an even older white male also wearing glasses and a suit. Race, sex, or class are never the apparent subject of this strip, nor are the inequalities of students and teachers or of teachers and the principal often intentionally examined. This lack serves to uphold the values of the dominant culture in which nonwhite men and women of all races do not constitute an important aspect of the status quo, and conflict with the existing institutions is seen as social rather than political. Almost all is reasonable in this high school, with plot complication arising from poor music lessons,[16] Les the nerd, confronted with his own inability to fit in, the home lives of teachers (Woodstock remembrances), dumb cheerleaders (always drawn with sparkles around their eyes), and air-guitar contests.

Diverging from this reification of the standard narrative of school as a generally good though flawed institution is the student hall monitor in the high school, who sits in a desk in the hall behind a machine gun, and the disgruntled graduation speaker made famous first by Gary Trudeau in *Doonesbury* in the early 1970s. In the Doonesbury graduation speech, Harvard's president stands before the assembled multitude and asks them a pointed and inspirational question: "Well, gentlemen . . . what about tomorrow? This is the fundamental question you must now ask yourselves!—*What* will you be doing this time *tomorrow*?" A voice from the crowd of graduates answers, "Smoking a lot of grass."[17] The crowd breaks in loud applause. In the *Funky Winkerbean* graduation speech, the school superintendent is addressing the crowd of graduating high school seniors. Clothed in his doctoral robes and mortarboard, Superintendent Shoentell addresses the graduating class of 1989: "I'm looking at a group of people whose sheltered and privileged existence is about to come to an end, as you cease being a tax burden and begin contributing to *my* retirement! Now it's *your* turn to put up with all the *garbage* . . . Jerk bosses, backstabbing peers, nagging spouses, inappreciative offspring and the *IRS!!* And I'm glad! You hear me!? Glad!!!" Then he breaks into maniacal laughter. Pointed social commentary like this, which exposes unequal power relations of any kind, is exceedingly rare in any of the mainstream comics.

Aside from this sort of occasional critique of power relations within school and society, *Funky Winkerbean* perpetuates the dominant ideology of American schooling: though there are serious minor problems, school is a positive institution and generally a good place to work and to grow up.[18] The minor flaws described in the institution merely serve to point out its generally positive function, exceptions that prove the rule. Drawn from the point of view of a middle-class, white, male kid, Funky, whose picture appears daily in the heading or title to the strip, it concerns the culturally constructed, accepted social interactions that occur within the uncritical liberal vision of the institution.[19]

Though the strips are represented in a similar pictorial and narrative point of view coming from the middle-class, white, male kid, this "realistic," unexamined, or unconscious rendering is substantially different from the children represented in Watterson's *Calvin and Hobbes* and Groening's *Life in Hell.* In both of these strips, boys (human and animal) are main characters who, for part of the time, exist apart from their relations to adults. Calvin is the personification of childhood or "Everyboy." He is white and blonde, and comes from understanding, ironic, and humorous middle-class parents. Unlike Batiuk's drawings of children, Calvin is drawn differently than his parents. In contrast to them, his character is raw, appearing both incomplete and scribbled into constant motion, a punk kid drawn from thick lines, with wildly jagged hair, big feet, and a completely fluid face. Hobbes, Calvin's "straight man," is Calvin's tiger—stuffed when there are other people present and real when he and Calvin are alone together.

Calvin's days are spent involved in the "standard rituals of childhood" from resisting bathing to resisting eating to resisting going to school to being afraid to go to bed. Within this context, he often involves himself in Bakhtinian grotesqueries of gorging and making horrible faces much to the chagrin of his parents and his teachers.[20] While his interactions with authority figures are never positive (Calvin routinely tells his father how poorly he is doing in the parent popularity polls), school is his nemesis.[21] Calvin reacts to the constant intrusion of school into his imaginative life by daydreaming himself away in violent science-fiction fantasies, landing only when the teacher intrudes to humiliate or punish him. While in school, Calvin is Space Man Spiff, superhero, fighting horrible monsters (his teacher) with death-defying deeds in alien territory (school).[22] Saved within his daydream world in the nick of time by his own brilliance and bravery, Calvin the schoolboy often ends his interactions with his teachers in the principal's office.[23]

The narrative focus of the comic is only on a single young boy's experiences of the world created by Watterson; his interactions are exclusively from Calvin's individual point of view, and, as such, seldom explore the social construction of relationships except within the context of his family and his occasional interaction with a "slimy" girl. Watterson uses Calvin's experience of childhood to describe its unequal power relations and the lack of democratic practice available to children.[24] While the persona of the artist in this strip is not specified, the narrator seldom consciously examines the unequal power relationships between women and men, mothers and fathers, or girls and boys—only that of parents and child or child and school. Told from a narrative point of view similar to Calvin as seen from an adult perspective or to Hobbes, the experience of the white male kid is the normative experience in the strip, and, effectively, portrays *the* meaning of childhood.

Groening explores different elements of life in his strips, with school being the latest in a series of remarkably funny, biting narrative and analytical critiques of love (comparative chart of whether its better to be homo- or heterosexual: one of the advantages of the former—sharing clothes), dating, marriage, and deciding whether to have children; and the alienating nature of work, which analyzes the repercussions of the unequal power relationships and dull, boring jobs. Groening's characters are all animals made human, and the main ones are rabbits: not funny, soft, cuddly, cute bunnies, but thin, bipedal, wired, frenetic, bug-eyed and unhappy. The adult rabbits are beset with fear, indecision, alienation, anomie, and unhappiness; their offspring is not merely a copy of themselves but mutant, not only smaller but possessed of one large ear instead of two on the top of his head.[25] Bongo, the young rabbit, is not only alienated from all the other characters but also self-loathing and completely bitter about it. In a one-frame strip, Bongo is sitting bound, gagged, and shackled in a child-sized chair in the corner of an empty room. He looks very small. Looking through the observation slit in the closed door of the room are a large pair of eyes obviously belonging to an adult. The speech balloon coming from the slot in the door reads, "Don't be bitter."[26]

Bongo's experiences at school, far from the imaginative flights of fancy that give Calvin's schooling a value through his ability to resist indoctrination, are tortured and isolating (see figure 10.1).[27] Calvin, undaunted hero of his own imagination, can come home to his tiger-friend, Hobbes. All that Bongo comes home to are parents who exacerbate his isolation and punish him for being himself. In one strip, Bongo is sitting in a school desk listening to the pronouncements of the teacher, one pronouncement for each frame:

> "Be the master of your habits or they will be the master of you.
> "Don't let your parents down. They brought *you* up.
> "The only place where success comes before work is in the dictionary.
> "Why do you think they call it dope?
> "To keep peace, we must prepare for war.
> "Choose only a date who would make a good mate.
> "The government is your friend.
> "Be humble enough to obey. You may give orders some day.
> "Premarital sex can blow your legs off."

Overcome with rage, Bongo stands up at his desk and yells out, "LIES, LIES, LIES." In the next frame, he realizes his mistake and covers his mouth with his hands. His eyes are very large. He is then pictured with the teacher, a large dog or bear, standing beside his desk, glowering down. In the last four frames, the young rabbit is sitting bound and gagged in his desk. After one frame of silence, more pronouncements follow from the disembodied voice above him:

> "There are a few rotten apples in every barrel.
> "A bad school record will follow you forever.
> "You'll thank me for this some day."[28]

Groening does not state Bongo's race or sex, and these categories remain unexamined in a strip focused on the alienation of people without regard to their race or class. All the rabbits in the strip are

LIFE IN HELL
© 1987 BY MATT GROENING
ANY QUESTIONS, CLASS?
WHY IS SCHOOL RUN LIKE A JAIL?
HOW COME YOU'RE SO BORING?
WHY ARE THERE SO MANY STUPID RULES?
HOW COME THESE DESKS ARE SO UNCOMFORTABLE?
WHY DO WE HAVE TO USE SUCH BLAND TEXTBOOKS?
HOW COME THERE IS SO MUCH EMPHASIS PLACED ON ROTE MEMORIZATION?
WHY ARE WE GIVEN SO MUCH POINTLESS BUSYWORK?

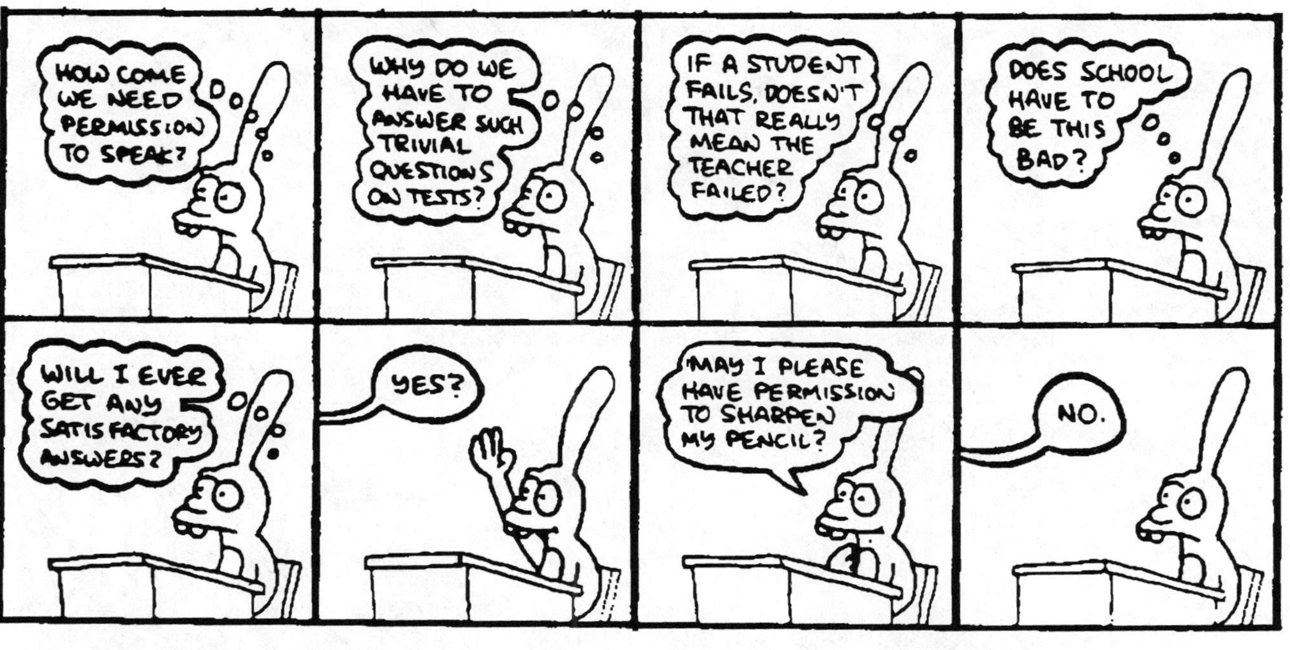

Fig. 10.1 © 1987 *School is Hell* by Matt Groening. All rights reserved. Reprinted by permission of Pantheon Books, a division of Random House, NY.

BREAKING POINT
66
©1989 BY ALISON BECHDEL
MO'S HAVING A CRISIS.
DING DONG
HARRIET! THANK GOD YOU'RE HERE!
!
MO, WHAT'S WRONG!? DID SOMETHING HAPPEN?
I... I DUNNO! AT FIRST I THOUGHT I WAS JUST PREMENSTRUAL.. THEN I THOUGHT MAYBE IT WAS A FOOD ALLERGY. Y'KNOW, LIKE FROM THAT GLAZED DONUT I ATE MONDAY
BUT NOW I THINK IT MUST BE MY SATURN RETURN!
WHAT IS? WHAT ARE YOU BABBLING ABOUT?!
MY LIFE, HARRIET! WHAT AM I DOING WITH MY LIFE?!
ALL THE YEARS OF BE... SOCIALLY RESPONSIBLE, STRUGGLING FOR PEACE AND JUSTICE, WORRYI... MYSELF SICK ABOUT ... WORLD... WHERE HAS IT GOTTEN ME?

Fig. 10.2 "Dykes to Watch Out For," from *New, Improved! Dykes to Watch Out For* by Alison Bechdel. All rights reserved, Firebrand Books, Ithaca, New York, © 1992.

white. As in *Funky* and *Calvin*, the experiences of the white rabbits maintain unequal social relationships through their lack of examination of issues of race and sex. While an occasional, obviously female character is depicted, Groening's point of view (male as either adult or child) is maintained throughout: Women are objectified and viewed only as "other." There is no solution to the relations between male and female rabbits and no solution for the interactions of kids and school. Despite his brilliant critique, Groening is completely hopeless. There are no answers. Rather than carnivalesque transformation, the reader is left in despair in a nihilistic universe.

CONCLUSION

Comics as carnivalesque suggest an alternative world that calls on readers to recognize, name, and laugh at the dominant discourse about schools as places of learning and childhood as either innocent or good. Their visual representation and narrative form create the opportunity for students to understand and analyze critical readings of existing social institutions and the potential for resistance and critique of the forms of schooling and popular culture. As we watch Calvin being sent to the office and Bongo preparing for years of therapy, the process of schooling and its effect on children is evoked, examined, and found lacking in a variety of ways. Like the liberal *Funky*, they seem to say that this is just the way it is; they're resigned to it.

What is missing from these texts, however, is the potential for creating alternative visions of ideologies examined therein. These do exist in both the invocation of the experiences of women or other subcultures as the subject of the text and through alternative readings of the cultural constructs presented as "normal" in mainstream comic art. Feminist critique, for example, is liberating to our cultural construct of what it means to be a "woman" through the inclusion of the values and attitudes our culture designates as "feminine": care, nurture, physicality, power, political sexuality, reproduction, and wildness. This is also evident in Nicole Hollander's *Sylvia* and Alison Bechdel's *Dykes to Watch out For*. In addition to its critique of various cultural institutions, *Dykes*, for example, depicts a subculture largely unfamiliar to many students which exposes politics as integral to both sexuality and lifestyle (as it also is in the unexamined world of the dominant culture), values difference, and articulates a lived feminist consciousness (figure 10.2).[29] It gives many students a rare opportunity to see the world from the "other's" (the outsider with whom most undergraduate education students seldom identify) point of view, and it normalizes that point of view.

Because of the involvement of the reader in their interplay between visual and written text (and their other potentially resistant aspects), comics hold the potential for human agency in the institutions they depict. The alternative comic representation in Calvin's fantasies, and *Bloom County*'s occasional lapse into the surrealistic universe of *Crazy Cat* and the philosophical problems analyzed within a contrasting universe, are some examples of how such a process might and does work, as is the intervention of the artist or the process of creating art demonstrated by ink intentionally spilled on the character or deliberate redefinitions of the genre through the introduction of incongruous action or characterization. These and other heretical interactions between the artist and subject/text suggest a genre that is open to questioning established practices of comic art and existing institutions.[30]

Through the critique of the comic artist and your own reading of the strips, you might find, in Calvin's escapist fantasies and Bongo's "lessons for children" resistance and subsequent empowerment, the potential to transform the schools. Simultaneously, you might find, in the recapitulation of hierarchy, order, and domination which the strips depict, a tacit acceptance of the ideology which prohibits alternative readings of the world and denies the potential for interrogation, revision, and renewal. Comics, with their wide circulation and varied readership, suggest many more studies in which form and content—visual art, written narrative, and the interplay between those forms, their function as subtext within the newspaper, their pretended audience in contrast to the real audience, the exclusionary norms embedded in the characters, and the stories depicted within them, the conventions and tropes of the texts as art and literature, and the various forms of comics in relation to each other and to the reader—are examined. In short, comic texts, like the carnivals from which they derive, mediate the official world in opposition to them. Within this medium, official culture is contested and debated in dialogues between a variety of contexts in the spirit of play, thus forming the potential for critique of, and opposition to, the dominant ideology. Such is the function of the carnival in Rabelais and the dialogic novel to Bakhtin. Popular-culture texts, in all their variety, carry the potential for laughter in which hierarchy, discourse, form, and ideology are constantly questioned, analyzed, and drawn anew, suggesting potentially alternative visions about the nature of class, race, gender, ablebodiedness, ideology, and democracy through the construction of critical understanding, political consciousness, and dialectical process.

NOTES

1. Comics included as illustrations are indicated by a figure number.

2. I use the term "(de)volved" in a deconstructive mode. In this case, I am playing with the resonance between the words *evolve* and *devolve.* In this instance, as in many, what one might assume to be progress may, in fact, be less good, true, or beautiful than that which came before (essentially, the postmodern condition). Contemporary celebrations of carnival are greatly diminished and watered down since their apex in Medieval Europe.

3. "Chivarie" (also *charivari* and *shivaree*) is the ritual burlesque serenade performed with tin horns, pots and pans, and kettles which would accompany a newly married couple on their wedding night. It was customarily performed by drunken friends of the bride and groom. Its darker side, for peasants, was that the lord of the manor would at that time take the bride to his bed before the groom could. This custom has devolved in modern times to the painting of the car of the bridal couple with "Just Married" or "Going to Florida to Get a Little Son," the car chase, and the ritual filling of the couple's suitcases with rice or shaving cream.

4. Michael Holquist, Prologue to *Rabelais and His World*, by M. M. Bahktin (Bloomington: Indiana University Press, 1984), p. xvii.

5. Krystina Pomorska, Foreword to *Rabelais and His World*, by M. M. Bahktin, p. x. This idea of the dialogue as anti-authorian text is also found in some readings of Plato which insist that the reader pay attention to the dialogic interchange between Socrates and his students as *dialogue*. Rather than knowledge, Socrates is proposing a process and not truth itself.

6. Holquist, Prologue, p. xxi.

7. Jean-Francois Lyotard disparages the scientist who disregards narrative form which is supposed to exist only within the realm of the nonofficial language of the unempirical, subjective world of women and children, concluding that even scientific knowledge is ultimately exchanged and legitimated through narrative, from scientist to the state and from state to people, and disparages the scientist who conceives of narrative as "belonging to a different mentality: savage, primitive, undeveloped, backward, alienated, composed of opinions, customs, authority, prejudice, ignorance, ideology. Narratives are fables, myths, legends, fit only for women and children." Jean-Francois Lyotard, *The Post-Modern Condition: A Report on Knowledge*, trans. Geoff Bennington and Brian Massumi (Minneapolis: Minnesota University Press, 1984), p. 27.

8. I use the terms "objectivity" and "subjectivity" because, in both academic and wider cultures, men define meaning and purpose: White men are the reason and object of all endeavor. Women and other disempowered groups are subjected to and subjugated by the desires and needs of the culture as it is defined by rich white men. For example, women put on makeup and shave their legs to be feminine, thus making themselves objects of men's notice and desire. Without this, they are undesirable and outside the mainstream. Men are masculine in their

unadulterated state; they "naturally" define the norm. Women, *only* when we are enhanced, are worthy of men's notice or able to participate in the public world. Women are still not part of the reason for political, economic, or social endeavor. We cannot begin to participate until we have "objectified" ourselves, but merely objectifying ourselves is never enough to participate fully. The work of reproduction, which falls to women and other disempowered people, is not the subject of our economy, our politics, or our history. (I can chase my one-year-old daughter all day, wash clothes, cook, etc., and still have done "nothing" either professionally or economically valuable as defined by our culture or that will be remembered historically.) Family leave, childcare, a living wage, protection against sex discrimination, freedom from harassment, and prevention of rape are denied by our government. This government was created, and is maintained and perpetuated, by white men who see these basic human rights as unnecessary to our social and political existence or, worse, who see women's oppression as necessary. Disempowered groups are the subject, not the object, of "our" cultural existence; the subject of laws, not protected by them; the subject of business, art, pornography, and religion, not its object.

9. Don Thompson and Dick Lupoff, Introduction to *The Comic-Book Book: Recalls the Great Comic-Book Features of the Past*, ed. Don Thompson and Dick Lupoff (Cralstadt, NJ: Rainbow Books, 1977), p. 10.

10. Richard Marschall describes the long history of the representation of children in American strip comics in "Oh, You Kid: A Strip of Leviathan Quality, An Appreciation of Calvin and Hobbes," *The Comics Journal: The Magazine of News and Criticism* 127 (February 1989): 72–77.

11. The concept of PCCTs is defined by Paul Smith: "The artifacts and objects produced for us by capital must then be seen simultaneously as sites of our interaction and as objects for which we are consumers; they are popular-culture-commodity-texts (PCCTs)." Paul Smith, "Pedagogy and the Popular-Culture-Commodity-Text," *Popular Culture, Schooling and Everyday Life*, ed. Henry Giroux and Roger Simon (Granby, MA: Bergin & Garvey, 1989), pp. 31-46. The concept of the comic as a PCCT is particularly ironic for the strip *Calvin and Hobbes*. Bill Waterson has refused to licence his strip, which means he is unwilling to give up the artistic rights to it so that it can be made into dolls, T-shirts, or stuffed animals: "I have no aversion to obscene wealth, but that's not my motivation either. I think to licence *Calvin and Hobbes* would ruin the most precious qualities of my strip and, once that happens, you can't buy those qualities back. . . . At that point, you've transformed him into just another overpriced knickknack. I have no interest into turning my characters into commodities. . . . Instead of rampant commercialism, we ought to be asking, 'What justifies it?' Popular art does not have to pander to the lowest level of intelligence and taste." Richard Samuel West and Bill Waterson, "Interview: Bill Waterson," *The Comics Journal: The Magazine of News and Criticism* 127 (February 1989), pp. 68–69.

12. Trudeau, *The Doonesbury Chronicles* (New York: Holt, Rinehart & Winston, 1975), p. 61.

13. Charles Schultz, *Peanuts*, 4 June 1989.

14. Tom Batiuk, *Funky Winkerbean*, 11 August 1989.

15. Batiuk, 27 August 1989.

16. Batiuk, 21 May 1989.

17. Batiuk, 28 May 1989; Trudeau, *Doonesbury Chronicles*, p. 50.

18. Batiuk, 13 November 1989.

19. Tom Batiuk's comics in this chapter are taken from the *Atlanta Constitution*, from November 1988 through September 1989. They are copyrighted by Universal Syndicate and may not be reprinted without the permission of the syndicate.

20. Bill Watterson, *Something under the Bed Is Drooling: A Calvin and Hobbes Collection by Bill Watterson* (Kansas City, MO: Universal Press Syndicate, 1988), p. 116.

21. Watterson, "Interview," p. 69.

22. Watterson, p. 70.

23. Bill Watterson, *Calvin and Hobbes* (Kansas City: Andrews and McMeel, 1987), p. 14.

24. Ibid., pp. 28, 53.

25. Matt Groening, *Love Is Hell* (New York: Pantheon), p. 24.

26. Matt Groening, *School Is Hell* (New York: Pantheon, 1987), p. 35.

27. Ibid., p. 42.

28. Matt Groening, *Childhood Is Hell* (New York: Pantheon, 1988), p. 34.

29. Alison Bechdel, *New Improved Dykes to Watch Out For* (Ithaca, NY: Firebrand Press, 1990), pp. 94–95. I would like to thank Steve Hodge for his suggestion of this point.

11 Educational Cartoons as Popular Culture: The Case of the *Kappan*

Eugene F. Provenzo, Jr., and Anthon Beonde

Cartoons represent an important element found in many American magazines and newspapers. Over the years, magazines such as *The New Yorker* have come to be associated with the cartoons of figures such as James Thurber and Charles Addams as much as with the essays and stories included in its pages.[1] No major American newspaper—with perhaps the exception of the *New York Times*—is without an editorial cartoonist.[2] In the field of education no single magazine has been more closely associated with cartoon humor than *Phi Delta Kappan* magazine.

The *Kappan*, which is sometimes referred to as the "*Time* magazine of education," is the journal for the national education fraternity, Phi Delta Kappa. The magazine is published monthly and had an average circulation in 1991 of 150,000. In addition to regular monthly columns, it includes feature-length articles dealing with different issues facing elementary and secondary schools in the United States. Publishing in the *Kappan* is considered highly prestigious in the field of Education. With perhaps the exception of the *American School Board Journal,* or the *Executive Educator*, no monthly or bimonthly educational magazine is more widely read and followed.

The cartoons included in the *Kappan* are among its most popular features. Robert Cole, a *Kappan* editor, has commented that, in trips across the country to various local chapters of the fraternity, he is regularly approached by people who tell him that the thing that they like best about the magazine is its cartoons. Cole's response is that "the editor part of me—that part that wants the *Kappan* to be a valued source of information is always a bit dismayed by this inevitable comment. But that part of me that reads the cartoons in *The New Yorker* before anything else understands completely—and secretly nods agreement."[3]

It is the assumption of this chapter that the cartoons included in the *Kappan* reflect the interests of its readers as well as trends and concerns about American education that have developed over the past thirty or forty years. In this context the total corpus of cartoons published by the *Kappan* can be read as a social text and popular-culture source—one meriting serious critical analysis.[4]

The first issue of the *Kappan* was published in 1939. It was not until the late 1950s that cartoons began to be regularly included in each issue. In most instances, the early cartoons had been previously published in magazines such as *The Saturday Evening Post, Colliers*, and *The Saturday Review*. They were created by professional cartoonists, and appeared at the rate of less than one cartoon per issue.

The number of cartoons included in the *Kappan* increased significantly by the late 1960s. In volume 45 (1963–64), a total of eight cartoons were included in the magazine. In volume 49 (1967–68), the number reached thirty-three. By volume 67 (1985–86), the number of cartoons had reached two hundred, or an average of twenty cartoons per issue. Volume 72 (1990–91) included one hundred forty-nine cartoons, or an average of approximately fifteen cartoons per issue.

One assumes that the exceptional popularity of the cartoons found in the *Kappan* is a result of the fact that they tap into not only amusing but meaningful issues and themes found in the experience of teachers and administrators and the more general culture of the schools. As the research for this study progressed, it was clear that certain themes were emphasized over and over again throughout the forty-year period that we studied. Low teacher salaries, for example, is a theme that can be found throughout the entire publication history of *Kappan* cartoons.

Many of the early cartoons that appear in the *Kappan* confront issues that are still with us today. an anonymous cartoon from the January 1961 issue, for example, shows two soldiers looking down the wall of a battlement at a Trojan horse on the side of which is labelled "Merit Pay." The caption beneath the cartoon reads, "Here comes those damn Greeks again bearing gifts."[5] A few months later, another anonymous cartoon shows a sleepy-looking dog with eyeglasses. The collar around his neck is labelled "Curriculum," and a tag tied to his tail, "Athletics." The body of the dog is moving back and forth while the tail remains perfectly still. The caption asks, "Is he really wagging?"[6]

In 1965 a female teacher in tattered clothes drags herself across her principal's office floor. Grasping the side of the principal's desk, she reaches up towards the principal, who, with folded hands, comments, "Ah, Miss Thornbury. I see that you have come to discuss the salary

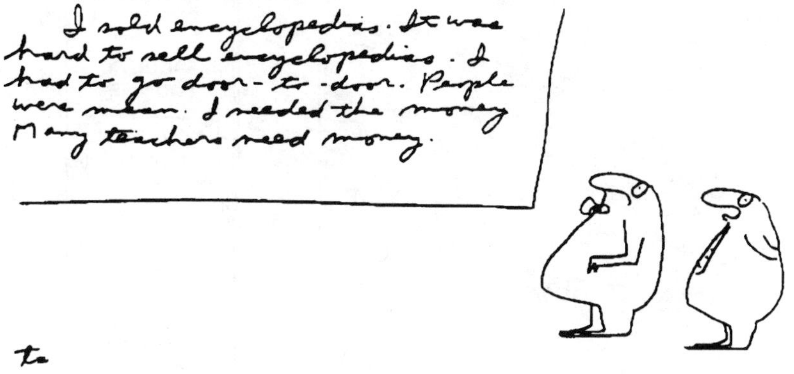

"Mr. Cosgrove must be trying to tell us something. No one asked him to write a theme on how he spent his summer vacation."

Fig. 11.1 Reprinted, with permission, from the *Kappan,* September 1975.

schedule."[7] Irony often pervades the captions of the cartoons dealing with salaries. A 1973 cartoon, for example, shows a man talking to a women with the caption: "I showed my folks what I am earning as a teacher. Now they're mad because I won't go to school and get a job."[8] In a 1975 cartoon, a female teacher says to a colleague, "When I compare the wages of Education to the wages of sin, I'm tempted . . ."[9]

The theme of inadequate salaries can be seen in another 1975 cartoon in which two individuals look at theme written on blackboard by a teacher that says: "I sold encyclopedias. It was hard to sell encyclopedia. I had to go door-to-door. People were mean." I needed the money. Many teachers need money." One of the observers comments: "Mr. Cosgrove must be trying to tell us something. No one asked *him* to write a theme on how he spent his summer vacation" (figure 11.1).[10] In a 1980 cartoon, two female teachers are talking to each other by themselves in a classroom. One of them says, "Since there's no money for a teacher raise, maybe we could get the reduced lunch for us."[11] A variation on this same theme is found in a 1983 issue: A male teacher stands in front of a female colleague seated in the cafeteria. He says, "As you know, Miss Henson, the school board has had to stretch its resources rather thin. Could I have some of your lunch?"[12]

Problems experienced by teachers in the cartoons go beyond simply salary. Physical violence and vulnerability is a theme that becomes fairly common in cartoons beginning in the 1970s. Teaching as

Fig. 11.2. Reprinted, with permission, from the *Kappan,* September 1977.

self-inflicted punishment is suggested in a 1974 cartoon in which two women stand in front of a shelf of books dealing with careers. One shows a book on teaching to a smaller and, one assumes, younger woman, saying, "Here's a rather forthright one on the teaching profession. It's called 'So You Want to Be a Masochist.'"[13] A 1977 cartoon shows a sign taped to the door of the faculty lounge that reads, "Recovery room" (figure 11.2).[14]

In 1972, the first of a series of cartoons about violence and the teaching profession appear in which as comically drawn, physically battered teacher sits behind a desk and says to a student, "'We don't take mischief lightly here, Tommy. I want you to go to the blackboard and write 500 times, 'I must not pistol-whip my teacher.'"[15] A 1978 cartoon shows the window of the Ace Karate School with this sign prominently displayed: "Discount for Teachers."[16] A cartoon appearing a few months later shows a teacher sitting in her classroom swathed in bandages, while a child stands behind her on the blackboard writing over and over again the statement "I will not knife Mrs. Glyn" (figure 11.3).[17]

Questions of teacher vulnerability and legal liability also begin to appear in cartoons during this period. A 1973 cartoon shows a young student holding a tape recorder in front of a vice-principal while he explains, "It's only fair to warn you, Mr. Flint—everything you say is being recorded for my ACLU lawyer."[18] A 1975 cartoon shows a student in show-and-tell talking about her day in front of a group of teachers, saying, "'My Day.' I went to school. Teacher read 'Gingerbread

Fig. 11.3. Reprinted, with permission, from the *Kappan,* March 1978.

Boy." The teacher recited 'The Man in the Moon." Then we sang "This Old Man." After recess, I went to the school board to report teacher's antifeminist leanings" (figure 11.4).[19] A 1979 cartoon shows a teacher with a child standing next to her. She tells the principal, 'He fell in the hall. I kissed his boo-boo. That didn't make it feel any better. Now he wants to sue me for malpractice."[20]

Teachers are not alone in being vulnerable. Superintendents and administrators are clearly subject to attack as well. In a 1965 cartoon, two men stand outside a superintendent's office. The superintendent's secretary announces into the intercom, "It's the Ad Hoc Committee To Beat the Superintendent's Brains Out, sir."[21] A 1974 cartoon shows a superintendent, at an after-dinner speech, swathed in bandages with a broken arm and a black eye (figure 11.5).[22] Back in 1965, a cartoon shows a male character pointing to the mess on the bottom of his jacket, explaining that it is "just a little tar and feathers left over from my last job as superintendent."[23]

Many of the cartoons included in the *Kappan* showed teachers having to deal with a changing culture and society. A 1975 cartoon shows a blindfolded teacher pointing to a blackboard as students look on. One of the students comments, "We're ready for elementary sex education. Our parents are ready for elementary sex education. But I wonder if Miss Finstrom is ready for . . ."[24] Another cartoon from the same year shows a teacher listening on as a young female student reads a

"'My Day.' I went to school. Teacher read 'Gingerbread Boy.' Then teacher recited 'The Man in the Moon.' Then we sang 'This Old Man.' After recess, I went to the school board to report teacher's antifeminist leanings."

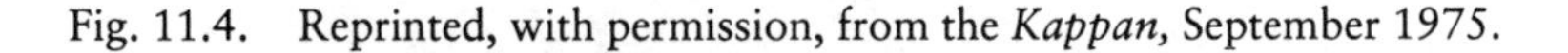

Fig. 11.4. Reprinted, with permission, from the *Kappan,* September 1975.

"We're grateful Mr. Alford could take time out of his busy superintendent's schedule to give us his views on the state of our school system."

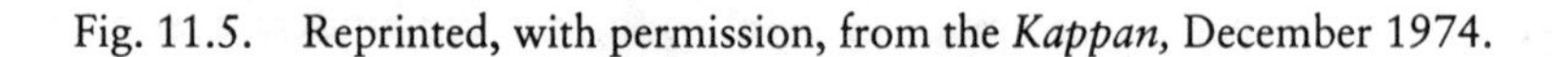

Fig. 11.5. Reprinted, with permission, from the *Kappan,* December 1974.

"'My Summer.' by Elizabeth Pennypacker. I spent the early part of my summer in Rochester, N.Y., with my daddy while he switched jobs, the middle part of my summer in Reno with my mom while she switched husbands, and the last part of my summer in Denmark with my big brother while he switched sexes."

Fig. 11.6. Reprinted, with permission, from the *Kappan,* September 1975.

report: "'My Summer,' by Elizabeth Pennypacker. I spent the early part of my summer in Rochester, N.Y., with my daddy while he switched jobs, the middle part of my summer in Reno with my mom while she switched husbands, and the last part of my summer in Denmark with my big brother while he switched sexes" (figure 11.6)[25]

Machine metaphors and teachers having to compete with television and computers for the attention of students is a theme that shows up throughout the cartoons included in the *Kappan.* A 1963 cartoon shows a child's blackboard drawing of "Teacher," in which a roboticized figure has the head of a typewriter or perhaps teaching machine.[26] In a 1967 cartoon, a large tape recorder sits a the head of a class, while smaller tape recorders are at the students' desks. No one is in sight. The caption reads, " Good morning, students. This is Tape One of your first lecture in Biology 276."[27] A teacher in a 1969 cartoon addresses the

"Jim claims it triples their attention span."

Fig. 11.7. Reprinted, with permission, from the *Kappan,* April 1981.

classroom, "Good morning, boys and girls . . . and fellow machines."[28] In the same year, a cartoon shows a blackboard with a student's drawing of a television and the word "Teacher" pointing to it.[29] A student talking to his father after school in a 1977 cartoon says to him, "It isn't Miss, Mrs., or Mr., Dad. My teacher is a machine."[30]

Related to machine metaphors and teaching are a large number of cartoons about computers and the impact of media such as television on the work of teachers. The extent to which there is a generational shift resulting from the introduction of new technologies into the schools is seen in a 1986 cartoon in which a student stands in front of a group of seated teachers, explaining: "We will now begin our computer training workshop for teachers."[31]

The theme of competing with television as a medium is seen in numerous cartoons. In a 1981 cartoon, a teacher provides a lesson in fractions by holding flash card while standing inside of a phony TV screen. A teacher, or possibly an administrator talks to another individual at the door of the classroom and explains, "Jim claims it triple their attention" (figure 11.7).[32] This cartoon recalls an earlier 1977 cartoon with much the same theme, in which a teacher introduces multiplication lessons to students as though she were the hostess of a television game show.[33]

Despite jokes about teachers and schools competing with television for the attention of students, the message is clear that they are no match for the media. A 1985 cartoon, for example, shows two fourth graders walking out of their classroom with one of them making the comment: "Mrs. Morley's all right for a couple of hours, but then I get the urge to start changing channels."[34] Another cartoon from December of the same year shows an elementary school child talking to a teacher, explaining, "I don't have anything against homework. Its just that I'm always tied up during prime time."[35]

Those connected with the education field and the work of teachers are frequently portrayed in negative ways in the cartoons found in the *Kappan*. A 1973 cartoon shows what are evidently two professors talking to one another, one of them saying: "Who cares about communicating with my students! I just want to impress them with my educational jargon.[36] In a 1977 cartoon, a professor of education is shown talking to a university dean. The professor explains that "I couldn't do anything else so I became a teacher. When I found out I couldn't teach, I became a professor of education."[37]

Educational jargon and obscurity in language is commonly associated with education professors, as well as with federal bureaucrats. A 1977 cartoon shows what is evidently a university professor lecturing, with a book in front of him: "We come now to the problem of finding viable teaching strategies for coping with diminished student motivation engendered by altered environmental conditions extrinsic to the teaching-learning situation. Or, as we might put it, how to get through the last two weeks before the Christmas holidays" (figure 11.8).[38] A virtually identical cartoon published two years later by the same cartoonist (Ford Button) includes this caption: "We come now to the problem of creating viable teaching-learning strategies for maximizing student development of conceptual and manipulative abilities in the areas of basic passive and active language arts skills and systematic comprehension. Or, as some have called it, teaching the three Rs."[39]

The use of educational jargon is not limited to professors of education. A 1976 cartoon, for example, shows an individual doing a

"We come now to the problem of finding viable teaching strategies for coping with diminished student motivation engendered by altered environmental conditions extrinsic to the teaching-learning situation. Or, as we might put it, how to get through the last two weeks before the Christmas holidays."

Fig. 11.8. Reprinted, with permission, from the *Kappan,* October 1977.

simultaneous translation of "educationese into English" at a state education convention.[40] In a 1980 cartoon, a women shows an advertisement to a superintendent of schools, explaining, "It's an ad from a new consulting service. They translate federal guidelines into English."[41]

Sports are consistently portrayed throughout successive issues of the magazine as contradicting the academic mission of secondary schools and, in particular, colleges. A 1961 cartoon, for example shows an administrator sitting behind a desk and explaining to a husband and wife who are evidently asking about scholarship money for one of their children, that he's sorry, but "our scholarships all go to six-foot, 220-pound students.[42]

The fact that athletes are somehow set apart from other students in the schools is seen in a number of cartoons. A 1965 cartoon shows a professor talking to another colleague while looking at an athlete who is leaning against a tree reading a history book that he is holding upside down. The professor comments to his colleague, "I'm afraid the athlete is a marked man."[43]

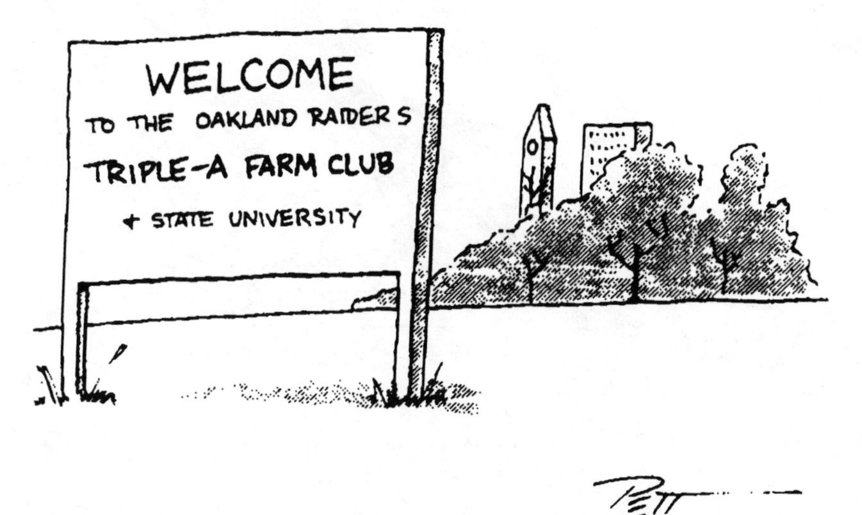

Fig. 11.9. Reprinted, with permission, from the *Kappan,* September 1980.

The corruption of universities as a result of their emphasis on sports is a theme found in many of the cartoons. A 1965 cartoon shows one football player talking to another saying: "Some school. It says in my scholarship I gotta choose between an Austin-Healy, a luscious blonde, and passing grades in English."[44] The notion that athletes warrant special treatment appears in a 1969 cartoon in which a football player says to a teacher, "About that low mark you gave me—is that any way to treat a boy in uniform."[45] A 1980 cartoon shows a university off in the distance, and a sign in the foreground that reads, "Welcome to the Oakland Raiders Triple-A Farm Club & State University" (figure 11.9).[46]

The inherent conflict between academic goals and athletic goals is repeated over the years throughout many of the cartoons. A 1969 cartoon shows a father speaking to his son, saying, "Son, I want you to win that college scholarship. Therefore, no studying until you've completed your football practice."[47] A 1972 cartoon shows a student carrying books talking to woman and commenting: "My scholarship? Oh, I lost it I became so absorbed in my studies that I neglected football."[48] A somewhat more ambiguous cartoon shows an administrator, or possibly a professor, in academic robes making a speech: ". . . and we are working diligently to make this a university our football team can be proud of" (figure 11.10).[49]

". . . . and we are working diligently to make this a university our football team can be proud of."

Fig. 11.10. Reprinted, with permission, from the *Kappan,* March 1980.

THE *KAPPAN*'S CARTOONS AND THE IMAGE OF SCHOOLING

Olga Skorapa, in her essay "Carnival, Pop Culture, and the Comics: Radical Political Discourse" (see chapter 10) makes a powerful argument that

> comics as carnivalesque suggest an alternative world that calls upon readers to recognize, name, and laugh at the dominant discourse about schools as places of learning and childhood as either innocent or good. Their visual representation and narrative form create the opportunity for students to understand and analyze critical readings of existing social institutions and the potential for resistance and critique of the forms of schooling.

Such an interpretation certainly fits the educational cartoons published over the years in the *Kappan* which have provided the basis for this study. The cartoons included in the *Kappan* can also provide us with another type of information—in this case, a popular-culture text that reflects changes and social forces at work in the culture.

Schoolteachers Amidst Forces of Change, by Eugene F. Provenzo, Jr., and Gary N. Mc Closkey, describes at length the emergence of a new *paideia* that has come into being since the mid-1960s—one that has significantly shaped the ethos of schooling and the experience of teachers in their day-to-day work. Essentially, the authors argue that the growth of higher education, massive population shifts, the movement of women into the labor force, the changing character or work associated with postindustrial society, the civil rights and women's liberation movements, and television have contributed to the definition of a new *paideia*—one that has profoundly affected the experience of teachers and the work they do in the schools.

In reviewing the cartoons published in the *Kappan* since the early 1950s, it seems clear that they reflect the emergence of this new *paideia* and the social changes that have occurred in American culture. In this context, a popular-culture source such as the *Kappan* cartoons becomes an important indicator of social forces at work in the culture—ones that, by virtue of their popularity and inclusion in such a magazine, are probably highly reflective of the historical moment they represent, as well as the tensions experienced by the teachers and administrators whose lives and works they portray. What, in fact, can we learn from these popular-culture sources about American education and culture? How do they give us a sense of forces and issues at work over the past twenty or thirty years?

What emerges from the cartoons is a sense that teachers are underpaid and underappreciated. Together with school administrators, such as superintendents, they are legally and often physically vulnerable. The teachers in the *Kappan* cartoons are profoundly influenced in their day-to-day functioning by larger changes at work in the culture, such as divorce and the need for students to receive sex education. Recurring references in the cartoons to the increasing influence of television and computers on children, and the necessity of teachers to compete with various forms of media for the attention of the students in their classes, is also highly suggestive of forces of change that are affecting teachers. Finally, the portrayal of the university professoriate and an educational bureaucracy that is not connected to the reality of the schools, as well as the hypocrisy found in sports programs, suggest very real issues that are to be found in the educational system and the culture at large—one which is obviously connected to the lives and experience of teachers. While issues such as teacher salaries and violence against teachers and administrators are found as recurrent themes in American educational history, the growth in legal liability of teachers and administrators, the competition provided by new forms of media such as television, the growth of the educational bureaucracy, and other themes are reflective of a new *paideia*.[50]

In conclusion, it can be argued that popular-culture sources, such as the cartoons found in the *Kappan*, represent ways of reconstructing both tensions and issues found in American culture. In addition, the cartoons represent forces and problems that speak to a reality experienced by teachers and administrators, who find the cartoons not only funny but meaningful.

NOTES

1. For background on the cartoon and graphic humor of *The New Yorker* see M. Thomas Inge, "The *New Yorker* Cartoon and Graphic Humor," in *Comics as Culture* (Jackson, MI: University Press of Mississippi, 1990). Inge notes that, in the prospectus issued for the magazine before its first publication, Harold Ross explained that "*The New Yorker* will be a reflection in word and picture of metropolitan life" (p. 109).
2. For a general introduction to caricature and cartoons in American culture, see *The Image of America in Caricature & Cartoon* (Fort Worth: Amon Carter Museum of Western Art, 1976).
3. Robert Cole, Foreword to *Recess Time: The Best Cartoons from the Kappan*, ed. Kristin Herzog (Bloomington, IN: Phi Delta Kappan, 1983).
4. The idea of cartoons and, more specifically, comic books as history is developed in Joseph Witek,*Comic Books as History: The Narrative Art of Jack Jackson, Art Speigelman and Harvey Pekar* (Jackson, MI: University Press of Mississippi, 1989).
5. *Phi Delata Kappan* [hereafter referred to as *Kappan*], 62(5): 162.
6. *Phi Delta Kappan*, 42(7): 274.
7. *Kappan*, 46(5): 226.
8. *Kappan*, 55(1): 52.
9. *Kappan*, 56(7): 485.
10. *Kappan*, 57(1): 44.
11. *Kappan*, 61(6): 397.
12. *Kappan*, 65(3): 196.
13. *Kappan*, 56(3): 184.
14. *Kappan*, 59(1): 56.
15. *Kappan*, 53(10): 627.
16. *Kappan*, 59(5): 330.
17. *Kappan*, 59(7): 508.
18. *Kappan*, 54(8): 543.
19. *Kappan*, 57(1): 42.
20. *Kappan*, 60(7): 526.
21. *Kappan*, 46(9): 458.
22. *Kappan*, 56(4): 280.
23. *Kappan*, 46(5): 245.

24. *Kappan*, 57(1): 50.
25. *Kappan*, 57(1): 29.
26. *Kappan*, 44(6): 272.
27. *Kappan*, 48(5): 205.
28. *Kappan*, 51(3): 146.
29. *Kappan*, 51(4): 209.
30. *Kappan*, 58(6): 492.
31. *Kappan*, 67(10): 747.
32. *Kappan*, 62(8): 593.
33. *Kappan*, 58(5): 404.
34. *Kappan*, 67(2): 146.
35. *Kappan*, 67(3): 214.
36. *Kappan*, 54(8): 547.
37. *Kappan*, 58(19): 750.
38. *Kappan*, 59(2): 108.
39. *Kappan*, 60(9): 668.
40. *Kappan*, 58(3): 255.
41. *Kappan*, 61(5): 354.
42. *Kappan*, 42(7): 281.
43. *Kappan*, 46(7): 317.
44. *Kappan*, 46(7): 310.
45. *Kappan*, 50(10): 572.
46. *Kappan*, 62(1): 15.
47. *Kappan*, 51(2): 83.
48. *Kappan*, 54(2): 142.
49. *Kappan*, 61(7): 491.
50. Note that the subjects that are considered humorous for teachers and adminisrators in the cartoons such as those found the *Kappan* are not those found for other professions. Cartoons about poorly paid doctors, physically threatened lawyers, or unrespected actors or sports celebrities are not included as part of the coda of American cartoon humor. The fact that such issues are included in the context of cartoons about teachers and school administrators is highly revealing.

12 Education 1st!: Using Television to Promote the Schools

Lynn Nations Johnson and Gunilla Holm

For one week in the spring of 1991 (15–21 April), major television networks and cable channels promoted programs that addressed the topic of American education.[1] Newspaper accounts[2] at the time touted the effort, dubbed "Education 1st! Week," one declaring it to be a "history-making 75 hours of programming . . . committed by network and cable TV executives to pro-educational themes."[3] As another suggested, "Even commercial channels, sensitive to criticism that their shows often have more appeal than homework does, are responding this month to what they call a national crisis in education with a special week of 'pro-education' programming."[4]

What was Education 1st! Week, and why does it warrant a closer look? In this chapter, we explore these questions and consider the significance of what Education 1st! Week reveals. Education 1st! Week was proposed in the fall of 1990 by two former teachers who are also the founders of Education 1st!, a nonprofit group well connected to the Hollywood entertainment industry and established for the purpose of promoting education. According to one of their flyers, Education 1st! is

> composed of concerned and influential individuals in the film, television and music industries, in print media, and nationally recognized educators and child development specialists. Education 1st! was created to gather and use the resources of the entertainment industry and the media to communicate the realities of the current crisis in education and the positive solutions to ensure a functionally literate, productive work force by the year 2000.[5]

This passage helps to situate the organization. While Education 1st! is a nonprofit organization, its link to corporate concerns overarching the entertainment industry is apparent in the emphasis on the economic goals of education and the rhetoric of concern about the role of schooling in producing a productive work force. The organization's assumptions regarding the realities of the current crisis are broadly representative of contemporary views centered on economic competition and productivity.

Education 1st! has an impressive board of advisors including the presidents of the NEA, the national PTA, and the Carnegie Foundation for the Advancement of Teaching. One of its guiding principles is a commitment

> to ensuring that the entertainment and communications industries acknowledge and continue to take responsibility for their increasingly powerful influence on our national culture, including our attitudes toward education.[6]

This comment indicates that Education 1st! represents a high-profile instance of a group seeking to exercise what Joel Spring calls ideological management within a form of popular culture[7]—endeavoring, that is, to shape attitudes of the general public, in this case, with regard to crisis in schooling. The organization states in its promotional material that it wants the media to portray teachers and successful students as heroes, parents as involved in their children's education, diverse cultures in the school as something positive, and learning as fun.

The publicity created around this proeducation week aligned the networks with concerns being voiced by many Americans. The central purposes of the Education 1st! organization were adopted by the networks, which pledged to boost the ideas that education is important and that there are admirable educators and students who deserve greater respect and attention. The networks proclaimed their commitment in the struggle to get the "right" kinds of messages out to the public.

From the standpoint of ideological management, such an effort to shape the public's attitudes toward education through a week of network and cable-sponsored education-oriented television programs surely makes sense. Watching television is the most common form of popular culture that people engage in today. People from every age group, as well as from every occupation and social status, watch television, with the total household viewing time averaging more than seven hours a day.[8] In this chapter, we explore the way television programs included in Education 1st! Week construct images and ideas about schooling. The manifest and latent content of a sample of the programs is examined in order to assess how the programs sought to promote education and achieve the goals of Education 1st! Week. These analyses are then placed in relation to the sociohistorical context from which Education 1st! Week emerged and came into view.

PROGRAM ANALYSIS

According to news media reports, there were some seventy-four programs slated for the Education 1st! Week, thirty-seven on network television and thirty-seven on PBS and cable networks. The pieces reviewed represent programs broadcast by both the commercial and cable networks.[9] For this study, we reviewed three cartoons or animated children's programs, three documentaries, four movies (two of the movies, *Lean on Me* and *She Stood Alone* being cinematic biographies), and fifteen sitcoms/variety shows/psychodramas (see table 12.1). In interpreting the messages and portrayals about teachers, students, and schools, we include examples from all four types of programs. Although the four types of programs have different audiences, the implicit messages about education included in each program remain largely the same, independent of the type of program.

SCHOOL BOOSTING

In many programs the proeducation message is explicit and unmistakable. Several programs strive to boost perceptions of the importance of education, emphasizing positive aspects of school experience and tales of exemplary teachers and students. A representative instance of the networks' goal to live up to Education 1st! Week's proeducation publicity is found in the animated children's program "Captain N and the Adventures of Super Mario Brothers III." This segment's adventure comes to an end with Julio and Captain N saving the people in a town from being controlled by Mother Brain's use of text hypnosis. In this context, the illiterate Julio is told that learning to read is important, and he even asks his newly employed father to help him learn to read. In this way, the program is structured to send the desired proeducation message to its young viewers and to reassure their parents and the concerned public that the show supports educational goals.

One of the goals of the Education 1st! organization is to portray teachers and students who are successful. Nearly two-thirds of the programs that feature teachers include clearly positive images and portrayals. Teachers appear who are sensitive, intelligent, and strongly committed to their profession and students. The documentary *American*

Table 12.1 Education 1st! Week programs analyzed

Program type	Program title	Network
A. Animated children's programs	1. "Captain N: The Adventures of the Super Mario Brothers 3"	NBC
	2. "Morris Goes to School"	Disney
	3. "Paddington Goes to School"	Disney
B. Documentaries	4. *American Teacher Awards*	Disney
	5. "America's Most Wanted"	Fox
	6. *Take Me to Your Leaders*	Disney
C. Feature Films	7. *Children of a Lesser God*	HBO
	8. *Lean on Me*	HBO
	9. *She Stood Alone*	NBC
	10. *Stanley and Iris*	HBO
D. Psychodramas, variety shows, sitcoms	11. "Guns of Paradise"	CBS
	12. "Life Goes On"	ABC
	13. "Carol and Company"	NBC
	14. "In Living Color"FOX	
	15. "A Different World"NBC	
	16. "The Cosby Show"	NBC
	17. "Designing Women"	CBS
	18. "Doogie Howser"	ABC
	19. "Evening Shade"	CBS
	20. "The Fresh Prince of Bel Air"	NBC
	21. "Golden Girls"	NBC
	22. "Growing Pains"	ABC
	23. "Parker Lewis Can't Lose"	Fox
	24. "Roseanne"	ABC

Teacher Awards further celebrates teachers and their accomplishments. A variety of teachers, female and male, white and minority, are featured. The consistent theme in the teachers' speeches is that learning has to be both fun and practical. It is the love students express for them that makes teaching rewarding and worthwhile.

The most comprehensive picture of a single teacher shown during Education 1st! Week was the movie *She Stood Alone,* a biography of the Massachusetts teacher Prudence Crandall. Crandall, an important pioneer in black education, established the first all-black girls' school in the 1830s after failing to teach both black and white students in the same school. A fictitious romance with a man in town who has political aspirations[10] and allusions to a second romance obscure the educational theme to some extent, but the movie succeeds in depicting Crandall as an independent and heroic woman and teacher. She stands up against the men in the town, one of whom declares at one point, "You are a woman, an unmarried woman. You have no rights." She even goes to jail for her convictions and actions. Nonetheless, her actions serve to empower the black girls who learn to withstand the intimidation of the whites in the courtroom and the town.

Similar valor is depicted in another film, *Lean on Me,* celebrating Joe Clark's work as a high school principal. This film depicts Clark as involved in heroic struggles to turn around a school that had become an urban jungle. Clark's charisma eventually wins over teachers and students alike. This is the only program reviewed that explicitly portrays a school reform process.[11] The theme of charismatic leadership suggests that ordinary institutional and professional efforts are few and pale in comparison.

Among other strong images of teachers included in Education 1st! Week programming is a tough but dedicated visiting teacher in a black history class in "Fresh Prince of Bel Air," a show also featuring a quote from Malcom X about the importance of education. Another strong image of a teacher is the character John Leeds in the film *Children of a Lesser God.* Leeds, a teacher who is knowledgeable, lively, and caring, manages to motivate his hearing-impaired students in ways that open up a new world for them. Television teachers appearing in several other programs ("Golden Girls," "Doogie Howser," and "Morris Goes to School") are shown working hard to motivate students. They win small but satisfying educational victories, such as the moment when Vincent, a reticent student in "Doogie Howser," agrees to learn French following an adventure with his French teacher.

Students are occasionally depicted in the process of coming to find school knowledge relevant or of becoming motivated and beginning to take action required for school success. An example of the latter is "The Cosby Show," where Pam, a young relative living with the Huxtables, learns that studying hard pays off. Higher grades and the potential for going to college are the rewards. Pam is challenged by her male friends, who wonder what she will do with all her Bs. They doubt that she will go to college, because she does not have money like her wealthier relatives. When the possibility of earning a scholarship arises, the boys mockingly inquire if she plays football, but do not dissuade her from pursuing her ambitions. Here students are implicitly encouraged to think of their futures in new ways. Hope is given; it is possible to go to college if you want to, but you have to ignore certain kinds of friends. In the "Fresh Prince of Bel Air" episode, two initially reticent African-American students are surprised by the enthusiasm of their classmates in exploring black history. Their teacher (who is also the mother of one of them) helps them recognize and overcome their arrogant but uninformed, self-defeating views.

Highly motivated, achieving students are also featured in the documentary *Take Me to Your Leaders.* This program features elementary and secondary students who are said to have leadership ability, such as ten-year-old Audrey, who took a school tree-planting campaign to the state level and now is working to make it a nationwide, and possibly an international, program. Another example is Dan, who, at age thirteen, recruited one hundred young people to work on a congressional campaign and, at the age of fourteen, recruited thousands of students to register the elderly and handicapped to vote. Also featured in this program is Leadership America, a five-week problem-solving seminar for young people, which is described as not being "about the pursuit of knowledge, [but] about the pursuit of significance . . . leadership is found wherever someone cares to find a new solution to an old problem." It is worth noting that all these examples, in *Take Me to Your Leaders,* of highly motivated students obtaining valuable knowledge center on activity taking place outside of school. The school does count for something in other cases, however, as in the cartoon "Morris Goes to School." Everything delights Morris the moose when he learns to read. The relevance of the learning is underscored in the story: He can no longer be fooled, and he knows which store to go to in order to buy candy and how much it will cost him. Likewise, a feature film also concerned with illiteracy, *Stanley and Iris,* explores the importance of being able to read. Stanley is fired from his job as a cook, putatively because his inability to read labels might lead to the poisoning of restaurant customers. He is portrayed as a good man who finds himself unemployed and a social outcast because of his illiteracy. The pivotal event in this story involves the efforts of Iris, his former co-worker, to teach him how to read. Stanley's striving pays off, and, after his success and joy in learning to read is vividly portrayed, he goes on to become successfully employed. This represents precisely the connection Education 1st! sought to emphasize between the triumphs of teaching and learning and the prospect of productive employment.

SCHOOL BASHING

As we have suggested, Education 1st! Week featured numerous examples of programs engaged in school boosting. More common, however, were varieties of school bashing in which schools, teachers, and students were skewered, mocked, or maligned in some way. At times, this occurs in programs that contain ambiguous messages, typically with proeducation ideas tacked on to stories containing contrary notions.

Recall Julio, for example, the main character in "Captain N and the Adventures of the Super Mario Brothers III," who is lectured on the importance of learning to read and, in turn, seeks help in doing so. Within the main action of that episode, Julio avoids being hypnotized precisely because he is unable to read the text that Mother Brain uses to take control of people's minds. Because Julio is not hypnotized, he and Captain N are able to rescue the others, all readers, by dehypnotizing them. This type of ambiguous message is quite common in the programs we analyzed. Often, the message about education is bleaker still.

Our analysis of the school bashing during the Education 1st! Week focuses on issues that fall into four categories: distractions, portrayals of practitioners, marginalization of school knowledge, and how television copes with race, gender, and social class.

Offering Distractions

Despite the professed proeducation purpose, the programs reviewed often focus on matters quite distinct from education and schools. Educational concerns are often overshadowed by a variety of powerful distractions. For example, in "Doogie Howser," the central event of the program concerns a teacher's delivery of a child in an elevator; in "Designing Women," the plot is built around sexual harassment; in *She Stood Alone* and "A Different World," it is romance; in "Guns of Paradise," it is the pursuit of a bank robber; in "Evening Shade," it is when a sensual and provocative woman steps in as a teacher and excites student attention; and so on. Even in the documentary *America's Teacher Awards,* much of the excitement that is generated centers on the presence of celebrities introducing particular categories of award-winning teachers, such as Oprah Winfrey introducing the Elementary Teacher of the Year. While short clips of the teachers at work were presented, the program's appeal centered as much on the lineup of celebrities as on the celebration of teaching.

In many cases, proeducational themes represented small segments of larger programs. For example, in the simulated television documentary "America's Most Wanted," an education program in a jail is one of seven stories featured. In the satire "In Living Color," a few minutes spent making light of a literacy program in a prison constitutes the sole reference to education and reason for including the program on the Education 1st! list. Those programs that did feature a sustained focus on schools and education—such as "The Cosby Show," *Lean on Me,* and "Morris Goes to School"—were clear exceptions in their respective genres.

On the basis of the programs reviewed, one must conclude that it is difficult to make enticing programs that focus on education. To the extent that many viewers, adults and children alike, believe that education is inherently boring and of marginal interest, the programs of Education 1st! Week did little to dislodge that perception.[12]

Potshots at Practitioners

As we have indicated, it was an avowed purpose of Education 1st! to encourage the airing of positive images of good and caring educators, and clear instances of such images did, in fact, appear. But they were not alone. Several other teachers in the sitcoms and cartoons are depicted as boring, incapable of motivating students, or intolerant of student creativity. This type of image echoes the widespread belief that a major problem in education today is incompetent teachers. Three of the five male teachers portrayed in the programs we analyzed are in this category; a fourth teacher, a male professor in the sitcom "Designing Women," engages in sexual harassment. In the program "Evening Shade," a white math teacher puts athletes to sleep with his monotonous droning voice. His students, who are failing algebra, do not revive and learn until he is replaced by an attractive townswoman who uses sexual metaphors to capture their attention and to make math "relevant" for them. The teacher in "Guns of Paradise" is a white male teacher with a tendency to persecute children who do not learn easily. He goes so far as to beat a child severely for fighting on school grounds. In "Paddington Goes to School," the male teacher is portrayed as boring and insecure with regard to how he should handle a capable and witty student (the bear). Exasperated, he even sends the bear out on the town to do some shopping. The teacher's trials end only when, to everybody's relief, it is discovered that bears do not have to go to school after all, and Paddington can simply be offered a diploma. A similar pattern of intolerance of student creativity is found in "Life Goes On," where an art teacher—in this case, a woman—fails to appreciate the innovative work of two students. She expresses her hostility, saying, "In my class, when I give an assignment, I'm not interested in any avant-garde interpretations."

Finally, while we have noted above the portrayal of a heroic Joe Clark in *Lean on Me,* the film is ambiguous in its message. Clark's energy and passion are set in contrast to other educators depicted in the film. A key aspect of Clark's work has to do with overcoming a prevailing pattern of teacher recalcitrance and apathy. Other principals who come into view during the week are cast in a different light. Some of these characters, like the Joe Clark character, have scant respect for the teachers who work with them and the efforts they make, but, unlike Clark, they are not presented as heroic in their efforts to transform teachers and schools. In "Golden Girls," for example, a principal expresses a dismissive attitude toward Dorothy's struggle to maintain academic standards for athletes. Another, in *Children of a Lesser God,* criticizes John Leeds's innovative ways of teaching hearing-impaired children (only coming to appreciate Mr. Leeds after parents have demonstrated their support for his work with their children).

Marginalizing School Knowledge

Schooling and school knowledge are commonly portrayed as irrelevant for students. In "Evening Shade" and "Golden Girls," student athletes find mathematics and English boring and irrelevant, in contrast to the life they find in sports. In "Doogie Howser," Vincent is asked to give his teacher a reason why he chose to attend the class, since he is not interested in French. He offers the following reasons: "My girlfriend was in the class, it's a beeline to the cafeteria, and it's close to my locker," an answer that infuriates the teacher who therefore threatens to fail him in the course. In "Parker Lewis Can't Lose," Mikey hates school and decides to drop out to play in a rock band instead. He exclaims that he feels like a "free man" when he leaves school. The principal, who has given up on him but still does not want him to leave, lamely states, "I would consider it a professional favor if you did return"; she is concerned about keeping the number of drop-outs low, not any good it would do him as a person. Finally, Mikey decides to return, saying: "I don't miss Musso [the principal], I don't miss cafeteria food. I don't miss high school. What I do miss is you. I miss the buds thing. I miss the dudes, the Park, us. I even miss Jerry [the class nerd] a little." As the program comes to a close, Parker offers this comment: "I say rock 'n' roll should live forever. It's the soundtrack of high school, of hope, of growing up. And for my pal, Michael Randall, it's the second most important thing in his life."

Friendship is the most important thing in Mikey's life. In fact, student characters are often portrayed as viewing school as an important place to maintain friendships, be cool, and impress members of the other sex. Sometimes this attitude is encouraged by adults, as in this episode of "Growing Pains": The father argues that his son should not be taught at home by his mother but should go back to school, because he needs to be with his friends, who might otherwise call him "a mama's boy." The centrality of peer relations in schooling is also the subject of "Life Goes On," as Becca and her friend Maxi are pressured into drinking alcohol in order to be cool and impress their new friends from school. Romance, too, is presented as a major reason for going to school. Girls who consider learning more important than romance are considered outcasts. In "A Different World," for example, a young woman committed to her university studies is accused of having "no life" because she is concerned about the impact of dating on her classes and has refused to date a young man who wants to go out with her.

Earlier, we noted those programs that rather straightforwardly present a positive image of the advantages that follow from learning to read and write, such as the cartoon "Morris Goes to School" and the film *Stanley and Iris.* The cartoon "Captain N and the Adventures of Super Mario Brothers III" (as described earlier) and the satire "In Living Color" convey messages that are much more ambiguous. The segment of "In Living Color" focuses on three incarcerated criminals who are a part of Barbara Bush's campaign against illiteracy. Learning to read is sarcastically portrayed as being of negligible value or only helpful in committing further crime. One inmate says, "Thank you, Mrs. Bush. Before I could read, I was forced to rob convenience stores for a living. But since joining your literacy program, a whole new world has been opened up to me: embezzlement." This segment of "In Living Color" is a fascinating entry in the Education 1st! lineup. It is penetrating in its derision of the speciousness of arguments that education can solve deep social problems. Indeed, its central message deconstructs the very idea of Education 1st! While this is itself potentially educative, it scarcely reinforces the idea that education is the answer to serious social problems.

Anti-intellectual sentiments are visible in many programs portraying the school either as an impediment to real life or simply a place for socializing. After an argument with the principal during the episode of "Roseanne," for example, Roseanne seizes the school's intercom to announce, "Attention, all students taking Latin: you're wasting your lives." This was something she said she had always wanted to do. The implication is that school knowledge should be practical, and the comment reveals a certain hostility toward those who choose to spend their time studying esoteric and less utilitarian subjects such as Latin.[13] "Carol and Company" featured a skit portraying different kinds of students, in which one, referred to as "Miss Perfect," is characterized as an outstanding student wanting even greater challenges in school. As Miss Perfect points out a spelling mistake in a textbook or says that the teacher has not graded her extra-credit project, Carol comments to the audience, "Couldn't you just puke?" Miss Perfect is diligent and focused as a learner, and is therefore a target of contempt. As the programming of Education 1st! Week suggests (with a few exceptions), it is rarely advisable or desirable to demonstrate strong commitments to learning.

Coping with Gender, Race, and Social Class

It is widely acknowledged that issues involving gender, race/ethnicity, and social class are deeply implicated in problems found in American education. How do such topics arise in the programs reviewed here? Are schools portrayed as institutions where equality among students is supported and encouraged or where stereotypes and inequalities are reinforced and reproduced. First, with regard to gender, it is difficult to decipher the proeducation messages for females in the reviewed programs. These messages are buried in programs emphasizing romance, sexual innuendo, and the pursuit of popularity. The satire of "In Living Color," for example, is peppered with sexually suggestive content. Sexual harassment takes center stage in the proeducation segment of "Designing Women" when Charlene is harassed by her professor. His behavior is excused, however, because he is a lonely man who has not developed his social skills enough for appropriate behavior with women. As his student and assistant, she has a professional relationship with him, but the message here, as he looks her over from head to toe, is that men relate to women's bodies instead of their minds. Sexual harassment also provides a subplot during the episode of "Golden Girls" as well.

In addition to sexual innuendo and harassment, several programs give ambiguous messages about female intelligence. In the episode of "Designing Women," Charlene's friends express surprise that she has been accepted to college. While Charlene reports having always wanted a degree, she expresses her belief that an education at the "right" institution and in the "right" field of study will enhance her social status among her acquaintances and friends. In "Parker Lewis Can't Lose," female students are portrayed as losing all control when they hear Mikey play his guitar after he has dropped out from school. In "A Different World," as described above, bright women are considered as not having a life if they focus on school instead of on being popular with men. The second story line in "A Different World" centers on Dwayne challenging Whitley's intellectual capacity. He believes she is not bright enough for an academic bowl competition. The competition for which she is not considered bright enough turns out to be an academic trivia bowl, and Whitley is, in fact, very knowledgeable about the subject matter covered in the competition.

For young females, Education 1st! Week's programs often appear to affirm stereotypes. If they are intelligent and focus on their studies, they might be harassed, or they risk becoming unpopular. Especially for teen-age girls in coeducational schools, being considered attractive is of great importance, and social success is often believed to be incompatible with academic success. The female students in the programs reviewed were generally not depicted as challenging this mindset, and were also unlikely to pose major problems for teachers, parents, or themselves. The exceptions are Becky, who flashed her middle finger in the class picture in "Roseanne"; Carol, in "Carol and Company," as she gets into a fight when the teacher leaves the room; and Becca and Maxi in "Life Goes On," as Maxi gets drunk. Sarah, in *Children of a Lesser God*, is the only female character shown who actively resists learning. Far more often it is the males who want to leave school, who are uninterested in school and learning. This kind of disengaged male student is portrayed, for example, in "Evening Shade," "Growing Pains," "Doogie Howser," and "Parker Lewis." Along with this seemingly negative image of male students comes the attention they receive and, frequently, their eventual turnaround as they return to school, pass an exam, or at least promise to master some subject matter. Story lines seem to play on the hopes of an audience more inclined to worry about the lack of interest young males show in education. Female students receive much less attention of this kind.

With regard to issues of race and ethnicity, a similarly uninformative and conventional approach is evident. Virtually all of the comparatively few minority students portrayed in the Education 1st! Week programs are black, except for a male Latino student who is an inmate and Julio, who is an illiterate but successful Latino student in "Super Mario Brothers III." The black students are either upper-middle-class students, as in "The Cosby Show," or they represent the urban underclass, either attending threatening schools of the sort depicted in *Lean on Me* or, as in the case of "Fresh Prince of Bel Air," as a kind of emissary from the street. Very few working-class or lower-middle-class black students exist in these programs. Pam, the poor niece of the upper-middle-class Huxtable family, is one exception in the programs reviewed. With few minority students appearing, the programs in no way reflect the fact that about 30 percent of American students now come from African American, Latino, Asian American/Pacific Islander, or Native American background.[14] These findings are consistent with the findings of a study conducted by the National Commission on Working Women of Wider Opportunities for Women, which shows that few minorities have roles in prime-time television programs.[15]

This tendency is evident with regard to the question of social class as well. The focus of the majority of the programs is on characters representing middle-class or upper-middle-class students and families, such as the well-to-do boarding school students in *She Stood Alone,* or even the bear who comes from a home with a housekeeper in the cartoon "Paddington Goes to School." There were eight programs that included main characters from working-class or poverty backgrounds. The characters portrayed in these programs are often shown engaging in antisocial behavior or anti-educational behavior. As described above, one of the daughters in "Roseanne" is accused of making an obscene gesture in the class picture. In the simulated documentary "America's

Most Wanted" and in the satire "In Living Color," the students are prisoners.

Principals and parents are characterized as interacting differently depending on the social-class background of the parents. The principal in "Roseanne" is rude, treats the parents as children, and implies that they are not good parents. As Roseanne points out when she is asked to visit the principal because of her daughter's action, she feels like she is in trouble and is concerned about missing work. In contrast, the middle-class parents in "Growing Pains" carry on a constructive, concerned conversation with the principal regarding their son. The result of the conversation is their decision to instruct their son at home. They are in control and making important decisions about their son's education.

Upper- and middle-class parents of handicapped or black students are portrayed as working with the school by instilling the importance of education in their children. The affluent mother in "Fresh Prince of Bel Air," for example, stresses the importance of broad knowledge in an ethnic-heritage class. Similarly, in "The Cosby Show," the upper-middle-class family shows Pam the value of good study habits and good grades. In other words, the well-to-do show the poor the road to success. Middle-class parents and, in particular, affluent black parents are portrayed as more supportive of and assertive regarding their children's education than are working-class parents.

Social-class issues intersect with gender as well in several programs. In "Growing Pains," the middle-class mother decides to teach her son at home after he experiences serious problems at school. The father remembers that the son's problems started when the mother started working, suggesting that her career may be a detriment to the son's education. Education is implicitly portrayed as more important for upper-middle-class students, especially girls. There are few programs portraying working-class or poor girls, except for "Roseanne." The only program featuring students in poverty is the film *Lean on Me.* In this case, the most prominent female student becomes pregnant and struggles to stay in school. Some of the working-class boys in "Parker Lewis Can't Lose" and "Golden Girls" confine their school concerns to contemplating dropping out or worrying about not being allowed to play football—problems that are, as is usually the case, resolved in the end.

In short, the education of the poor is conspicuously absent from the programs shown during the Education 1st! Week, and messages regarding the education of females and minorities are muddled at best. Most clear is the message that it is the well-to-do who best appreciate the value of education and understand how to help their children succeed.

DISCUSSION

Through the promotion of Education 1st! Week, the networks proclaimed an interest in responding to, and reaffirmed common perceptions of, the present crisis in American education. It is a crisis that, according to promotional material distributed by Education 1st!, is tied to issues such as uninvolved parents, illiteracy, low respect for teachers, and the diversity of the student population. To the extent that this is so, the networks' treatment of educational matters obfuscates more than it informs. Fundamental issues that influence educational success are scarcely evident in the portrayal of schooling during Education 1st! Week.

How then does Education 1st! Week relate to the problems for which it offers itself as a balm? First, it is clear that serious social and structural problems require long-term solutions and tend, therefore, to be skirted or ignored by those unwilling or uninterested in pursuing the process of significant change. Quick-fix solutions to profound structural problems are often advocated as an alternative to critical and open debate. This tendency is exacerbated by deeply rooted anti-intellectualism in American society.[16] Public skepticism of advanced academic study and of expertise in general, low teacher prestige, and a lack of financial support for educational programs are symptoms of this sentiment, making substantive deliberations on education problematic.

Education reform is difficult to accomplish in such a climate and within the context of a public unwilling to consider the complexity of education and its problems. As Cremin argues, the discussion about educational reform has

> been seriously flawed by a failure to understand the extraordinary complexity of education—a failure to grasp the impossibility of defining a good school apart from its social and intellectual context, the impossibility of even comprehending the processes and effects of schooling and, in fact, its successes and failures apart from their embedment in a larger ecology of education that includes what families, television broadcasters, workplaces, and a host of other institutions are contributing at any given time.[17]

Discussing educational problems and educational reform apart from the social and intellectual context of education is symptomatic, therefore, of a lack of critical vision. In this regard, the networks delivered programs unequipped for and uninterested in contextualizing educational problems. Such programming could scarcely do more than reaffirm prevailing views about education within the public eye. Educational matters were often marginalized. Frequently, parallel plots drew attention from the educational theme, or educational matters were overshadowed by unrelated events such as child birth or sexual harassment. In several programs, the proeducation segment constituted a minor part of the total program. One might argue, of course, that sitcoms and other entertainment programs, by their very nature, are not the best vehicle for discussing complex social and educational issues. As Cremin points out, however, television "educates and miseducates relentlessly . . . and . . . offers models of behavior through soap operas and sitcoms."[18] Others have also argued that television has multiple functions. Television networks seek to entertain, but they might also provide information and space for debate about societal decision making.[19]

The failure of Education 1st! Week to provide a more comprehensive, meaningful, and consistent set of images and ideas regarding education and its problems is, in the end, quite revealing. For one thing, the effort by network executives to gather numerous education-related programs into a one-week period provides an opportunity to take stock of ways in which schools and educational matters are routinely portrayed in various television formats. In addition, the efforts that led to Education 1st! Week—efforts to manage and shape what television offers with regard to education—suggest how strongly television is tied to interests other than those that are strictly educational or focus on the public good that education seeks to provide.

One constraint the television networks have to contend with is economic. They must hold an audience in order to make a profit.[20] Marcus refers to this type of popular culture as "the commodified culture-for-the-people organized by the leisure sector of the capitalist market."[21] The commercial and cable networks, as profit-making organizations, could scarcely retreat from their imperative to choose programs that would appeal to the largest possible audience, the rhetoric of Education 1st! Week notwithstanding. The imperative to keep and build its audience goes beyond matters of content alone. As Gary Day[22] argues, the television industry strives to homogenize the culture by not only controlling what is experienced but also how. This is evident, as we have seen, when proeducation content is at times sprinkled into programs whose format effectively engulfs and dilutes it. The audience for most of the programs, after all, does not look to television to satisfy needs for serious reflection on complex issues; its desires are on a different order altogether.

Beyond this, television not only fulfills a variety of needs[23] but it also creates new needs which cannot be fulfilled. And as Day suggests, the media also provide "distractions from the present, a means of shutting it out. This suggests that where there is no remedy for the dissatisfactions of the present there is at least escape."[24] However illusory this escape may be, the need for it might explain the fascination with the rich and famous, or at least the prevalence of the middle-class families, who dominate not only the programs of Education 1st! Week but television programming more generally. In this context, Fiske and Hartley comment that

> television performs a function of 'anticipatory socialization', whereby people use the mediated view of status groups higher than their own . . . as models they can emulate. The idea is that people can then learn the characteristic language, behaviour, and habits of the aspired-to status group in order to gain entry and then adjust to that group.[25]

To the extent that television routinely performs such a function, its doing so involves a deep tension insofar as the goals of Education 1st! are concerned. Consider, for example, the strong commitment articulated in Education 1st! promotional materials with regard to cultural diversity. One of the guiding principles of the organization reads, "We are committed to an America which recognizes and values diversity of its many cultures, races, and religions."

The Education 1st! organization also provided to the networks (through its promotional materials) statistics about drop-outs and illiterates among minorities. Such details were overwhelmed by the tendency of television to feature the trappings of 'anticipatory socialization.' The lack of cultural diversity evident in the programs aired during this week contradict the explicit goal of Education 1st! to promote sensitivity to cultural diversity. The organized efforts' failure in this regard is not surprising in view of the way diversity is portrayed within prime-time television more widely. As Paul Harris, citing a recent study conducted by the National Commission on Working Women, has noted in *Variety*:

> On TV almost all minority characters are black. . . . Nine out of ten minority characters are middle-class or wealthy. . . . Almost three-quarters of all minority females on TV are featured in sitcoms, the only genre in which they have leading roles. TV's world is one of racial harmony. The workplace is an egalitarian one with no hint of bias, even though whites are almost always in charge. Most programs reduce injustice to individual conflict, denying the reality of oppressive social structures. Only a few shows present a multicultural world.[26]

These tendencies account for the way Education 1st! Week skirted issues concerning minority groups and the poor. Statistical information and demographic trends regarding cultural diversity have little impact on how programs are designed, including those selected for Education 1st! Week.

It could be argued that, with regard to the type of programming included for Education 1st! Week, we exaggerate the significance of the program content and the power of television network executives and program producers to manipulate the mass of viewers. Ultimately, the meaning of the programs is created through the viewer's interpretation of them. However, this analysis of Education 1st! Week suggests the degree to which television both reflects and contributes to the reproduction of the culture in which schools, including schools in deep trouble, reside. The high degree of what we have called school bashing provides a context, and influences the conditions of possibility, for widespread, thoughtful analysis of educational problems. Disinclined or unable to address the underlying social-structural problems of the schools—such as the devastating effects of poverty, for example—television tuned into topics of personal interest but marginal importance, such as suspension from school for making obscene gestures or temporary peer rejection. A crisis in education was once again proclaimed but not explored. In this way, the promotion of Education 1st! Week trivialized educational problems and concerns. With the television industry's imperatives to offer programs that make audiences feel comfortably at home, new insights concerning education in American culture were largely beside the point. The week could do little more than echo existing beliefs, stereotypes, and attitudes about schooling and its problems.

The point here is not to demean the intentions of those behind Education 1st!—their intentions matter little in the end. Rather, one gathers that, in order to achieve its goals, Education 1st! would need to do no less than change the face of television, allowing educational values to take precedence over the commercial interests of the entertainment industry. Since no such coup transpired before the banner was unveiled, we are left to reflect on what the promotion means. More than anything else, the programs of the Education 1st! Week underscore the way entertainment values take precedence over educational concerns and the public need to reflect on the state of the schools. It is the irony of Education 1st! Week that it reveals how far from first education is among the concerns of those who make what we see on TV.

NOTES

1. The participating networks were CBS, NBC, ABC, HBO, Fox, Disney, PBS, TBS, TNT, A&E, Lifetime, Nickelodeon, MTV, E! Entertainment, The

Learning Channel, and Univision. We examined the programs listed in table 12.1.

2. Articles on Education 1st! Week appeared in several newspapers—for example, "Networks Band Together to Show School Is Cool," *U.S.A. Today* (20 March 1991); "Nets Launch Week of Education 1st!" *Hollywood Reporter* (16 April 1991); "What's On TV," *Kalamazoo Gazette* (13 April 1991); "Attempting Integration in 1830's Connecticut," *New York Times* (15 April 1991).

3. "What's on TV," *Kalamazoo Gazette* (13 April 1991), p. D2.

4. Bill Carter, "Teaching on the Tube," *New York Times* (7 April 1991), p. Ed 22.

5. *There Is a Crisis in America* (pamphlet issued by Education 1st!, Los Angeles).

6. *Education First: How to Be a Perfect Ten!* (booklet issued by Education 1st, Los Angeles).

7. Joel Spring, *American Education. An Introduction to Social and Political Aspects.* (New York: Longman, 1991); and Joel Spring, *Images of American Life: A History of Ideological Management in Schools, Movies, Radio, and Television* (Albany: State University of New York Press, 1992).

8. Nancy Signorielli, *A Sourcebook on Children and Television* (New York: Greenwood Press, 1991), p. 2.

9. We selected a sampling of popular programs from networks available in our area. However, some of the programs could not be taped and analyzed because they were not shown by our local stations. Others did not air at the times they were listed, therefore, taping was not possible.

10. See Susan Strane, *A Whole-Souled Woman: Prudence Crandall and the Education of Black Women* (Glendale, CA: Norton, 1990).

11. For a more in-depth analysis of *Lean on Me,* see chapter 7.

12. It is important to note that, as we spoke with them, the Education 1st staff indicated that they only solicited network commitments to air proeducation programs; they did not participate in final program selection. They served in an advisory capacity only. Television network personnel made the final program selections.

13. This could be seen in opposition to the social-class structure of the school system, but ABC considers it proeducation.

14. L. Paine, *Orientation Towards Diversity: What Do Prospective Teachers Bring?* (Michigan State University: National Center for Research on Teacher Education, 1990).

15. Paul Harris, "TV's a White Man's World: New Study Supports Claims by Women, Minority Orgs.," *Variety* (30 August–5 September 1989), p. 73.

16. Richard Hofstadter, *Anti-intellectualism in American Life* (New York: Alfred A. Knopf, 1974).

17. Lawrence A. Cremin, *Popular Education and Its Discontents* (New York: Harper & Row, 1990), p. viii.

18. Ibid. p. 56.

19. Robert J. Blakely, *The People's Instrument: A Philosophy of Programming for Public Television* (Washington, DC: Public Affairs Press, 1971).

20. For a discussion on the economic and profit-making history of television, see Raymond Williams, *Television: Technology and Cultural Form* (New York: Schocken Books, 1975).

21. Greil Marcus, *Lipstick Traces: A Secret History of the Twentieth Century* (Cambridge, MA: Harvard University Press, 1989), p. 148.

22. Gary Day, ed., *Readings in Popular Culture: Trivial Pursuits?* (London: Macmillan, 1990).

23. E. Katz, M. Gurewitch, and E. Hass, "On the Uses of Mass Media for Important Things," *American Sociological Review* 38 (1973); M. De Fleur and S. Ball-Rokeach, *Theories of Mass Communication* (New York: McKay, 1975); Arthur Asa Berger, *Media Analyses Techniques* (Newbury Park, CA: Sage, 1982).

24. Gary Day, ed., *Readings in Popular Culture,* p. 7.

25. John Fiske and John Hartley, *Reading Television* (London: Methuen, 1978), p. 106.

26. Paul Harris, "White Man's World," p. 73.

LIST OF CONTRIBUTORS

Anthon Beonde is an Assistant Professor in the College of Education at Florida Atlantic University. His research interests are in science education and the sociology of knowledge.

Jeanne Ellsworth is an Assistant Professor of Educational Studies at the State University of New York College at Plattsburgh. Her research interests lie in the history of education and teacher education.

Andrea Ewart has her Master's degree from the Graduate School of International Studies at the University of Miami. She works as an administrator in the field of international education.

Paul Farber is an Associate Professor of Education at Western Michigan University. His work in the philosophy of education centers on applied ethics and the politics of teaching.

Gunilla Holm is an Associate Professor of Education at Western Michigan University. Her research focuses on gender relations, popular culture, and the education of girls.

Lynn Nations Johnson is an Assistant Professor of Education at Western Michigan University. Her research centers on issues related to multicultural education and classroom dialogue.

Okhee Lee is an Assistant Professor in the School of Education at the University of Miami. Her research interests include science education, classroom teaching and teacher education, and issues dealing with cultural and linguistic diversity.

Gary N. McCloskey, O.S.A. is Associate Professor of Education and Degree Program Coordinator for the M.S. in Elementary Education at St. Thomas University (Miami, FL). His research interests include the impact of perceptions of teachers and teaching on the development of educational programs.

Eugene F. Provenzo, Jr. is a Professor in the Social and Cultural Foundations of Education at the University of Miami. He has written books on a wide range of topics related to schooling and culture including *Video Kids: Making Sense of Nintendo* (Harvard University Press, 1991).

Arlene S. Sacks is Professor at the Union Institute (Miami, Florida). Her research areas include early childhood special education, educating the mentally handicapped and children with learning disabilities. In these areas she focuses on parent and community advocacy in the education of students with special needs.

Michael B. Salwen is an Associate Professor of Communication at the University of Miami. His research interests include the social effects of mass communication and the role of the mass media in influencing public opinion.

Olga Skorapa is currently pursuing her radical feminism through lived experience outside the bounds of academia.

Robert Stevenson is an Associate Professor at the State University of New York at Buffalo. His main research interests focus on student perspectives on schooling, action research and professional development, and the assumptions in educational policy about how teachers acquire and further knowledge of their practice.

INDEX